Joe Dante

Edited by Nil Baskar and Gabe Klinger

Österreichisches Filmmuseum
SYNEMA – Gesellschaft für Film und Medien

A book by SYNEMA ≡ Publikationen
Joe Dante
Volume 19 of FilmmuseumSynemaPublikationen

This book is jointly published with Slovenska kinoteka, Ljubljana

© Vienna 2013
SYNEMA – Gesellschaft für Film und Medien
Neubaugasse 36/1/1/1, A-1070 Wien

Design and layout: Gabi Adébisi-Schuster, Wien
Cover photo: © Felipe Lima
Printed by: REMAprint
Printed and published in Vienna, Austria.
Printed on paper certified in accordance with the rules of the Forest Stewardship Council.

ISBN 978-3-901644-52-8

Österreichisches Filmmuseum (Austrian Film Museum) and SYNEMA – Gesellschaft für Film & Medien
are supported by Bundesministerium für Unterricht, Kunst und Kultur – Abteilung V/3 FILM
and by Kulturabteilung der Stadt Wien.

Table of Contents

Preface

Believe it or not, the present volume is the first comprehensive critical appraisal of Joe Dante's work in the English language. While not exactly a household name, the director of such iconic films as *Piranha, Gremlins,* and *The 'Burbs* is undeniably one of the great filmmakers of contemporary Hollywood cinema, and his body of work should have generated any number of serious books by now (*Cahiers du cinéma* and the Locarno Film Festival's publications that appeared in French and Italian and Frank Lafond's French language *Joe Dante: L'art du je(u)* are notable exceptions). Starting out as a reviewer for monster magazines, Dante became deeply conversant in genre filmmaking and went on to make some of the smartest fantasy, horror, and sci-fi films of the last four decades. A fierce satirist whose political awakening came in the countercultural years of the late '60s, he also understood early on cinema's ability to powerfully and meaningfully effect change.

As much as Dante's oeuvre is inspiring for its originality and sharp insight, he's often overshadowed by the more financially and critically successful work of his contemporaries (Steven Spielberg, Robert Zemeckis, Tim Burton, and Ron Howard, among them), which might begin to explain the lack of an in-depth appreciation such as the one attempted here. To better understand the enigma of Dante's (non-)reception – to "make the illogical logical," in the words of *Gremlins* inventor Rand Peltzer – we should consider the (mis)fortunes of his embattled relationship with Hollywood.

Dante's integrity and humility, and consequentially, his disinterest in self-promotion, situate him within the particular phenomenon of a "post-cult cinema," as Jonathan Rosenbaum has termed it. A commitment, in other words, to his subjects and audiences, to formative cinematic traditions, however lowbrow they might appear, and a particular ethos which has, against all odds, retained much of the unbridled, collective enthusiasm of Roger Corman's paradigm-shifting New World Pictures production, of which he was an essential part.

Of course, the insolubility of Dante within the studio system has always been a question of his explicitly political choices. From the originating salvo of *The Movie Orgy*, his and Jon Davison's carefully curated cinematographic leviathan which remade the detritus of postwar American pop culture into a critique of the unholy trinity of consumerism, nationalism and organized religion, to the late and unhinged *Looney Tunes: Back in Action*, Dante has maintained an effortless, indiscriminate and often painfully funny critique of the whole Western political spectrum from its top-level classes down to those they exploit. In the course of this trajectory, his work has knowingly straddled the cheap thrills and laughs of "B" cinema, and, often within the space of the same film, affectionately rendered the bygone eras and milieus in which cinema offered a mirror to the scary world of global politics. These are some of the currents and strands of the Dante-esque universe explored in these pages.

The collection of essays is bookended with contributions by John Sayles and the writing partners Michael Almereyda and Jim Robison, who, respectively, have played a role in Dante's beginnings and things (hopefully) to come. Further on, Bill Krohn rediscovers Dante, or rather the New World incubator, through the premise of an *avant la lettre* slasher cinema. More discoveries await in a career-spanning conversation that attempts to solve a number of Dante-related riddles. In Dušan Rebolj's essay, Dante's body of work, usually seen through the prism of satire, politics, and genre, is reformulated as essentially humanistic and marked, in equal parts, by irrepressible hope and horror. Shedding bright light on both the iconic original and its sequel, J. Hoberman's historical dissection traces the *Gremlins* phenomenon as it progresses on its rampage from Main Street to Wall Street. Reconnecting facets of his ongoing critique of militarism and America's interminable wars on fronts both foreign and domestic, Dante's politics at their most articulate are also investigated in an essay on the so-called war trilogy. In *Looney Tunes: Back in Action*, the corporatization of mass culture, cinema, and history are packed into an exhilarating, Luddite spectacle, securing Looney Tunes their "proper place in the history of arts," as Christoph Huber argues in his contribution. Finally, in essays by Violeta Kovacsics and Mark Cotta Vaz, Dante's work is addressed in the rich diversity of its contexts and practices, such as his intriguing serial work in both cinema and television, and his imaginative and often groundbreaking special effects collaborations. In the hope of making all these approaches as substantial as possible we include "A Dante, Esq. Chronology" authored by Howard Prouty and Gabe Klinger, a complete filmography with extensive annotations, and a veritable treasure trove of stills, storyboards, drawings and other artifacts from the archives of Renfield Productions and the collections Dante has donated to (and which are carefully preserved at) the Margaret Herrick Library of the Academy of Motion Pictures Arts and Sciences.

The publication coincides with the Joe Dante retrospectives in Vienna and Ljubljana in autumn, 2013. We would like to express our deep gratitude to all the authors who contributed to this book; our colleagues from the Austrian Film Museum, Alexander Horwath, Regina Schlagnitweit and Andrea Glawogger, whose help and guidance can hardly be overpraised; Gabi Adébisi-Schuster, who has created another in a series of her beautifully designed publications; Jurij Meden and Ivan Nedoh from the Slovenian Cinematheque, who gave this project enthusiastic support from its origins; Markus Keuschnigg of the */slash* film festival, who partnered on the retrospective and offered initial support on the book. We are greatly indebted to the teams of all the institutions involved. Special thanks are due to Felipe Lima, who coordinated and digitized much of the visual content of the book and created wonderful new photographic elements (including the cover portrait); Howard Prouty and Jeanie Braun of the Margaret Herrick Library, who lent their assistance on research and digital imaging tasks; Mark Alan, Elizabeth Stanley, and Joe Dante, for his time, patience and good humor over the last several months as we attempted to piece together his brilliant and unpredictable career.

The Editors

John Sayles

A Soldier in the Field

The first time I ever looked through a movie camera was on Joe Dante's set. It's the late '70s, and I had written three or four movies (unproduced) at that time and seen hundreds of them, either on TV or at the drive-in, but I was not a film school grad and movie cameras were not so easy to get a hold of. I'd read the two or three film books, Germanic and theoretical, that existed back then, and grown up associating movies with their starring actors, not their directors (with the exception of Hitchcock). I'd parlayed a brief career as a novelist into getting a screenwriting agent in Hollywood, and the first assignment they threw at me was a rewrite of the script for *Piranha*, a *Jaws* spin-off being made at Roger Corman's New World Pictures. As I remember it, I did two drafts before Joe was tapped to be the director, and had some minimal phone contact with him before he was sent off (with less than a million dollars) to make the movie. There was a drought in California that year, the rivers so low that the bulk of the shoot was moved to San Marcos, Texas (not far from the LBJ ranch), where they still had enough water to put fake carnivorous fish into.

I do remember a conversation with Joe about those fish – their resemblance in profile to J. Edgar Hoover, the option of cutting the lips off the real thing to show their teeth and

make them look more scare-worthy (an option Joe rejected quickly, fish anesthesia or no). I visited the set once when they were still in Los Angeles, where the combination of Karo-syrup blood and live aquatic plants for underwater action scenes had turned the water in the USC pool (where Johnny Weissmuller had wrestled rubber crocodiles) something close to black, and then was invited to do a walk-on part ("Sentry Number One") in San Marcos. As it turned out, this also had something to do with me rewriting around the fact that the bloody finale was supposed to take place at a brand-new amusement park, while the rides at Aquarina Springs (home to Ralph the Swimming Swine) looked suspiciously old and funky.

I was impressed on that field trip by two things: just how much Joe had to get done in so little time (I don't remember him getting to Take Three the whole time I was there); and how little everything looked through the eyepiece of the camera (this was before video assist had become commonplace). I had pretty much written out every shot, angle by angle, in the screenplay, assuming that whoever they got to direct it would ignore whatever they didn't like, but wanting my employer, Mr. Corman, to see if the movie would "play." What I realized watching Joe work at Aquarina Springs was that he not only saw the movie in his unique way, but that he had it, every little piece of it, in his head. There are directors who, given the time and money, discover a film while shooting much more than will eventually make it onto the screen, like a sculptor chipping a human-sized statue from a giant block of stone. Nobody who worked for Roger Corman got to shoot that way. Joe started in the New World editing room, cutting trailers, where every good moment in a film is employed (and repeated several times if there aren't too many available). You quickly learn what works and what doesn't by cannibalizing the finished film. The idea of a director's "vision" sounds pretentious, but it really is only that specific movie he or she carries in the mind, and shooting your vision on a low budget and tight schedule is often more compromise and salvage work than discovery.

The other thing clearly evident to me was Joe's affection for the genre. One may make a successful movie – right time, genre, and cast – while condescending to the material, but rarely a good one. Joe has a knowledge and feeling for movies that is analytical without being academic. He's an aficionado in the best sense of the word, a fan who can take a movie apart and tell you how it works.

What was less apparent on my visit was the aspect of Joe's work that developed over time, picture after picture – essentially, the concept of tone. Though they all started making movies for Roger, a Francis Coppola movie is not a Jonathan Demme movie is not a Peter Bogdanovich movie is not a Monte Hellman movie is not a Joe Dante movie. It isn't a question of signature camera movements; it's the way they see the world, or rather it's the world they choose to create and present to us in their films. Joe has worked in monster flicks, horror, sci-fi, comedy, but there is a tone, an attitude toward the people and creatures in his stories that is unique. There is more suspense than shock, more storytelling than stimulus, and there are always characters who you'd like to hang out with (as opposed to the haunted house or summer camp filled with assholes you can't wait to see skewered). There are fond references, at times, to films and filmmakers that preceded us, sight gags out of cartoons, and the recurrence of Dick Miller.

Joe's movies are classic matinees: laugh, worry about the hero and heroine, toss your popcorn when the thing jumps out, and leave the theater feeling good. His movies are also self-aware. I remember a conversation with Joe and producer Mike Finnell when I was rewriting *The Howling* for them. We agreed that the next step in werewolfery was to have characters *who have seen a horror movie*, and thus do not wander back into the house where six of their friends have been brutally murdered to search for their cat.

Wearing nothing but their undergarments.

I got to see Joe's *The Movie Orgy* on tape a few years ago, watching the whole thing in one viewing (no, I was not stoned), and it made me wish I'd experienced the thing in a crowded theater back in the late '60s. Without the need for narration, it doesn't only contextualize '50s movies, but explains the psychic and political life of the era. Joe's editing skills are already apparent, layering flying creatures, fellow-traveler aliens, vindictive, glandular females, public service admonitions from the straight and narrow, and Madison Avenue sales campaigns into a kind of found-object cultural epic. The result is too meaningful to be campy and too much fun to be taught in school. And truly amazing that it was put together before digital sampling and offline editing (but alas, not before copyright litigation).

Joe is also the first person I ever saw operate an upright Moviola editing machine, a device requiring the use of both hands and feet and notorious for chewing film into little bits if you're not careful. An upright is (was) the perfect thing to cut a trailer on, able to handle thirty seconds to two minutes of material without spitting up ("crashing" in those days entailed expensive reprints). A true editor's touch is needed to put together an exciting (or even competently coherent) action sequence from dozens of shots of hand-puppets, rubber figures (I think of them as Gumbys with attitude), guys in monster suits, real (and therefore uncooperative) animals, children (often worse than the animals), and actors pretending that shit not even visible on the stage is about to eat them. Joe's action scenes are terrific, and given the budgets he's worked with, he's usually dealing with frames of credible film action, not seconds. He knows that if you can't make the creature lunge at the camera you can at least make the camera lunge at the creature, and that you should never despair of a ripping-flesh-to-shreds sequence till you've laid the sound effects into place.

These pictures are hard enough to make when everybody is pulling in the same direction, but Joe has often had to deal with capriciousness bordering on sabotage and the shifting sands of studio control. Threadbare as it was, working for New World had a stability built into it; there was only Roger Corman and his right hand woman, Frances Doel, to answer to, and you knew they were going to be there tomorrow. A film director is, in most cases, an employee, and Joe has made the best of a bad situation more than once.

Nonetheless, Joe has been a soldier in the field, making memorable pictures despite the obstacles. I've learned a lot over the years working with him, both as a writer and as an actor (I think I did hit Take Three once on *Matinee*, but that was John Goodman's fault). I suppose, in light of a whole book being devoted to him, it's time to reveal his deepest secret: the gremlins are real. He keeps them in a self storage locker in Tarzana.

(But they're a bitch to direct.)

July 11th, 2013

NATIONAL SCREEN SERVICE
COLOR
NSS
NATIONAL SCREEN SERVICE
WITH FEATURE
PICTURES RATED
The Band Around the Proper Trailer
The Band Around the Proper Trailer
WORK PRINT

Gabe Klinger & Joe Dante

A Conversation

GABE KLINGER: When do you remember movies impacting you for the first time?

JOE DANTE: Well, I'm actually old enough to have been a child of radio. We didn't have a TV when I was a kid, and I remember listening to the radio with my grandfather. The first movie I saw was either *Peter Pan* (1953) or *Snow White* (1937). Now, I don't think I really got the movie bug until we moved from Morristown, New Jersey, to the neighboring town of Livingston and there was a theater that was literally within walking distance from my house. And every Saturday they would have a special matinee for kids that consisted of ten cartoons and two movies. My ritual was mainly to watch the ten cartoons and leave because the movies all had adults in them and weren't that interesting to me. But then one day I stayed to see *It Came from Outer Space* (1953) and I got the impression that these movies with adults could be okay. We used to count when the names came on at the beginning to see how many girls there were in the cast – and I thought, as many girls as there were, that's how many trips for popcorn we were gonna be making.

There was nothing more magical than a Disney cartoon, for me, in the theater. There were gradations: kids applauded Disney and Warner cartoons when the logos would come up. Then it would get a little iffy – they wouldn't applaud Woody Woodpecker cartoons; we tolerated him but we didn't applaud for him. And then when you got down into the dregs, like *Heckle and Jeckle* and *Casper the Friendly Ghost*, they would actually get booed, because [Casper] was such a wimp. In the beginning, it was lots of great cartoons, and I guess, as the rentals got higher or whatever, they would start sneaking in these crappy Paramount cartoons and after a while it was *Herman and Katnip* and stuff, and it was like, "Christ, this is really terrible."

But we did form an aesthetic watching these cartoons. They made a real visual impact. It was much later that cartoons other than really early silents were sold to television. I remember we got our first television and the cartoons were all Paul Terry cartoons from the 1920s like *Farmer Al Falfa*, and they were all silent. You could literally hear the needle drop on the record when the station would run it. And the music never sunk [synced] up to the picture. And that was still fascinating in its own way… but it was the black and white Warners cartoons that were released in the early '50s that made a big impact. I became quite a cartoon connoisseur and it sort of led me into live-action movies, because it was the thrill of being in the dark and watching a big, exciting image on the screen.

And then I was very big on Westerns 'cause Westerns were very big and there were a lot of color Westerns then. Universal was making a lot of them and our theater, for whatever reason, ran a lot of Universal stuff. I wasn't mad about war pictures – they seemed so grim to me. I wasn't big on series Westerns either. I didn't like watching Roy Rogers because I knew that he and Gene Autry would always come out at the end and there was no suspense, whereas if I was watching an Audie Murphy picture maybe they might kill him.

GK: I heard that you wake up every day watching ENCORE Westerns.*

JD: I do. I find it relaxing. It's comfort food for me, you know? And there's a tremendous number of Westerns. I mean, people don't realize how many fuckin' Westerns there are. And that's not even just B pictures on hand – in the '50s they must've made hundreds and hundreds of Westerns from all these different studios, all these different directors, all these different actors, and not all of them are on the radar and certainly not all of them played in my theater. So I'm constantly finding things that I've never heard of, like *Dawn at Socorro* (1954), which it turns out I saw as a kid but had completely forgotten. There's a couple of pictures I saw when I was a kid that had indelible moments that I've been trying to find over the years and I keep wondering, "Maybe this is the one?"

GK: It just clicks like that and you remember?

JD: There are moments that you take away when you're a kid that are indelible for whatever reason, because they're too scary or shocking, or because they're just something you haven't seen before. There's a trailer for an unknown movie, probably from '54 or '55, where the trailer says, identifying the characters, "The Coward," and it's a color movie and this guy is on a ledge outside of a building and the ledge collapses and he falls. And I've been looking for that movie ever since. I don't know why it resonated with me but there was another picture which I finally did identify. People are chasing each other in the arctic and falling through the ice, and that turned out to be a picture called *Dangerous Mission* (1954) with Victor Mature and Vincent Price, which I finally saw. And some of the other movies that I had that reaction to are movies that I'm now so familiar with that I can hardly place myself far away, like *This Island Earth* (1955).

It's hard to recapture exactly the magic impression that movies make on you when you're

* American cable television channel specializing in western film, serial, and TV programming

Pages 17–20:
Details of Joe Dante's shoebox theater

young and unsophisticated and uncritical. Many times you revisit a movie that you thought you loved as a kid only to discover to your horror that it's really inept. And you try to connect with the part of you that related to it originally and usually it's something in the fantasy or science fiction vein where it's the images that you hadn't seen before and concepts that you hadn't thought of that won the day, and later on you realize that this was so derivative and there were other versions of this that were better but you just didn't get to see them.

GK: Initially, your ambition was to become an animator.

JD: I was going to be a cartoonist of some sort, but animation was a little daunting. I figured maybe I could do a strip. And then I realized, of course, that you had to do a different joke everyday for the strip, and I went, "Oh my God, I'm not going to be able to do that." So it was comic books that really got me. I was a huge Carl Barks fan and he was writing and illustrating the better Donald Duck and Uncle Scrooge comics and they were of a literary quality that really dwarfed all the other comics, which were just one-shot gags. Here was a guy who used historical basis for some of his stories, and legends and fantasies from other places, and they were bigger than life, those stories. I was not alone: Spielberg and a lot of other people were very into Carl Barks. Nobody knew his name at the time, he was only known as "The Good Artist Who Paints the Ducks Best." And the mythos was different in the comics than it was in the cartoons: in the cartoons, Donald Duck was simple, quick to anger, and he had his little nephews who would get him out of scrapes, but that was about it, whereas the character in the comic books was much more sophisticated and much more interesting and multi-dimensional. I think that's what I really aspired to. Then when I finally did make my Carl Barks movie, *Explorers* (1985), it was very conscious on my part that I was replicating Huey, Dewey, and Louie with these kids building their spaceship.

GK: Was the shoebox theater the first creative manifestation of your ambition?

JD: No, I used to draw comic books and they would be many pages, and in black and white – it was too much trouble to color them in. I had my own stable of characters; Wilbur Cat and Ducky Dog and all these characters that were sort of rip-offs of other characters that I had seen. I would place them into different stories and draw the comics and leave them at my grandma's. I don't think any of those survived. But when my brother came along – he was six

WRITTEN, PRODUCED AND
DIRECTED BY
ANONYMOUS SAM

Scribbly-International presents
AN
OUTER SANCTUM
MYSTERY

LIFE
ANNOUNCING AN EXCITING
NEW SERIES OF BOOKS
WHICH ONLY LIFE COULD DO - THE
LIFE NATURE LIBRARY
You Are Invited to Reserve a Copy of
the First Volume -- THE SEA -- for
Free Examination, with the Option to
Purchase It at a Very Special
Pre-Publication Rate
...the articles ever published in LIFE, the most acclaimed

A
MYOPIC
PICTURES
Re-Release

STARRING
ROVER CAT
WITH Duffy Dog
Wally Furd

turned into
ature!
And---it's---all---your---fault!
AGH!
Good grief.
That came from the lab back side

SCRIBBLY INTERNATIONAL PRESENTS
"FORT DEATH"
A MYOPIC PICTURES RE-RELEASE
PLENTY GUTS!

INTERNATIONAL
TH"
NOW RE-RELEASED IN IT'S ORIGINAL UNCUT FULL-LENGTH VERSION!
They're in!

FOR WESTERN THRILLS ...SEE...
"FORT DEATH"
NOTHINGCOLOR • KATORAMA
A MYOPIC PICTURES RE-RELEASE

is Gorak. He turns up
many of these low-grade
horror movies. Kill, Gorak!

Oh, no
you
don't!
ACID

years younger than me – I got the idea of turning these comic books into little movies. And I would draw them on a pad and I'd tape the pictures together on a roll, on a pencil, and I'd roll it through a shoebox that had a screen cutout on it, and I would show it to my little brother.

GK: He was your only audience?

JD: He was my only audience. And nobody else ever saw them. And I didn't even use my own name. I was building anonymous sand. But again, I had a hierarchy of characters I would use, and I would star them in one and then they would just appear in the other. Sometimes they were rip-offs of movies, sometimes they were original ideas that were very simple – the equivalent was one panel equaled a minute. So, sometimes the panels would run ninety panels and sometimes they would run only sixty panels. It just depended on whether it was a B picture or an A picture.

GK: So you were already, at that point, very aware that there were people making the movies, there were studios, there were different styles…

JD: Yes, I was my own studio. I released them as from Scribbly International, which was the distributing company, and the production company was Pencil Pusher Productions. And it was in "Schmechnicolor" or a made-up wide-screen process; I made up all sorts of stuff. It was all very inside – for me. I basically just did it for me.

GK: What was the next progression of that?

JD: I did these shoeboxes from 1960–1963, maybe. Then I sort of lost interest because my brother lost interest and I didn't make any more of 'em. Later I did the high school newspaper comic.

GK: Do any of those survive?

JD: I hope not. I was a very unhappy high school kid who didn't fit in. It really wasn't, as with most kids, until I went away to college that I started to figure out who I was. And of course it was the mid-'60s, so there was a lot going on, culturally. I went to art school because my math grades were so bad from having polio when I was in third grade and missing multiplication tables that I wasn't really going to be able to get into any kind of fancy college. So I thought, "I'll go to art school and I'll take cartooning." Little did I realize that that's not an option, cartooning is not considered an art. And after taking a year of basics they'd say, "No, take something else, you can't take cartooning." So I took film, because this was the era of the fledgling film school movement. There were, like, three cameras and thirteen students. You would do assignments but you wouldn't do them until the week they were due, and then everyone would scramble to get the cameras. Luckily, very few of those things [films] survive; I have a couple under lock and key. I don't think I expressed any particular affinity for making films when I was in film school, but I did get into writing about films. I had been following British magazines like *Sight & Sound* and *Films and Filming* that were taking a somewhat more scholarly approach to writing about film. And you have to remember around this period, there were very, very few serious books about film; it was considered frivolous. If it wasn't just a bio of David Niven or something, there really weren't a lot of books like *The Loftiest Art* or the Parker Tyler book, and if there were they were very dry. And they didn't take any genre stuff into consideration; it was never about that. And so, these British magazines were much more free-wheeling in their ability to discuss and take seriously the kind of things that weren't really talked about in America.

When I got out of college, my attempts to enter the film business were via working for Ralph Lopatin, a local Philadelphia industrial filmmaker making films where they tell you how to fix your TV or how to upholster a chair. They were soul-deadening.

GK: I'm wondering about your political background.

JD: My political background is that I didn't have one until 1968. I was not particularly interested in politics and then the riots at the Democratic Convention radicalized me to a point where I took a tremendous interest in politics. *The New York Post*, which believe it or not used to be a liberal paper, was a great paper, and *The Village Voice*, of course, was a great paper, too – and so instead of just reading the movie section, I was now reading the politics section. And I wouldn't say that I became an activist, but it became clear to me that there was a need to try to right wrongs. If movies could right wrongs, the world would've disarmed after *Dr. Strangelove* (1964) came out. And we know that that doesn't happen. But I think that you can influence people, change minds, and particularly in a genre setting you can make more effective arguments than you might be able to in a Stanley Kramer kind of setting.

GK: Are there any examples which made you realize that about genre films? Or is it something you discovered organically, through making films yourself?

JD: I think more of the latter. I mean, yes, there were movies that were subversive that I had seen – Frank Tashlin movies were subversive, though not in a political way. That kind of sneaking the message in appealed to me more than an overt message movie, although there were overt message movies that I thought were great, but it always helps if you agree with the message.

GK: Did you see things like *The Incredible Shrinking Man* (1957)?

JD: Yeah, movies that have an innate critique of society in them – science fiction is perfect for that, since the genre really divides itself into right-wing movies and left-wing movies, and there are many more right-wing science fiction movies than there are left-wing ones. Even so, the politics of *The Thing* (1951) are not my politics, but I think it's a great movie, one of the great science fiction movies, and I can watch it putting myself in that mindset and enjoy the movie. Which is something I can't do, for instance, with *The Green Berets* (1968); it's just so overtly mindless that it's wrong.

GK: When you were getting into college, would you say that you already had a film history basis?

JD: Yeah, I knew a lot about films. I knew more about films than most of my friends, from whatever limited sources I could get. And you have to remember that this is a period when the entire panoply of older movies from the '20s through the '50s were on television routinely. I mean, this was the general fodder – you haven't got anything to run, you ran an old movie. I was very fluent in film culture and what had been done and who was doing what, and when the Shock Theater pictures hit TV in the late '50s and all the old horror films from the '30s started to appear, these were brand new to us, we had never heard of some of these people. That gave rise to the *Famous Monsters of Filmland* phenomenon, which became sort of a cultural force that united a lot of kids who thought they were just dweeby and didn't have any friends who liked the kind of stuff they did. Then they realized that there was actually a network of people out there who were like them. And so once these magazines came out, and there were quite a few of them by 1958, there was a real movement that grew. It was a monster movie movement but it was more importantly a film movement because it involved film history and learning what had been done.

GK: Is this the time that you met Jon Davison?

JD: Jon was a formative contact although he was still in high school. I think I met him in '65. I lived in a basement apartment – it smelled terrible 'cause all the garbage was right outside the door. And he knocked on the door and introduced himself. He had read about me, in *Castle of Frankenstein*, and he invited me to a science fiction convention that was going on in Philadelphia. Eventually, I went over to his house and met his parents – and he had a film collection! I had never heard of such a thing – a 16mm film collection – and he got me into spending my hard-earned shekels on my first 16mm print, which I paid $50 for.

GK: What was it?

JD: *The Gamma People* (1956). Which I still have. And eventually I got hooked. It's hard to imagine in today's video era, but the idea of having a movie in your house was unheard of. They had souvenir versions, 8mm movies that you could get silent versions of, and I certainly had a lot of those, but that wasn't the same as actually having the real movie with the sound. And when I first met Jon, he lent me a whole bunch of pictures that I took home to New Jersey and I ran them on my ceiling and I just thought, "This is *great*." You know, when I had polio, I was laid out and one of the things I kept thinking about was, "Wouldn't it be great if I could just look up and watch *The Deadly Mantis* (1957) right on my ceiling, right now?" And not only that, as the years went on, and you go to college, you can say to a girl, "Hey, wanna come over and see *8½* at my house?"

GK: With Jon, your first collaboration was taking bits and pieces of films you were collecting and fashioning them into what the two of you eventually called *The Movie Orgy*.

JD: Yes, that happened about two years after I met him. He was very close with people who were running film rental places that would rent to schools, convents, prisons, etc. They would often get prints back and they'd be beat up, so they'd have to send away for replacement footage, and these places had a lot of stuff that they had cut out of the prints that they were going to throw away, and Jon and I would always end up with these scraps. We had this box of odds and ends; we didn't even know what some of them were.

In 1966, Columbia re-released the 1943 *Batman* serial that they had made, which was like fifteen chapters, and they ran it all at once, from 8 'til midnight or 1 or something like that. And it became a phenomenon because it was very funny, and very campy, and very dated, and very racist. And also, it cheated: at the end of every episode, you'd see something like Batman getting run over by a steamroller. Cut to the next episode and you'd see there's a shot they didn't show you before where he dodged the steamroller. The kids weren't supposed to remember from week to week what they had seen. We had a bunch of stuff like that and thought to put on a show. We got a serial, called *The Phantom Creeps* (1939), with Bela Lugosi, which was at least as funny as *Batman*, and we interspersed it with a bunch of other stuff, much in the way that we change channels – this whole ethos is actually based on changing channels. And we ran it to some success at the Philadelphia Culture Bar on a couple of projectors, and we'd cut off one projector and put on something from this one and then go and put the other one back on… It kind of got us thinking, you know, "We can do this better if we have more films." So we decided that if we use several different features, we can cut randomly between them and tell five stories at the same time. We eventually put together a version that ran about seven hours at NYU and we charged admission. It was phenomenally successful. When we came home, Jon lifted up his sweater and he had all this money in his shirt, which he immediately put in the freezer. So we ran it at Columbia University, we ran it at the Fillmore East, we ran it at a whole bunch of places… It got a sort of underground reputation. At one point, a guy from Schlitz Beer saw it and said, "We would like to give you guys a hundred bucks a shot if you'll go and fly this show to various colleges and we'll sell beer." It sounded like a good deal to us. It was a rather arduous process though, because to run seven hours of film and just constantly be threading the projector –

GK: It was a performance piece.

JD: And like an Andy Warhol movie, it would be different depending on when you cut out of the reel and which piece you use from various films. So no show was exactly the same. And it was really a pain because at the time we were renting the features legitimately and then interspersing them with other junk. And finally we realized that it was very limiting and that it would be a lot easier if we just bought the features and cut them up ourselves. Then we would at least have ten reels of stuff that's just our stuff and not twenty reels of all sorts of stuff. So we did that and we got a little scared once a guy from the *New Yorker* magazine appeared and said, "This is great! We gotta write about this!" and we didn't own anything.

Now today, the doctrine of fair use might cover us, but who knows. And eventually, when I came out to work for Roger Corman, after Jon had already come out to work for Roger, we realized that there was no way we were actually going to be able to physically do this ourselves, so we contracted our friends and we'd pay them some money and they would

Out 1
(1971/1990, Jacques Rivette)

take the stuff to the various places all around the country. And I mean *all around the country.*
GK: When we showed *The Movie Orgy* in Chicago, it occurred to me that the storytelling in the film is pretty sophisticated, and that people like Jacques Rivette were taking similar approaches when it came to long-form narratives.
JD: [*Laughter.*] That's the first time that *The Movie Orgy*'s been compared to Rivette. Like, *The Movie Orgy Belongs to Us*, that kind of thing?
GK: You guys obviously weren't working in that more lofty register…
JD: Well, no, we weren't working in a lofty register at all, but we *were* working on the idea that you should think anything can happen. And that we can do anything we want with this footage, and we can make you think the ending of this movie is really the ending of a different movie. And because some of the actors would play the same parts, like Morris Ankrum always would play the general, you could intercut several different movies with him. So there were a lot of things we sort of seized on while we were doing it. Every night was an opening night. Because if we tried something new and it didn't work, we'd take it out. And so we were con-

stantly using all these screenings as test screenings, refining the job…

A tremendous amount of the appeal of the show was that it reacquainted the audience with material that they were unaware they even remembered. Things that they saw when they were kids that they'd completely forgotten. In particular, the kids' shows, which hadn't been on for years and all of a sudden it's like, "There's Froggy the Gremlin, I haven't seen that show since I was a tadpole and I have only a vague memory of it but now it's flooding back to me and, boy, this is even sillier than I thought it was when I was a kid."
GK: This aspect really fascinates me about *The Movie Orgy*: not only does it channel old memories, but it creates something new, putting these relics into a new and interesting context. I guess what I'm trying to lead into is that maybe *The Movie Orgy* gave you a working concept for the films that you would make later.
JD: Every time I see an old movie of mine, I see incredible influences. There are many pieces in *The Movie Orgy* – it's like a compendium of tryouts for movies I eventually made. And I've incorporated not just the editing style, but the actual footage into my films. I guess I would say, today, that it was a major work of mine – and it was a lot of work – but at the time it was cer-

The Movie Orgy
(1966–2009)

tainly not something I took seriously. I mean, we were just trying to get a laugh.

GK: How did this experience lead you to cutting trailers for Roger Corman?

JD: You gotta remember, the first film that I ever cut was *The Movie Orgy*. And by "cutting," I mean it's an assemblage. And it's an assemblage of optical soundtracks. Optical tracks don't cut off at the picture cut – they hang over. And so in many ways that was helpful to us, because we got laughs out of something that you would ordinarily nix, 'cause we couldn't nix anything. And I gained some facility with the equipment – I certainly became very good at repairing sprocket holes. Then when the time came to do trailers for Corman at New World Pictures, I had never worked with 35 mm, but I did house an innate sense of how to do a trailer. As far as the actual mechanics of making a trailer, I was basically like all Corman people: I was put in a room with equipment and a film and expected to come out with something. And the only way I could do that was by going down the hall and asking other people questions like, "What's this synchronizer for?"

GK: How did you get the job in the first place?

JD: I got the job because Jon Davison had come out [to Los Angeles] to work for Roger and worked his way up to head of publicity. Roger wasn't having much luck with trailer editors and Jon suggested that he hire me. If the trailers were good, he'd leave me on and I'd keep making trailers for him. So that's what happened – I came out and did a trailer for *Caged Heat* (1974), Jonathan Demme's first movie. I went way over-budget on it, and Jon managed to hide that fact. But *Caged Heat* made money and Corman said, "This kid did the trailer, maybe [he's] okay." Which led to *Candy Stripe Nurses* (1974) and some other surefire titles that you can't screw up. When that was working out, there were more trailers than I could handle, and so Allan Arkush came on and we became the New World trailer department. We did the trailers for every picture for the next couple of years.

The trick with trailers was that you first went through the film and took out all the pieces that you thought were gonna be good. Then you had to piece them together, you had to write a narration, and you had to figure out a concept for what you were going to sell. Around the time that we did that, there were a lot of exploitation pictures coming out, and a lot of very envelope-pushing images. And so, we got away with a lot because we pushed the envelope so far that the trailers became parodies of trailers for those kinds of movies. There's a trailer we did for *Cover Girl Models*

Joe Dante and Roger Corman
(right), *The Howling* set

(1975) that is nothing but voiceover jokes and juxtaposition jokes that weren't in the movie. Now, our intended audience never seemed to mind, because the trailers did what they were supposed to do.

But more important than the trailers were the TV spots, because X number of people may see a trailer but everybody was seeing these TV spots, and they were doing saturation booking in towns. They wouldn't make that many prints. And they would go to a particular region and blanket the place in TV spots, and they would run all the prints they had for a week or two, and then they would take the whole she-bang and go to another part of town. Some of these movies took a year to play off, and we'd always be making new copies of the trailers because they would get beat up really quick. It was fun and it was a lot of work, but we really felt that we were making little movies. We got to choose the fonts, we got to choose the opticals, we got to choose the music…

GK: What is your first memory of meeting Roger Corman?

JD: I had been a huge fan of Roger when I was in high school. I divined that this was the guy I would want to meet and maybe write for or maybe get a script made. Actually, all the kids in school had Jean-Luc Godard buttons on; I had Roger Corman buttons made up. So I sent him a couple and he replied with a letter saying what great taste I had. Then, I got a distribution service, Hurlock's Cine World, to make a page in their catalog devoted to Roger's Filmgroup movies – *The Creature from the Haunted Sea* (1961), the Jack [Nicholson] movies – and they offered them as a package, and Roger thought that was pretty cool, too. And so, he was going to come to New York and I was supposed to meet him but it didn't work out for whatever reason and I never actually met Roger until the day I had to run my very, very poor rough cut for the *Caged Heat* trailer at the Nossic Screening Room in California.

Caged Heat (1974, Jonathan Demme)
Hollywood Boulevard (1976)

I didn't drive then – don't drive now – so I took the bus. On the trip, I had my reels – the sound reel and the picture reel. One of those reels fell while I was getting off the bus and rolled down Santa Monica Boulevard and actually went into an open manhole, like in a Tashlin movie. When I finally got there, I was late, of course, and I'm amazed that the stuff even ran through the projector. And Roger's first words to me were, "If I were you, young man, I'd get to these things on time." I thought, "This is it, it's over, I'm going back to New Jersey."

And then I ran this footage, which was just as I recall, a mess of meaningless exploitation stuff, all the exploitation stuff in the movie – the people being zapped, and topless girls, and beatings over the head, you know – and he said, "Oh, okay, I think we can make this work." So I managed to make it into a decent trailer with a good voiceover – we had this guy named Ron Gans at the time, who had this big, deep, mellifluous voice and he would go, [*Imitating bass voice*] "*Caged Heat*: they're hot young women behind cold prison bars," you know. You look at it today and it looks like a parody, but it worked. The rest was history. Allan and I harbored the view that if given a chance we could make a picture *at least* as good as this. And Jon also had produced a movie called *Big Bad Mama* (1974) for New World, which made some money. Jon said, "Let the trailer boys make a picture," and Roger said, "Okay, but they have to do trailers at night while they're making it, they've only got 10 days, and it's got to be the cheapest picture we've ever made here." And so we wondered how could we possibly make a movie that was releasable for 50, 60 thousand dollars. Then we hit upon the idea that if we used footage from the other movies that we had been doing trailers for, we could have action scenes, and they're action scenes bigger than we could ever imagine doing on our own. But how to put them all together in a story?

We drafted Chuck Griffith, who had authored *Little Shop of Horrors* (1960), to write what was then called "Free Popcorn," and it contained the seed of what it was that we were eventually going to make: a movie set on a movie set. We figured that's the cheapest thing we can do – we can use our crew as the crew and dress up our actors like the people in the clips from other movies that we have. We came up with what was then called "The Starlets." Roger had been making nurse and teacher pictures, and always three girls would get in trouble and take off their clothes and have left-wing adventures, and this was going to be a new variation on that. So we actually made the picture under the title "The Starlets" with both of us directing. I did the sound and Allan did the non-sound, which was mostly action. While shooting my scene, Allan would be setting up his scene and vice versa. Our motto was, "Two directors, no waiting." And we did manage to somehow put this thing in the can in 10 days. But we sort of had an ace in the hole: we knew we didn't know enough to do this properly, so we put Paul Bartel and Jonathan

Kaplan into the movie, in the cast, so they could tell us when we were fucking up.

I was shooting a scene and I was about to go on, and Jonathan would say, [*in a fevered voice*] "Get a close-up. If you don't get a close-up you can't cut these two scenes together." Sure enough, he was right.

Roger saw the movie and he actually thought it was surprisingly good. I don't know what he expected, but he thought it was very funny. Roger was very logical about stuff, and there was one scene where we had some sky-diving footage from a movie and we decided that we would try to use it because the girls get a job making a movie in the Philippines. So we figured, okay, what we'll do is have the girls fly over in an airplane and come out in their sky-diving suits and land in the Philippines. And Roger said, "How would they get through customs?" [*Laughter.*] I mean, it's the kind of question that Roger would routinely overlook in a movie. The picture came out and it didn't particularly do well. One reason it didn't do well was that, for some reason, he didn't want to call it "The Starlets." He actually wanted to call it "Hollywood Hookers." Allan and I both felt that it was a better movie than that and we went on to call it *Hollywood Boulevard* (1976), because it was a block down from Sunset Boulevard, which was a very pretentious place for us. Anyway, for whatever reason, he said okay, and under that title it proceeded to die. We went back to making trailers.

GK: At this stage, we're getting into your next film, solo, as a director…

JD: Roger knew we were harboring ambitions to do other things, and there were two projects floating around. One of them was *Rock 'n' Roll High School* (1979) and the other was *Piranha* (1978). *Rock 'n' Roll High School* looked much more attractive to me than *Piranha*. However, Allan Arkush had been living his life for the moment when he could make a rock and roll film. So he got *Rock 'n' Roll High School* and I got the fish.

This was a *Jaws* (1975) rip-off that had waited too many years to happen. The script was a little dire – the writer couldn't figure out a way to get people into the water once they knew there were piranhas there.

The movie that John Sayles wrote is completely different than that script; the only things they share are piranhas and water. And people. That's about it. When Frances Doel, Roger's assistant, was in charge of reading all the new writers and trying to find people, she had read John's novel *Pride of the Bimbos* and suggested that maybe he'd like to take a crack at this. And

he did, and turned it into a more intelligent movie than it had any right to be. We added the political stuff to it, and I conceived it as a kind of spoof, because there was no way it could be taken seriously. All these other nature-goes-wild movies like *Grizzly* (1976) – William Girdler was making a lot of these things – seemed to me difficult to take without some tongue-in-cheek.

It was an arduous picture to make because you're not supposed to have special effects, kids, and water – and dogs – all in the same movie. We would not have made the movie if it weren't for the extensive tests that we did – Roger didn't feel it was worth making the movie unless we could have fairly convincing special effects. And in fact, Peter Fonda, who was offered the lead, turned it down because he said, "I don't think you can do the special effects." So we'd get on our wet suits, go down in the test pool, and find ways to photograph little rubber fish. We would shoot them fast, shoot them slow, put them on wheels, put them on wires, put them on whatever. And then we'd go back and look at them in the lab the next morning. They'd look terrible, and we'd go back and try again.

Somehow we managed to make it work. But the only way that I can think that it worked is

Piranha (1978)

that I spent all of my time in the cutting room when I came back. I lived in the cutting room. I would cut the piranhas to 8 frames, I would cut them to 2 frames, cut them to whatever. I was also convinced that the movie was terrible and I completely changed the structure of the picture to the point where when John Sayles saw it he didn't even recognize his own script. I was sort of desperate. I didn't even go to my own wrap party. But when the picture was released, it made a lot of money. I think Roger certainly came out of it very well and that got me the offer for my next picture from New World, *Humanoids from the Deep*. "I got this movie for you, it's about these underwater aliens who want our women." I replied, "You know, Roger, I think I just made that picture." And as it turned out, I did not make another picture for Roger. I was able to use my limited celebrity to get an agent, which I didn't have before, and Roger said, "Oh, that's good, he can represent you with everybody but me." I was offered *Jaws 3, People o* and *Orca 2*.

GK: Doesn't sound like much of a leap from New World.

JD: There was a lot of power play on *Jaws 3, People o*. It was the first time I'd ever been in a real Hollywood situation. I'd go to these meetings and there'd be all these different people in the room and somebody would say something and then I'd look and everybody's eyes would look around to everybody else to see what they thought of what was said. Could they endorse that? Was that something that they could buy? Did they have to take issue with that? It was like a Leone movie – all these sudden close-ups of eyes looking furtively around. And I realized that I was really in over my head because I was just the hired director.

When I had first come to the studio, they had given me a big flock of storyboards, already drawn from eye-level. Just like a Universal Television show. I suggested that there was a part that Orson Welles could play, and they said, "Orson Welles? We'd have to put him on the poster…" Also, during that period, Carl Laemmle, Jr., who was the guy who had ushered in all the Frankenstein and Dracula pictures in the '30s at Universal, had passed away. I went to the studio that day and I said to [studio executive] Ned Tanen, "Gee, shouldn't you guys be flying the flag at half-staff? You know, Carl Laemmle, Jr. died." And he said, "Who?"

It was very useful for me, because I had a concept that everybody in the business was aware of Hollywood history.

GK: So now we're getting into *The Howling* (1981).

The Howling (1981)

JD: The way that I came to *The Howling* was that it became quite obvious that *Jaws 3, People 0* was going to flounder. At the time, Mike Finnell – who had worked with me on *Piranha* and even on *Hollywood Boulevard* in the capacity of wading into a swamp to recover the one wooden hand grenade that we had – called and said that he was developing this werewolf picture and the director had fallen out, a guy named Steve Lane. It was being produced by Dan Blatt, who worked for AVCO Embassy,

and he asked if I wanted to read it. They sent me the screenplay and the book and, well, the screenplay wasn't good.

I hired a guy named Terry Winkless, who I think I met at Corman's, and we worked on an adaptation of the book that was a little better than the original script. But it still wasn't working. So I asked the studio if we could bring in John Sayles, because I knew he was already particularly adept at working with this kind of material.

John was working on *The Howling* concurrent with *Alligator* (1980), and the company that was making *Alligator* was paying him to fly out, and we'd pay him to fly back, and they'd put him up at this seedy motel on Santa Monica Boulevard. When we'd knock on the door of his room, he'd say, "Who is it?" and we'd say, "It's us." And then you'd hear pages being pulled out of the typewriter and the other pages being put in because he was always working on one picture or the other. At this point, I'm still convinced that one of our dream sequences ended up in *Alligator* and one of theirs ended up in *The Howling*.

We had to get a completion insurance and I had to talk to a guy named Lindsley Parsons, Jr., a pipe-puffin' guy who'd been in the business going back to John Wayne westerns, and his job was to make sure the picture wasn't going to go over budget. We had come upon this idea of doing the transformation [of the werewolf] all in one shot and at the time we were working with Rick Baker, and Parsons said, [*in grizzled old man voice*] "So, son, what are you going to do if you can't get it in one shot?" And I responded, "Well, I guess we'll have to do it the old way." And he said, *"That's* what I want to hear!"

Nonetheless, Rick had done some remarkable tests of masks that would start off in human form and morph into a werewolf face. But when John Landis heard that Rick was making *The Howling*, and not John's long-gestating *An American Werewolf in London* (1981), he called him up and said, "You've gotta make my picture." And Rick said, "But you don't have a picture." And he said, "Yes, I do!" And John went out and somehow put together the whole pie and package and got the picture made and so Rick said, "I'm sorry, I can't do the movie now, but I'll leave Rob Bottin, my protégé, and he can use some of the same techniques that I was going to use." And so, Rob did the whole show himself, and quite remarkably.

The picture came out and was a surprise success. It was one of those examples of seeing an audience react in the way that you want but to a much larger degree than what you imagined. When I went to this sneak preview in New York City at the Loews Theater on Broadway, they were running it twice, once upstairs and once downstairs, so you could hear this amazing audience reaction to something and then you could run upstairs and hear the exact same thing. That was a lot of fun.

Werewolf movies were considered at that time kind of passé and old-fashioned – they were something that you'd see on the late, late show, and we wanted the movie to be modern and hip and everything. So we intentionally made it look like a slasher movie. In the ads, there are no mentions of werewolves, and in the movie's beginning it looks like a story about a serial killer. Slowly we sort of snuck in the supernatural elements so that they would be accepted a little more readily by the audience. And then, oddly enough, that year, a whole bunch of other werewolf movies came out. Not just John's, but *Full Moon High* (1981) from Larry Cohen, and *Wolfen* (1981) from Michael Wadleigh.

GK: Did *The Howling* land you *Gremlins* (1984)?

JD: It turns out that Steven Spielberg had seen *The Howling* and cast Dee Wallace in *E.T.* (1982) based on her performance in it. Later, I discovered that he had also been instrumental in keeping Universal from getting an injunction against *Piranha* being released. So he kind of was aware of me. However, when I got the script for *Gremlins* sent to my office, my little cockroach-infested office on El Centro, I thought it was a mistake. I thought he'd sent it to the wrong address. It was a different version of the script – it was written originally as a sample by Chris Columbus that his agent had sent around. Spielberg saw it and at the time his company, Amblin, hadn't been created yet, but he was thinking of starting out with a low-budget horror film.

He wanted to shoot it in Oregon at the Osmond Film Studios for not a big budget – the kind of budget I'd been working with so that was why he sent it to me. During the discussions about *Gremlins*, I was brought on to do an episode in the *Twilight Zone* movie, which Spielberg produced. It turned out that the other guys' episodes were not as well written as mine, and so I got quite a career boost out of the movie. I guess it probably gave Steven more confidence that I would be able to do a good job on *Gremlins*, which was gestating in storyboards and rewrites during that period.

A puppet movie like *Gremlins* had never been attempted. We were having to do the research and development while we were making it. A lot of trial and error. But we did approach it smartly, saying, "Look, we'll shoot the large portion of the part with the actors, then we'll shut down and we'll gear up for the gremlins, and then we'll go back and shoot only a couple of minutes of gremlins." And it was very, very, very grueling to shoot with puppets.

We had a lot of interaction between the actors and the puppets while we shot, but the kind of detail work demanded on this type of project would be impossible to pull off with the crew just sitting around and waiting. So you really had to delegate all that stuff into a later part. We did bring Phoebe Cates back for the bar scene. But for the most part we shot without sound and we just shot gremlins. We shot them in slow motion, we shot them in fast motion, we shot in every speed. Every gremlin had at least three technicians on it, so for crowd scenes all the sets were built on stilts and underneath there was a little community of people looking at their monitors and moving their hands and trying to make the gremlins do something that was recognizably human. And it was quite the talent – it was certainly a talent I didn't have. There were a lot of people there and you got to know them quite well.

GK: I'd like to bring up a few people because we seem to be getting into another formative pe-

Joe Dante's episode in
Twilight Zone: The Movie (1983)

riod where your pool of collaborators is growing. I guess you encountered Jerry Goldsmith on *Twilight Zone*?

JD: Yes, I inherited Jerry, who had the job because he'd done *Poltergeist* (1982) with Spielberg.

GK: And then *Gremlins* was the next thing you made together. I think your collaborations with Jerry are some of the most extraordinary in the recent history of Hollywood movies.

JD: Oh, it's one of the reasons that I've been as successful as I've been: every single movie improved exponentially when Jerry's music went on.

GK: Can you tell me more about what you knew of him and how you worked together?

JD: I had been following Jerry for years. His first score was for a western called *Black Patch* (1957), and I remember noting the score even when I was a little kid. And then I would see his name pop up more and more and by the time he worked for me he was practically a legend. I could never actually quite get over the fact that the guy who made *Hollywood Boulevard* was now working with Jerry Goldsmith. But he was just a great guy – very critical of his own music, very critical of others' music. A bit of a curmudgeon in a way, probably in a Bernard Herrmann-like way. I would frequently use Herrmann in my temp tracks and Jerry would always go, "Ohh! Not Bernie again!"

Because my episode of the *Twilight Zone* was rather odd, Jerry saw it as an opportunity to have some fun. He used wacky Spike Jones kinds of instruments that hadn't been used in a while. A lot of the music that had to be played was re-orchestration of cartoon tracks by Carl Stalling, and these tracks are very fast and modern orchestras couldn't play them fast enough – they'd get lost. And so one of the bits we orchestrated was a piece from a cartoon called *Rabbit Rampage* (1955), and no matter how many times they tried, they would get lost. And it was something we could've used the cartoon track from, but we wanted it in stereo. As a result, it was a pretty wild and woolly session and it was a lot of fun and we really just hit it off and the music he did was great.

When it came time to do the *Gremlins* score, naturally I went to him, even though my previous two pictures had been done by Pino Donaggio, who I also got along great with. It was an interesting collaboration but I could never be there when the music was being recorded, since it was always done in Italy and then sent to me. And so I really enjoyed the collaboration with Jerry because if I needed it faster or I needed it slower or I wanted something different or a different horn or whatever, I could tell him and he could do it. So in that sense, it was much more collaborative than what I'd been able to do with Pino.

I remember going to his studio the first time, and he played me "The Gremlin Rag." This was before he'd gotten into electronics so he would just play it on the piano. The big change you have to make for yourself when you listen to something on the piano is to imagine what it's going to be like when it's orchestrated, a skill I hadn't mastered yet. He played it and I thought it sounded like circus music. So I said, "Are you sure this is what you want to do?" He said, "This is gonna be good, trust me." And of course, it was perfect.

GK: You worked with Goldsmith on eleven projects, including TV shows. How did that relationship change over time?

JD: He went into different phases and by the time we were done with *Gremlins*, he was into a heavy electronic phase. When I did my next picture, *Explorers*, it was all electronics. Toward the end, he was going back a little more toward the orchestral. But there were big gaps when I didn't work with him, where he was doing something else, or we couldn't afford him. And I was lucky enough to get him on his last movie, *Looney Tunes: Back in Action* (2003), which he was unable to finish.

GK: It's still such a beautiful score.

JD: It's a great score. I mean, it's much better than the movie deserves.

GK: How about your collaboration with him on *Matinee* (1993)?

JD: People who don't like that score call it a TV movie score. I think it's evocative of the period. What he didn't want to do was *MANT!* [one of the films-within-the-film in *Matinee*], because he thought it wouldn't be as good as using real tracks from the '50s. The tracks we used were from a 1958 Coral Record that Dick Jacob did of a whole bunch of themes, and it was orchestrated in a particular Universal heavy-on-the-horns way that was actually perfect. And also quite different from the music that Jerry wrote, so that the contrast was much stronger, and better. I think it's one of his best scores for me although it's hard to pick one out because I think they're all terrific, and in their own way they all do so much to help the movies.

GK: It's the mark of a certain progression in your work when you start collaborating with Goldsmith. A similar thing happened with Spielberg and John Williams.

JD: I think I got the best of it.

GK: I agree. How about your collaboration with John Hora, who became your go-to cinematographer?

JD: John Hora was recommended to us on *The Howling* by somebody who had done a nature film with him. We looked at the movie and he had done some beautiful nighttime outdoor photography. When I first met John, his Studebaker was filled with camera equipment and you couldn't get in because there was just no room. Then I went to go visit his house and he actually had to buy the house across the street to store all of his camera equipment. John was and is quite the character. He was really the perfect DP for *The Howling*. It's a gorgeous-looking movie and some of the nighttime stuff looks like Japanese paintings. We got along great. I managed to bring him onto *Gremlins*.

GK: Your stable of regular actors is starting to become apparent at this point. You've got Dick Miller, Robert Picardo, Kevin McCarthy –

JD: I used Kevin in *Piranha*, and *The Howling*, and *Twilight Zone*. Bob I don't think I worked with again until *Explorers* or *Amazing Stories*, whichever came first.

GK: But after that he comes up again throughout your work...

JD: Oh yeah. He's in my most recent *Hawaii Five-0* episode.

GK: Dick Miller's been your most consistent one.

JD: Dick I've had in almost everything.

GK: Whenever your fans see him on screen, they go nuts, like in Chicago when we screened *The Hole* (2009).

JD: It's absolutely the worst part I ever gave him. He was a glorified cutaway. I just needed someone to deliver the pizza. I was gonna do it myself, and then when we had to move part of the shoot back to L. A., I figured this was a good opportunity to get Dick into my picture. And it's so iconic that it's almost like the whole reason to get pizza is so Dick Miller could be in it.

GK: Going back to *Gremlins*, what's apparent now is that you're transitioning from the creative legacy of the '70s, where things kind of opened up in terms of making films for an adult

The Howling
(Dick Miller)

audiences, and *Gremlins* gets into the Reagan era – when you're making movies that are more…

JD: …family-friendly.

GK: Sure, but I don't necessarily want to glue that term to it. I think they give a more ample view of humanity, or it seems like you're growing up, as a person… that your view of the world is changing.

JD: Well, yeah, I should hope. I'm getting older. [*Laughs.*]

GK: Let's talk about *Explorers*.

JD: I was exhausted at the end of making *Gremlins*. The script for *Explorers* seemed to be a simpler movie because it was just these kids who build a spaceship. And I thought, how complicated can that be? Little did I realize what I was in for. It was a much more difficult movie to make than *Gremlins* had been, largely because the studio changed hands while we were cutting *Explorers* and they decided that they didn't need it to be finished; they just needed it to be released. And so we stopped. This was a very ambitious movie that we were finding in the editing room. I mean, there were a lot of aspects of the picture that just never made it into the movie because we literally froze where we were. And then we had a preview of the frozen version during which the audience completely turned off and just didn't want to see any more. And so the studio said, "Just dump it." So they opened it the day of the Live Aid concert when nobody went to the movies. They had an ad that looked like tar paper. And they had really no vested interest in it making money because it was the prior regime's movie. It was a tremendous bomb. And the ad line was, "From the director of *Gremlins*." It was disappointing to say the least. Because I did think that there was a good movie in there and I don't think that we were able to find it. I think that the last half of the movie just doesn't go anywhere. But people like it. People come up to me and say, "I saw the movie, I thought it was wonderful."

GK: It made a huge impact on me when I was a kid.

JD: Well, it's just that when you look up at the screen and what you see isn't what you intended, and it's not even because you weren't good enough to do it, it's just because they didn't give you the time… it's just a missed opportunity.

GK: But in a climate where you have *Porky's* (1982) and *Goonies* (1985), it's still a miracle that *Explorers* can exist. I recall you saying that *Innerspace* (1987) was your best experience.

JD: Up to then it certainly was. It was the most fun movie I ever made. The straight spy-fi script of what became *Innerspace* was written by Chip Proser. It was offered to me by [producer] Peter Guber after the success of *Gremlins*, but I didn't think it worked and took *Explorers* instead. Later I learned it had been rewritten as a comedy by Jeff Boam, and I read it and loved it. The concept was, "What if Dean Martin had been shrunk down and put inside Jerry Lewis?" But despite my earlier involvement, Steven Spielberg planned to get Robert Zemeckis to direct it. When he turned it down as too similar to *Back to the Future* (1985), I re-inherited it.

Starting from the failure of *Explorers* and remembering a comment made by my friend Scot Holton, who told me that I had to stop making films just for "us," I thought of *Innerspace* as my "mainstream commercial" movie, the one that would allow me to recapitalize on my *Gremlins* success. But when I was done with the film, it was just as bizarre and wacky as my other stuff. It played well in sneak previews but the studio created a hopeless ad campaign featuring a giant fingernail and no hint that it was a comedy. It flopped.

Still, this was probably the most rewarding experience I'd had up to that time, as I was left pretty much alone to fashion the tone. Martin Short and Dennis Quaid were perfect foils for each other, aided by a sound setup that allowed them to improvise throughout despite not being onscreen together. It was just so much fun working with that cast, in San Francisco, which is just a great place to make a movie. It's so photogenic and every time you turn around there's another great angle. And ILM's incredible pre-CGI interior body FX deservedly won an Academy Award. It's one of the few movies I'm completely satisfied with, even though it runs nearly two hours, awfully long for a comedy.

GK: I wanted to touch on something that I see happening in your films at this point. *Gremlins, Explorers,* and *Innerspace* all have a sentimental side and an emotional core to them that's not present in your earlier, more adult-oriented work. Maybe you're starting to connect back to your childhood?

JD: My inner child? That's that sense of wonder thing.

GK: It's obviously the maturation period of your work, when that sentiment begins to show up and climaxes with something like *Matinee*. Would you agree with that assessment?

JD: I think that makes sense. It's not the way I would have put it. But I wouldn't have put it.

GK: If you had to put it, how would you put it?

JD: If I was as introspective as I apparently should be, I would have a take on this. But for

Explorers

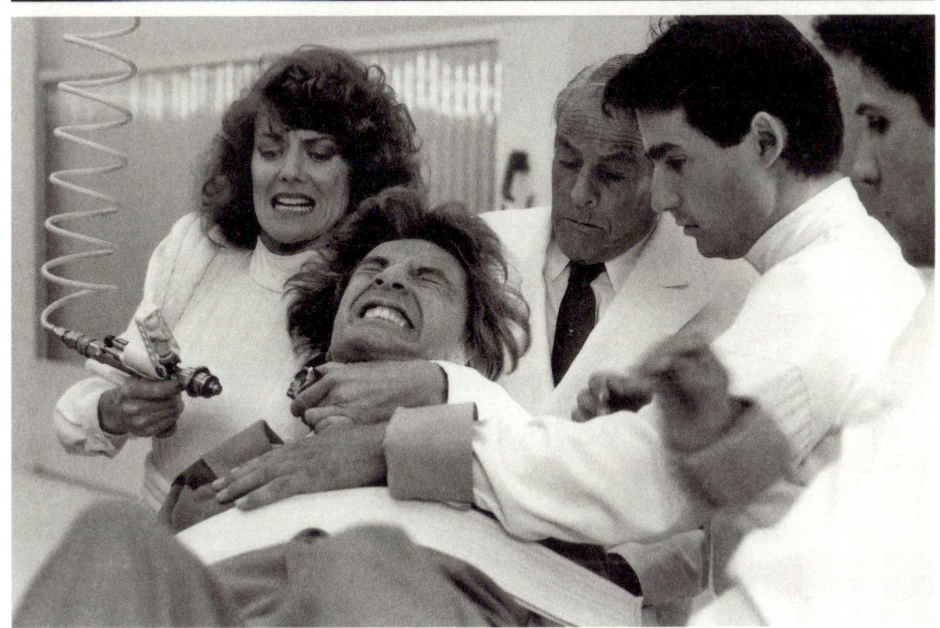

Innerspace (1987)

Ethan Hawke and Joe Dante
on the set of *Explorers*

me, the way that you evolve making movies is almost directly connected with the movies that you're allowed to make. And in-between the movies that I did make, there were always movies that I wanted to make, or tried to make, or worked on. The fact that they didn't happen affects you and turns the experience of making the movie that *does* happen into something different than it would have been. There were a lot of wrong turns and things that didn't quite happen. I was supposed to make an Italian western at one point called *Pizza and Tomahawks* with Luciano Vincenzoni, the guy who co-wrote *For a Few Dollars More* (1965). And Giancarlo Giannini was going to be in it. That didn't happen; there's just a lot of things that don't happen. And sometimes you invest a lot of yourself in them and then you discover that all of that enthusiasm has to be directed somewhere else that you may or may not be as connected to but that may have at least produced a movie.

GK: It's always interesting for an outsider to hear all of that because when I started to ap- proach your films intellectually there already existed a critical body of work around it. There were all these people – Kehr, Rosenbaum, Krohn – who were helping me appreciate your work as a sort of exception to the Hollywood blockbuster period that was so disappointing to so many of us for many reasons, and suddenly there was a saving grace, someone who could prove to us that Hollywood movies could be thoughtful and say something and that there were real ideas coming out of them, and you were one of the few. And so largely, for some- one like me who appreciates movies in that way, your career is an incredibly rich and suc- cessful one, despite all these things that you're saying were failures or didn't come out or that you had to adapt around. I know you've said that Dave Kehr was the only person who wrote a positive review of *The 'Burbs* (1989).

JD: It's true.

GK: Nowadays I find it hard to believe that was the critical climate of the time.

JD: That was the critical climate around *Explor- ers* too. It came out at the tail end of a whole spate of kid science movies and the reviewers were sick and tired of these pictures. It was like when Jonathan Kaplan made *Truck Turner* (1974), which is one of the best black exploitation movies – it happened to come at the very end of the cycle and it got pilloried. But in fact when you look back at it, it was one of the best ones they had done. But people couldn't see that because they were just inundated with the same things over and over. There were just so many and they were so similar.

GK: You get caught up in the werewolf wave with *The Howling,* then kid science wave with *Explorers…*

JD: Yeah, I missed the mermaid wave. [*Laughs*]

GK: At this point, you've already got a couple of TV things under your belt.

JD: Not many. I was asked to do *Police Squad!* (1982), which was my first television show and my first union job. And that was fun because I did it for the Zucker brothers, who I knew. And that show was a complete disaster. It went off after six episodes. The audience couldn't figure out that it was supposed to be a comedy because it didn't have a laugh track. And it was meticulously designed to look like a '60s TV show. So when they clicked the channel, and here was Leslie Nielsen on a '60s crime show, they just went, "Pfft!" and turned it off. They didn't even stay to see that it was supposed to be funny. And it's really clever – it's much better than the *Naked Gun* movies.

The next one was *Amazing Stories* (1985–87), which was less fun, although interesting. Spielberg had sold NBC on the idea of doing a series, I think largely because he wanted to use it as a jumping-off point to try out new talent. He did the pilot himself, and every episode cost, I think, a million dollars. It's probably the most overproduced half-hour in television history. The shows all looked great and the sets they built were so substantial that you could live in them. But the problem with the show was that Spielberg would come up with a gimmick and he would tell the writers what it was and they would slavishly follow that gimmick to the point where 10 minutes into the show you knew how it was going to end. So the bromide became, you could hear more amazing stories waiting in line at the post office than you could on the show.

From my point of view, I did an episode ["Boo!"] that Lowell Ganz and Babaloo Mandel had written, and I did it just because everybody was doing one. And the fun part was I got to work with Eddie Bracken and Evelyn Keyes and also to put Bob Picardo in as a sleazy film-maker. It was the first time I'd ever worked with Wendy Schaal, who was recommended by Bob, and who came in and made up this terrible song that she sang badly. And also it was very sexy. So it was a no-brainer. I got them to hire Bruce Davison, who I had always wanted to work with, and Andrea Marcovicci, who I knew slightly. It was a lot of fun, a really good cast, a pretty insubstantial story, a ghost story, but it was okay.

And then I came back the next season to do one that Steven was supposed to do, called "The Greibble," about a mom who throws away her kid's storybook and the storybook monster comes back. To me, this would have worked better with comic books than storybooks. I wasn't comfortable with a storybook at all. Because moms always throw out comic books but they don't really often throw out storybooks. Anyway, Hayley Mills was in it, and she was a lot of fun, and Rob Bottin had designed the monster. Because it was Rob, and he had done it for Steven originally, they were inclined to indulge and the episode went twice over the budget it was supposed to be. Took forever to shoot. Mick Garris wrote it. It suffered from not being comic books, I thought. And it was another one of the *Amazing Stories*.

Now, concurrently to *Amazing Stories* there was a *Twilight Zone* (1985–89) revival, which was done very, very cheaply. I did one for them called "The Shadow Man," which was about this shadow man who lives under your bed and he won't kill you but he'll kill everybody – I can't remember what the plot was. And it was interesting because you had to do it for really, really, really cheap. You had to make it look like this guy was literally a shadow. And I think Phillip Baker Hall did the voice and it was pretty good. It turned out much better, oddly enough, than either of my *Amazing Stories* simply because it was an imaginative idea that didn't wear out its welcome and it wasn't overproduced.

GK: And *Police Squad!*?

JD: *Police Squad!* was fast but no faster than a Corman. That was okay. The only problem with *Police Squad!* was that the Zuckers would come in and say, "Oh, we just thought of a better joke." And you'd say, "But I have to reshoot the reverse if I do that." Earlier the Zuckers had offered me *Airplane!* (1980) and I turned it down. One of the dumbest things I ever did.

GK: Wow. Can we talk about some of the other things you turned down? One of the famous anecdotes is that you were in contention for *Jurassic Park* (1993).

JD: Oh yeah. Each studio had a different director. I think it was me and Richard Donner and

Amazing Stories set

– was it Tim Burton? I can't remember, but there were four of us and each of us had it for a different studio and Michael Crichton called and talked to us on the phone. He gave it to Spielberg – big surprise! – who could give him a theme park. Also, I thought it was a mistake not to have the Richard Attenborough character be a villain.

GK: Backtracking a bit, it's interesting that you didn't have a good experience on *Explorers*. One would think, conventionally speaking, that you would be pretty free after making a $200 million box office hit with *Gremlins*…

JD: I gotta be fair: they did not hold me up while I was making the movie. The only problem was that they wanted it at a certain time. Jeffrey Katzenberg had said, "Wouldn't it be nice if it could come out in the summer?" This was in October and we hadn't started shooting yet.

We went on the sets, they weren't dry… we would sink into the cement. It was cobbled together to go as fast as possible. So in that sense, it was a harried project. Part of it was shot on location in Santa Rosa (where Hitchcock's *Shadow of a Doubt* [1943] was shot). And we had to find the kids and you couldn't work with kids for very long. And Bob Picardo was in this monstrous make-up that was so difficult to apply and was so heavy to wear that part of his performance is exasperation. And in fact when he tried to recreate the performance on a sound looping stage, he couldn't do it.

You've got to remember the one hit – *Gremlins* was my hit. This is the movie that I'm coasting on, as far as the rest of these pictures are concerned. I only did make a hit once. *Explorers* didn't hurt my career but didn't exactly help it. Obviously if I had made *Batman* (1989), which I was offered and also turned down, I would've had a different career, maybe a more remunerative one.

GK: Why did you turn down *Batman*?

JD: I considered doing it. I read Tom Mankiewicz's James Bond-ish script. I loved The Joker and had planned on casting John Lithgow for the part. But then I woke up in the middle of the night and said to myself, "I don't believe in Batman. I don't believe this guy wears a cap and lives up on a hill. I don't buy that. I believe in The Joker." I went to Lucy Fisher at Warner Bros. and said, "Lucy, I can't do this." And she said, *"What?"* They all looked at me like I'd lost my senses. And I said, "I can't do this. Somebody who believes in Batman has to do this picture. I don't believe in Batman. I believe in The Joker. If you want to do a movie starring The Joker, I'm your guy. But I don't think I can do this picture." And I swear, they were gonna have me committed.

GK: Did your agent want to kill you?

JD: Everybody wanted to kill me. Even Bob Kane wanted to kill me. I ended up doing *Explorers* instead, which was probably a more personal movie for me but not nearly what my career needed at the moment.

GK: I think that's really remarkable, especially given the way the Batman franchise has evolved. I don't know what you think about the Christopher Nolan incarnation of it, but I find it ideologically appalling.

JD: Ideologically, it's very unfortunate, yes.

GK: But in one way, that's part of what you were rejecting, right?

JD: Yeah, the vigilantism. But I've had ethical issues before.

GK: It doesn't sound like you were made for Hollywood.

JD: No, it certainly doesn't, does it?

GK: Yet, you did manage to make several more films within that system.

JD: Well, I think the achievement is staying in the business in whatever way you can manage.

GK: How did you approach *The 'Burbs*?

JD: They approached me. They had a script that was titled "Bay Window" and said, "We have a Hitchcock parody." I read it and thought, "Yeah, right, a Hitchcock parody – a guy looks out a window and suddenly it's a Hitchcock parody?" But it was intriguing to me personally because I had weird neighbors when I was a kid. I remember there was a house on the block that everybody always thought was full of weird people. The studio said the director originally assigned to the project wanted to do it for real in a suburb in Arizona or something like that. I said, as I had with the *Gremlins* script, "This can't be too realistic. You can't take these gremlins out and put them on a street corner and plop them down and expect it to look good." *Gremlins* had to be a stylized movie, we had to shoot it like an old-fashioned Hollywood backlot movie, and that's how it's gonna work – and it did. And this was the same thing – this was a stylized movie, this was not a realistic picture.

The studio had an issue with the writers' strike coming up and they wanted to make the

The 'Burbs (1989)

movie before a certain date. The most unlikely place in Hollywood right now was the new Universal backlot: they had taken the old one and had it moved up the hill – they'd moved all of these disparate houses from different movies and different periods and put them all together. *The Munsters* house is next to the house from *Harvey* (1950), which is next to the House of Seven Gables, and the Beaver Cleaver house. And now they're all together on one street. What's more, it's not even a street – it's a cul-de-sac. There's no backyards, it just falls off because it's a hill. I said, "It's really unreal but it looks real, it looks *movie real*. So I think we should shoot there." I got together with an art director friend of mine and we figured out a way to revamp the street and make it look like what we needed for the time we had. We shot it in the summer of '88. Just us, and the raccoons and the deer up there. Our raccoons.

Once we got Tom Hanks, we had Carrie Fisher, Bruce Dern, and Henry Gibson, and all these people who were pretty good. We told them that there's probably going to be a lot of improv here – because the writers' strike was on, we couldn't have the writer on the set to work. He was in the picture as an actor but he couldn't work with the director. So we said, let's shoot the picture in sequence so that if any ad-libs come along, if anyone wants to go into a different direction with their character, we can incorporate it into the story. And they agreed. To me it was a character piece and it was a behavioral movie. There's really not a lot of substance to the story but there *is* a lot of substance to the characters and the way they interact with each other.

We shot it and previewed it at Universal and they were laughing all the way through the movie. And then, just towards the end, someone shouted, "Boring!" and all of a sudden it was a bad preview. It just took one guy and it was a bad preview. So they lost faith in the movie completely and started to think that they could rewrite it so that Rick Ducommun's character was the killer and not the Klopeks. This was Ron Howard's idea. I said, "What?" And he said, "No, no, just watch the movie and just watch how suspicious he looks all throughout the movie." So we're watching the movie and he's eating food out of people's refrigerators and he's doing all this stuff that his character does. At no place does he look ominous or anything like that. And halfway through the movie they gave up that idea.

But we did, nonetheless, hire a bunch of writers, wrote a bunch of endings. We shot two of them, one of which had the trunk full of

Joe Dante and Tom Hanks
on the *'Burbs* set

cheerleaders and the other full of garbagemen. And then we ended up just using skulls. But the way it originally ended was that the Tom Hanks character is taken away by the Klopeks and it turns out he was right all along, they're crazy and they're going to kill him. As soon as they cast Tom they said, "You can't kill Tom Hanks." Okay. So now you have to explain all the stuff these people have been doing in the movie, which has been carefully constructed so that it doesn't have to be explained. We came up with some bogus, ridiculous explanation for what they've been doing with skulls and [*blows raspberry*].

Anyway, the picture came out and it was a modest success. Terrible reviews. But it has become this huge cult movie. And people love the movie – they quote it, they have websites devoted to it, they have screenings where they do the dialogue. And yet, it was basically considered a disaster when it came out. Vincent Canby wrote in the *New York Times* that it was

"as empty as a movie can be without actually creating a vacuum."

GK: The legend is that they gave you the keys to the palace with *Gremlins 2: The New Batch* (1990). Is that true?

JD: Well, it was the keys to the palace in the sense that they had been trying vainly to make a sequel to the picture for years. But they never liked the picture; they didn't really get it. When they first saw it, they said, "It's full of gremlins – it's full of these horrible gremlins blowing their nose on the curtains. It's disgusting." And Spielberg said, [*deadpans*] "Well, we can cut out all of the gremlins and call it 'People.'" I mean, it was what it was, and Steven to his credit stood by me and said, "It's his movie, it should be released the way he wants." And he had a lot of issues with things early on in the movie, he wanted to cut Dick Miller practically out of the movie, but he was ultimately OK with it.

So they come back to me and Mike Finnell and say, "We know that you must've had something to do with the success of the first picture because we can't figure out a way to make a sequel. And we really want one next summer. So if you guys will give us a movie by summer 1990," – and now there was nothing written, nothing – "you can do whatever you want." So we proceeded to do whatever we wanted. It was an assignment from them, but it really came directly from us. We hired Charlie Haas, who I'd known for years but don't think I'd ever worked with, and we came up with a new concept where the gremlins are in New York, and there's a smart building and all that stuff. We got it passed by everybody. Steven wanted to add a Sgt. Rock, an army guy who would come in and storm the building, but that didn't eventually pan out.

And so they let us spend $32 million to build a gigantic set for this ridiculous mall.

GK: $32 million doesn't sound like a lot anymore.

JD: Now it wouldn't be, but it was a lot then, considering the first one actually cost $11 million. The best thing about it was that the technology had changed so now we could have the gremlins doing things we could only imagine before: they could talk, fly, they can do all this stuff… We wanted Rick Baker to sign on, since Chris Walas had now become a director, and

he said, "I don't want to do a picture where I'm gonna have to work on someone else's designs." And I said, "If we create a genetics lab, then we can invent all kinds of new gremlins and you can design those." So we got Rick. It was a lot of fun to make, really, because we felt like we were being supported. They weren't being unduly critical about what we were doing because they couldn't be…

It was a very unconventional studio movie and probably my most Tashlinesque. Unfortunately, after coming to us and saying that they were so desperate for a particular date, they were faced with a summer where Warren Beatty's *Dick Tracy* (1990) was coming out and the scuttlebutt was that it was going to open bigger than *Batman*, which was Warner Bros.' biggest opening. They didn't want this to happen. *Gremlins 2* was scheduled for Memorial Day and there were ads already running. The studio called me in the projection room when I was timing the movie and said, "We've decided to move the opening to July 4th." I said, "July 4th is when *Dick Tracy* is coming out!" And they said, "*Dick Tracy* isn't tracking well with young kids." I said, "They're going to kill us. We've got no movie stars and they've got all the movie stars in Hollywood for this picture. It's a surefire property and even if it isn't a good

Gremlins 2: The New Batch
(1990)

movie it's going to be very successful. It's got Madonna in it, for Christ's sake." Basically they threw us under the bus so they could lower *Dick Tracy*'s opening gross. It didn't make the kind of money that a $32 million movie needs to make and was judged a flop. Which was very vexing. Every audience I saw it with thought it was hilarious.

GK: Maybe audiences weren't ready for it. It's such an anarchic non-story. And it's set in a much different media landscape than the first *Gremlins*.

JD: *Gremlins 2* is a movie about the coming decade. It's almost a futuristic movie in the sense that one of the gags is that there's all these cable channels dedicated to things like archery, which at the time was a hilarious idea. Now I'm sure there is an archery channel somewhere. But this was back before the huge explosion of television channels. The whole corporate plot of the movie, the whole idea of the smart building and all the futuristic devices like the videophone looked very cutting-edge. Now they just fit into the movie in a crazy pattern that doesn't seem that dated because it's set in a cartoon world – it's almost *Brazil*-like.

There was a part where the gremlins just keep changing the channels and it's like *The Movie Orgy* and all of a sudden there are these tiny muscleman movies…

GK: In *Matinee*, your next film, the theme of watching films represents almost the opposite of *Gremlins 2*. *Matinee* depicts kids who have not advanced into the age of passivity, of channel surfing: it's a world where movies can still make a lasting impression. Was it strange to go back to that idea?

JD: The genesis of *Matinee* was that I was at Warner Bros. and this writer had a script about a haunted movie theater playing a movie called *MANT!* It started with the kids as adults visiting the site of the theater, which is now a video store. Basically it was a sort of phantasmagoria where the projectionist is a vampire and there's a matron who's a hulky sort of scary character. It was more of a *Little Rascals* story, or Bowery Boys. We couldn't get that made anywhere, so I brought in a writer named Ed Naha, who's a friend of mine, and rejiggered the idea of the horror movie star who comes to the theater for his personal appearance. And that still didn't quite work. The issue was that we were trying to get the picture made at Warner Bros., and they funded Ed's draft of it, and it was just not something that they were ready to do yet. I think this was probably after I *hadn't* made *Termite Terrace*, my film based on Chuck Jones and

other animators, for them. We found international investors for *Matinee* who claimed that they would put up most of the money if Universal would distribute it, so at that point we had a deal. We brought in Charlie Haas and did a complete turnaround on what the movie was supposed to be about and came up with the Cuban missile crisis angle. That's where John Goodman's Lawrence Woolsey character came in, taking his very-unlikely-in-1962 giant insect movie to a preview in Key West, Florida, the same weekend. That seemed to give it some heft. It also added a lot of autobiographical stuff to the movie because I was exactly the same age as the kids during the Cuban missile crisis when we all thought the world was going to end. A lot of my personal feelings about that era – not to mention props and monster magazines and drawings – were all transferred over to the characters. It became this rather odd, not-really-a-genre-movie but it has a lot of genre elements in it and it's a coming-of-age story, I guess.

GK: The dream sequence is incredibly vivid and violent…

JD: Yeah, but that's the way we were really thinking. It seems so remote now but it was really very palpable.

GK: Where did that image come from?

JD: Of the H-bomb? That's a dream I think kids have. I mean, it was a nightmare and you didn't want to think about it much. But when you went to one of these movies that are all about Geiger counters and stuff, it kept reminding you that this could actually happen. And the surrogate atomic bomb monsters that are wrecking things – it's pretty blatant. I mean, *Godzilla* (1954) is a very poignant and moving picture, even in its American version. The fact that it became sort of a joke is interesting because as we became more remote from those feelings, it was easier to caricature. But at the time, the metaphor was inescapable.

GK: Can you talk about the last shot of the movie?

JD: That's not the original ending. The original ending was that the kids walk on the beach and they have some dialogue. We shot it but it wasn't very good. When it came time to end the movie, we filmed an extra scene with John Goodman and Cathy Moriarty in a car driving away, and we got a Sikorsky helicopter – the kind they used in Vietnam – as they went down to San Diego. In my view, a lot of those kids don't make it to adulthood – they end up in the Army and they end up going to Vietnam.

GK: It's so beautifully eloquent because it's not narrated.

JD: It was a very powerful image and I think a great way to end the movie. Without it, it isn't as good of a movie.

GK: I think it's your greatest ending. It's a real heartbreaker. And the music over the end credits…

JD: "The Lion Sleeps Tonight," which is Vietnam-era music.

GK: There's a gentleness to the movie, and then the violence of the social experience of the war and the Cuban missile crisis. It's such an interesting tone that you don't see in a lot of movies.

JD: Well, that's been my problem: tone. Ever since the president of AVCO Embassy looked at the first day's rushes of *The Howling*, which was the Dick Miller bookstore scene, he said, "Is this a horror movie or a comedy?" And I've also heard the phrase, "We're saving you from yourself." The tone of what it is that I'm doing is just inexplicable to some people that I work for, because it isn't any one thing – it's a mixture of things. Depending on what part of the mixture you're focusing on, it sometimes seems that the other part of it doesn't belong. I feel like I've lost jobs because of that.

GK: *Matinee* would seem to indicate the end of a certain period in your career.

JD [*Laughs*]: It was the end of the period where I got final cut, that's for sure.

GK: Right. And so you're migrating back to TV at that moment, you're between making studio features.

JD: I didn't think of *Matinee* as a studio picture at all. It turned out to be one but I thought of it as an indie. It really looks and breathes like an indie.

GK: I'd like to return to *Termite Terrace*.

JD: They did not want to do a serious movie about the people who made Warner Bros. cartoons. They wanted to do a silly movie, and so they did *Space Jam* (1996) instead.

Matinee (1993)

Chuck Jones had his story of how he got to Warner Bros. in the early '30s and started as a cell washer and worked his way up and all that, with all these colorful characters – Tex Avery and Bob Clampett and all those guys. Chuck wrote a memoir and Charlie Haas, Mike Finnell and I thought it might make a really good script. The names were changed, although obviously Chuck was the hero.

GK: Not even Chuck was named?

JD: No, we made up fake names, since it allowed us to go off topic and make up other stuff. So, Steven Spielberg read it and said, "This is a terrific script, what can I do to help you?" We got to a certain point with it and couldn't get any further because they just did not want to bring their characters back as extras in the story about somebody else. The merchandising department, as often happens at Warner Bros., wanted something to be able to merchandise these characters. So they made *Space Jam* and Chuck was appalled by it.

Termite Terrace is still a wonderful script. They own it, no one else can make it. Never, ever initiate projects based on characters you don't own – moral of that story. But it really would've been a good movie.

GK: *The Second Civil War* (1997) was a good deal for you.

JD: I think Barry Levinson was going to direct that picture and then he got interested in *Wag the Dog* (1997) and was probably afraid they were too similar. But he had a deal to make this one, so I got a call and read it, and at that point the script was like 200 pages long, like, really long. And it was very, very dense. Lots of characters. Lots of stuff – there was this huge wall of TV screens that played a major part and it was just impossible to imagine how you could pay for it on an HBO budget. Around this time, HBO was doing a bit of the politically-minded pictures. And because of their prestige, they could round up good casts without a great deal of money. So we worked on the script, shortened it, and tried to focus it a little more, and even so the movie I came up with was about two hours long and I had to cut 20 minutes out of it.

What was fascinating about making *The Second Civil War* was that every day we would read a news item and it would be something that was part of our movie. And the movie came out and it didn't make much of a splash. The picture really caught on when it played overseas theatrically. It came out on video but it was like a total secret – nobody knew. So it's not a very well-known movie. But whenever I go to festivals or retrospectives, I always ask

Joe Dante on the oval office
set of *The Second Civil War*

them to run it. Every time I see it, some different aspect of the movie is in the news. Whether it's spare parts for jeeps or immigration – whatever it is, the movie has had the longest shelf life of any topical picture I ever did. Everything that was wrong with the country is still wrong with it, if not more. The character types and the politics of it are never gonna change. Also, what I like about the picture is that there really aren't any villains in it, that everybody has their own reason for doing what they do and they think it's for a good cause, and as completely wrongheaded as they may be we never present them as caricatures.

GK: Aside from *The Howling* and *Piranha*, are there any real villains in your films?

JD: Certainly in *Piranha* there's villains. I don't even know if *The Howling* has villains. Who are the villains? The werewolves? They think they're justified. Villains? Well, you know, Daniel Clamp in *Gremlins 2* started out to be a villain but then he wasn't. I don't know, I guess

there really aren't any black hat guys in most of my movies. There's people I disapprove of.

GK: They all have their reasons.

JD: They all have their reasons, it's true.

GK: One of the most remarkable scenes in *The Second Civil War* is when you present the two newscasters, in two shot, with one following the script and the other saying, "I can't fucking believe this right now," and she goes off and has a cigarette and comes back. It reminds me of 9/11, when anchors just couldn't believe what they were seeing.

JD: There's a lot of missing subplots from the movie and one of them is about her. My favorite thing that we lost was a scene with Archie Hahn interviewing a woman who has been genitally mutilated. It's in front of the little wooden church in the Warner Bros. backlot because it's supposed to be Connecticut or something (because Connecticut now has a huge Muslim population). And there's this free-for-all where the Muslims are yelling at each

The Second Civil War (1997)

other and this woman is trying to get her story out. And it absolutely had nothing to do with the rest of the movie so it had to come out. I have an outtake reel somewhere in a vault.

GK: Following *The Second Civil War*, you embark on a studio picture that also manages to be fiercely political.

JD: Yeah, *Small Soldiers* (1998). I was one of the few people in Hollywood who do that kind of thing. Adam Rifkin had written a script that didn't get made. They'd been thinking about it for a long time, and then Stan Winston came aboard and he was going to make these puppets and it was going to be a kind of *Gremlin*-ish movie. Which is why they came to me – I thought of it as *Gremlins 3* while making it. The problem turned out to be – and I'd encountered this with *The Second Civil War* – that I didn't really have the control I wanted. It was a contentious relationship with the guy that was my superior and we went at it and the writer backed them, not me, which I thought was a suicidally stupid thing to do.

Amblin – this was not your father's Amblin anymore; this was DreamWorks. Steven had stepped away a bit from the kind of control he used to exert and he said to me when we started, "Don't come to me unless you absolutely have to." I was also admonished that for the picture to work it had to appeal to older teenagers. Because, as ["B" movie producer] Sam Arkoff once observed, a younger child will watch anything an older child will watch, but an older child will not watch anything a younger child will watch. So you have to try to go for the older kid in order to get the other kids. All of which was working fine, we're shooting the picture, and then Burger King wanted to do merchandizing. Merchandizing meant that the picture had to have a PG rating, or G, which would have been even better. The violence level had to be quite low. Here I am, making an edgy picture about kids putting toys down the sink and dismembering them, and I'm told that's not something we should do. There was a lot of tension about that. And then there was the fact that the script was constantly being rewritten while we shot. A lot of it was written on set by me and the script supervisor, Kathy Zatarga, because stuff just didn't make sense. No one seemed to know exactly what they wanted and it was technically a very complicated movie to make. Stan's puppets were very nicely designed and worked-over, and we assumed that we were gonna be doing a lot of puppetry. When it actually came time to shoot, it became apparent that the technology was not there yet to remove the puppeteers from the frame (as it is now). There were a lot of compromises you had to make to get these puppets to do anything (walk, jump, etc.) When they stood there, they were fine: they could be manipulated very well and we were very lucky in the fact that they were toys and they didn't have to look smooth or believable. We ended up, on more occasions than not, saying, "Take the puppet out, photograph the background, and send it to Industrial Light & Magic." In the end, 60% of the movie was CGI where 60% was gonna be puppets.

GK: That was your first experience with CGI, right?

JD: I did a commercial for Mars Bars employing CGI just because I wanted to see how to work with the new technology. So when I got to *Small Soldiers*, I had some background on it and it was easy to figure out how to do it. Now, I'm not so sure that the direction I took with the story was something they were approving or even aware of. But to me, the message of the story was just because a guy has a uniform, that doesn't make him a good guy. And just because a guy looks a little funny, that doesn't make him a bad guy. I thought this was an appropriate message for kids, if maybe a little subversive. But otherwise, the tone of the movie is pretty light. There's another corporate villain, played by Denis Leary, who's maybe a villain, maybe not.

In the end, we found ourselves doing things like shooting a scene where the puppets are lying on the ground and there are people with hazmat suits and they're picking them up like they're radioactive. And the kid who's in the movie said, "I don't understand this – I mean, if these guys need radiation suits, how is it that this scene is at the end of the movie? Shouldn't I be dead?" Once again, nobody had thought about it. So I sent the hazmat suits home and I shot the scene without that. I got in tremendous trouble for doing that because anytime I didn't do what they told me to do, they would get very angry with me. So it wasn't a very happy experience making the movie. I mean, I liked the kids – I thought the kids were great and I was happy with the cast and everything, but the tone was a little broader than I probably would have liked. Just working with Ernest Borgnine on the voice for his character was hilarious – such a funny guy.

GK: What I hear a lot from you is that you're always making compromises, but in the end you're getting things in that are little victories.

JD: And I think that's every filmmaker's story now – how much can you get past the gate?

GK: In a way it's the trajectory of an old studio

Small Soldiers (1998)

director more than a filmmaker today who might make a film more independently with fewer means.

JD: Well, the fewer means you have, the more freedom you have. As soon as you're spending money, you get all sorts of people interested in what you're spending it on. "Is this really what we want? Is everybody gonna love it? Are we gonna make a fortune?" I'm not knocking these concerns; I think these are reasons why people make movies. But that's not why I make movies. I make movies because I want to be able to express myself, and if I can't, then what am I doing here? People like Jonathan Rosenbaum have written very nice things on *Small Soldiers* and obviously some of the things I intended are there. I don't know if it made Steven very happy to read that it was a better picture than *Saving Private Ryan* (1998).

GK: We're up to *Looney Tunes: Back in Action* (2003) – there's five years in-between there.

JD: Five years in the wilderness. Now what was I doing?

GK: You're probably developing *Looney Tunes*.

JD: No, that's the interesting thing. They came to me with *Looney Tunes*. It was a script, it was already by the same guy and it was, I thought, a little rocky. I certainly didn't find it funny. But Chuck had passed away and I thought I really shouldn't let somebody do to those characters what had been done to them in *Space Jam*. I thought I have to be true to them and try to save them from Warner Bros. So I said, all right, I'll work on this.

GK: This is a very novel concept! A filmmaker coming in and saving a studio from itself.

JD: You know, *Space Jam* actually made a lot of money because of Michael Jordan. So this was not considered that far out then. They figure this is a license to print money. Which I think is probably one of the reasons they were willing to go with a script that didn't really have any

Small Soldiers set

jokes in it. There were a lot of studio politics involved and one of the studio people left and was replaced by another… Basically, what happened was that it was a very, very expensive movie.

GK: $100 million.

JD: More. They won't cop to the actual figure but it was quite a bit. They were willing to spend whatever they needed to get this movie done, that was never in question.

Creatively, there were two factions at the studio: one is the merchandising department and one is the actual people who make the movies. The merchandising department wanted this movie. The regular studio people were less taken with the idea. In fact, it was a movie supervised by people who would never cross the street to see it. And that is a problem when you're making something like this.

We shot for six months and we edited for a year. It was a movie they never really had much faith in to begin with and the first time we showed it to them, the reaction was, "We can't tell what this is. Just fix it." We might as well have run blank film for them.

Twenty-five writers ultimately worked on this picture, writing gags just to stick in when someone turns their back.

GK: How many worked on *Gremlins 2*?

JD: One.

GK: Just one gag writer for the whole movie?

JD: One movie, one writer.

At a certain point, the regular writer on *Looney Tunes* had pissed so many people off that he was kind of dispensed with, so they had these other people coming in. The same writer was trying to launch a series of new Warner Bros. cartoon shorts, which he was basically in charge of. He had this whole writing room full of people, gag people, and he produced, I think, ten shorts. None of which were ever released. They just had no faith in the movie. They mentioned this Academy Award-winning writer and they said they were gonna have him come in because he was a friend of theirs and he was going to fix it. So we go in a room with a big oak table and a TV down at the other end and all these executives with their pads and they're all gonna make notes. The picture starts and Mr. Academy Award-winning screenwriter has the remote. Bugs Bunny comes out and says, "What's up, Doc?" He pauses. "Stop! Does he have to say that?" That was only the first scene.

So we finish the movie. I went to the preview, which was a very elaborate affair at the Chinese Theater with the sound jacked up, you couldn't believe it. And I just slumped in my chair for 90 minutes thinking, "This is the kind of movie that I don't like. And I just made one. I just made it. It's got my name on it, and I don't like this kind of movie." It moves so fast that you can't get your bearings as to what's going on and it's the theory of, "Well, if you don't like this, something else is gonna come along." And my animation director, Eric Goldberg, was absolutely heroic on this movie, in the way he managed to be true to the characters, animate and voice them in way that I think match the late '40s and early '50s era, while being berated everyday by the producers and the writer. Insulted, even. It was a toxic work situation. In spite of the artists, storyboard, and effects people who really loved the idea of the movie and wanted it to be good, and really wanted to be able to contribute to it, there was just no way that it was going to come out as anything other than a mishmash of half-baked ideas that didn't bake.

GK: At the same time, it has glorious moments. The paintings, the Area 52…

JD: Area 52 was an early casualty because they *hated* that. They hated that more than anything. I don't know why they hated it so much. And so they made me shoot another replacement scene with Pepe LePew where they go to Paris. We previewed both versions and the reaction was exactly the same, so I said, "Being a director, I would prefer if you would release the movie with my name on it with my scene in it, you know?" And they begrudgingly grumbled and all of that. But also, it has a different beginning, a different middle, and a different ending. And they never previewed the movie. This is the thing that kills me. Because of the kind of picture it is and because of the fact that it's not finished-looking, they never showed it to anyone. Only themselves. And every single opinion they had on the movie was based on watching it in an empty room. With no audience. No feedback, no kids, nothing.

GK: I guess it's almost miraculous that the movie contains a pretty strong commentary on the idiocy of studios.

JD: The funny thing was, to their credit, that they didn't care about that. That wasn't on their radar. "If you wanna make fun of us, that's okay, do it, we don't care." But the fact that they wouldn't let the people they hired to do the job do their job is emblematic of what's wrong with the business today. Because this is not an isolated incident. This is an expensive incident. So many movies that come out have no bearing on what was originally intended. Hence the 25 writers and the 62 different endings. No wonder you can't find a thing to go see.

GK: But you put *Looney Tunes* next to *Space Jam* and it's a masterpiece.

JD: It's got a point of view, which *Space Jam* doesn't. But I'm sure they would've loved to have had another *Space Jam*. We even have a Michael Jordan joke in it. It's *Gremlins* 2-ish in the sense that there are lots of *Hellzapoppin'* (1941) kinds of gags. But that was another issue: breaking the fourth wall. *Ooooh boy*, did they *hate* that. Those cartoons all break the fourth wall, it's part of their DNA.

So anyway, that was the movie that made me think, "I don't want to do this anymore."

GK: That was your last studio movie.

JD: If this is what it's like to work at a studio, then I don't want to do it anymore.

GK: How does this compare to the climate of making movies for the studios in the '80s?

JD: It was completely different. When we made *Gremlins* – it's not fair to compare because I had the buffer of Steven Spielberg, which not many people had, but the guys who ran the studio, they were very supportive, even when they didn't understand the movie.

I mean, my big studio experiences are not all bad. But I think the climate now is not the same as it was in the '80s. It started to change for the worse in the late '90s. The corporatizing of movies has pretty much become complete and it's not the same business. The things made now are not made for the same audience – they're not even shot on film anymore. It's a different world. And if I was a young kid who wanted to make movies, and I wanted to break into the business, I don't know which movies would make me want to do that. When I was talking to kids in the '80s, it was all *Raiders of the Lost Ark*. That was the movie that made them want to make movies, which was of course kind of poetic because it's based on serials and things that made Lucas and Spielberg wanna make movies, and I can understand that kind of continuity. Now, I don't know if going to see

Looney Tunes:
Back in Action (2003)

Transformers 3 (2011) is going to make a kid say, gee, that's what I want to grow up to do.

GK: So now we're up to *Homecoming* (2005)…

JD: Which came from a place of anger. I was angry, Sam [Hamm, the screenwriter] was angry; we were pissed off about the political situation in America and the fact that everyone was being so cowardly about it. This unlikely opportunity arose. Because of the way that show was structured and in order to get people to work for cheap, they said they'd let you do whatever you wanted. We managed to sneak this thing by, which we never could've made for television and we certainly couldn't have made as a feature. It's agitprop, basically, and we got away with it. I sent copies of it to every right-wing nut and commentator I could think of and didn't get a single response. Either they just threw it away or it made them angry and they didn't want to publicize it. I didn't realize how potent it was until we went to the Torino Film Festival and got this ten-minute standing ovation, which I firmly believe is not necessarily because of the merits of the movie, but the fact that there was somebody saying that they hadn't all drunk the Kool-Aid in America.

GK: It seems even though you got burned by the studios pretty often, you still went back with the desire to reach a mass audience.

JD: *Homecoming* has got an audience but not a very big one. I'm sure *Looney Tunes* will always have a bigger audience than that because it's got Bugs Bunny in it. I don't think I'm going to spend the rest of my life on television, but I wouldn't mind having a series because that's the best way to do TV. You get in on the ground floor where you call the shots – like on *Eerie, Indiana* (1991–92), where you felt like you were part of the show and could really make a contribution. Unlike *Hawaii Five-0* (2010–) where you come in, get the script they hand you, do it, and go home.

GK: *The Hole* (2009), your latest film, could also be categorized as a horror film, though it's much gentler.

JD: When *The Hole* came around, it was a picture I did because I needed to do a picture. And of all the scripts I'd read, and in particular the horror movie scripts, this was the one that had the best writing and the best characters. I suggested doing it in 3D because it was such a small story and it only took place in something like five different locations and had six characters. I thought it could be enhanced by the use of depth. And surprisingly, they went for it. Ultimately that turned out to be its biggest problem – it was the reason it didn't get distributed.

The Hole (2009)

Joe Dante
on the *Hole* set

GK: Because there weren't enough theaters equipped to do it?

JD: There was a certain number of theaters, but by the time we were finished, they were all playing fake 3D movies with big stars and they all got held over and we lost them. It did well overseas but it didn't play theatrically in the States at all.

GK: Has your relationship to watching old movies changed?

JD: It has changed in the sense that I have seen so many of them so often that I'm only rarely seized by the need to drag one out and look at it. And I don't generally run 16mms anymore because the videos frankly come from better materials and are often not cut. The bane of collecting 16mm is that you would get a TV version that had been cut and censored and is missing pieces. Nonetheless, that's how I saw most movies.

GK: Would you say you're still bitten by the bug?

JD: I mean, *look* at that shit. [*Points to ceiling-high pile of DVDs and Blu-rays*] I'd say I'm bitten by the bug. It's easier to store and it's cheaper than buying a print. What amazes me is that there are still collectors who swear by prints and will pay up to $150 for a faded print of a picture that they could easily get in the correct ratio and in good color on video, and with a correct video system that picture is probably as good as 16mm.

GK: At the same time, your archive becomes a resource for institutions like film museums that are trying to preserve film prints.

JD: Yes, because as we know, digital is not an archival medium. Some of these pictures only exist in 16mm. We lend to archives and our prints are always in circulation. I think my and Jon Davison's print of *The Intruder* (1962) has run at festivals and archives more often than in its first run.

GK: I know it changes on a case-by-case basis, but who is your ideal audience?

JD: My ideal audience? Me! I'm the ideal audience and the one I make movies for. That's why it was so demoralizing with *Looney Tunes* to see that I'd made a movie that wasn't for me. I mean, it had elements of me in it, but I know that if I walked in from the street, I would say, "What happened to this movie? How did all of these disparate elements end up being thrown together like this?"

GK: It would be great to talk a bit about *The Man with Kaleidoscope Eyes*, your project around *The Trip* (1967).

JD: Hopefully that will get made someday. Tim Lucas, who edits *Video Watchdog*, and Charles

An "early Corman" reel from Joe Dante's trailer collection

Largent sent me a script which was something they'd written and they wanted to know what I thought of it. And it was about Roger Corman making *The Trip* and it was fairly well-researched. I said that I not only like it, but I thought maybe I would want to make it. So I showed it to Roger and got his okay and we went off trying to make the picture, which we've been doing off and on for five or six years. We got a couple of other writers involved, like Michael Almereyda and Jim Robison. And I think we improved the script.

Anyway, we made a little teaser which you can see online. The trick is the budget: it's a period movie, it takes place in the '60s, and that's not an easy period to do. So much of it takes place here in Los Angeles, so it's not like you can go to Canada and shoot it. Vancouver for L. A. doesn't work. It works for the Hollywood Hills, but not for L. A. So the trick is finding a place where you can afford to do it for the budget. It's got a lot of speaking parts with all these different people from that era. And it's got this special effects contingent because it has to be an acid trip. We haven't given up. It's an ongoing thing. But it's one of numerous ongoing things. In the old days, they would just call you up and say, "We've got a script, you wanna do it?" And you'd do it and okay, you're done, here's another job. But now you have to provide all these things on your own and do a lot of work that you're not paid for just to get in a position where somebody might say, "Okay, here's some money."

GK: Are there other things that you do parallel to filmmaking that we don't know about?

JD: I spend a lot of time on Trailers From Hell, which basically came out of my curatorial ambitions. This has been an effort to gather up a lot of like-minded filmmakers and basically introduce people to movies that they might not have heard of.

GK: Can you talk about the general concept of it?

JD: I had a trailer collection in 35mm that I wasn't running very often, and I thought maybe the Internet is the place to put it. This was back in 2007. And I thought, maybe I could talk over them, introduce them and do a little commentary. I did about five trailers, sitting in my screening room, and I put them up on the Internet for nobody in particular except some of my friends, who saw it and said, "Hey, I have a picture I'd love to talk about!" And so John Landis and Edgar Wright came on board. It started to grow. If we could find the trailer for it, we would do it. The trick was that we didn't tell them what to say: they can like the movie, they can not like the movie… What they can't do is say any factually inaccurate things. If they do, we correct them. But for the most part, it's anything you want to say for three minutes. We're now up to almost 900 trailers. I think it's like a mini-film school.

GK: Why don't you teach a class?

JD: You have to put together a curriculum and spend some time developing it – I just haven't had the time. I think you don't necessarily want to have a lesson plan, because I remember that the teachers I liked in college were more interesting when they were spontaneous. But the schools make you have one. I know I could probably teach a good class. I do like talking to students.

GK: It's always surprising to learn that film students today don't have much of a passion for film history. I wonder how we can inspire that. On one hand you could say, you've got the bug and you just keep going. But on the other hand, movies are a way to learn about the world, people… There are so many ways to approach it.

JD: What does Steve Martin say in *Grand Canyon* (1991)? "All of life's riddles are answered in the movies." [*Laughs*]

GK: Do you believe that?

JD: To a degree, yes.

This conversation with Joe Dante took
place over two days at his home in
Los Angeles, California, in March, 2013.
The author would like to thank
Patrick Wilson for his assistance in the
transcription of the interview.

Joe Dante in his home screening room, 2013

Bill Krohn

Dante's Slashers:
Hollywood Boulevard and Beyond

Not at all surprisingly, the blood-red artery running through Joe Dante's work – from *Hollywood Boulevard* (1976) to the interactive web series *Splatter* (2009) – is the low-prestige offshoot of serial killer cinema, the slasher, shading into the even lower-prestige "splatter film" at times. Here are some reasons to support this thesis:

1) his *nostalgie de la boue* would inevitably make him an adherent, conscious or unconscious, of the cheesiest available variant of a cinematic genre with noble antecedents like Hitchcock's *The Lodger* (1927) (parodied in the Dante-directed "Bullshit or Not" segment of *Amazon Women on the Moon* [1987], where Jack the Ripper turns out to be The Loch Ness Monster);

2) he started making films when slashers were exploding at the box-office in the long aftermath of *Psycho* (1960), which helped define Dante's moment (even though a rotten kid who'd read the book told him the surprise ending to spoil his enjoyment of the movie the first time he saw it);

3) *Piranha* (1978) is a cheap rip-off of *Jaws*, the game-changing hit that created the template for slashers in 1975;

4) slashers are avant-garde, or can be co-opted by an avant-garde filmmaker like Dante (or Stanley Kubrick), just as the French surrealists co-opted the Ur-serial killer Fantômas without even knowing his creator's name (a hundred years later, Dante knows all the names).

Calling slashers the "artery" of Dante's oeuvre raises interesting questions, if only because the "artery" metaphor is Dante's own, coined by him while we were working on *Joe Dante et les Gremlins de Hollywood*[1] to characterize my belief that the cinema of Edward L. Cahn was the "artery" of his oeuvre. But it may not be metaphor-making to apply the same word to a symbolic form in which arteries play such an important role.

INVENTING THE SLASHER

Not only is *Hollywood Boulevard* a slasher, it's a pretty early one, largely by virtue of the night scene where a masked killer in a black leather cloak stalks an actress through a fog-shrouded western set, transformed by filters and colored lighting into something out of a film by Mario Bava. Post-*Frenzy* (1972), post-*Sisters* (1973), post-*Black Christmas* (1974) and post-*Jaws*, *Holly-*

---

1 The volume was edited by Bill Krohn, in collaboration with Roger Garcia, Jonathan Rosenbaum, and Charles Tesson, Paris: Cahiers du cinéma, Locarno: Festival International du Film de Locarno, 1999.

Hollywood Boulevard

wood Boulevard arrived at the end of the long latency period before the slasher genre emerged full-blown, almost two decades after *Psycho* taught America to love murder, in John Carpenter's *Halloween* (1978).

Fortunately, Italian cinema had immediately set about exploiting and perfecting Hitchcock's discovery in *gialli*, beginning in 1963 with Bava's *La ragazza che sapeva troppo (The Girl Who Knew Too Much)* – a tradition that Carpenter, who readily acknowledges the influence of Dario Argento, pays tribute to less visibly than Dante because Carpenter is consolidating an invention that is still half-baked in *Hollywood Boulevard*. The fact that the film becomes a slasher in mid-stream has kept its role in the phylogenesis of the form from being noticed. It doesn't figure in any of the histories and encyclopedias of slashers that have appeared since the genre has achieved respectability through longevity. Instead critics call the murder on the fog-filled set the film's "slasher scene," as if slashers already existed in 1976 to be referred to.

Dante's co-director Allan Arkush filmed his own showy scene with a rock band, and *Hollywood Boulevard* didn't become a musical, but Dante and Arkush's mystery-comedy about people getting bumped off at a film studio – a plot that dates back to programmers like *The*

Death Kiss (1932), which the two directors happened to see on late-night TV – does become a slasher when Dante grafts his striking pastiche of the Italian maestro onto it, in the process displaying the underlying heterogeneity of the materials from which a new genre and a new way of making films were coming together in 1976. Of course, *Hollywood Boulevard* is entirely composed of heterogeneous elements anyway, so the Bava scene can stick out like a weirdly lit thumb after all those cutaways to New World films made in different styles, among which Joe Dante's poisonous Italian flower is just the latest cutting to be planted.

The new genre would continue to be marked by heterogeneity, obliging mostly anonymous legions of filmmakers to engage in feats of recycling *bricolage* that can be read off a title list: *New Year's Evil, April Fool's Day, My Bloody Valentine, Prom Night, Hell Night, Cheerleader Camp, Bones, Private Parts, The Temp, The Banker, The Stepfather, Drive In, Cheerleader Camp, Cabin in the Woods, Freddy's Revenge, I Still Know What You Did Last Summer, When a Stranger Calls, Bride of Chucky, Jason Takes Manhattan, Leprechaun in Space,* and so on. New slasher titles could be generated by a computer program using random numbers, much like the films being made at the fictional Miracle Pictures in *Hollywood Boulevard*. (The screenwriter of *Machete Babes of Mora Tau* explains: "When they gave me this assignment two weeks ago it was about Eskimo women battling dinosaurs in Alaska.") If that is a fault, it's one that characterizes the genre, which is rooted in exploitation films, whereas serial killer cinema broadly defined includes some of the masterpieces of film history.

BLOODY MARY

Echoing what critics usually say about serial killer cinema in all its forms, Dante told me during our discussion of *Hollywood Boulevard* that "when the plot does kick in an hour into the movie, it's pretty stupid." But the Bava scene was not an afterthought. In fact, everything in the film, which had to be tightly pre-planned, leads up to that ending. The idea of a stalking killer who is unmasked by a camera first appears in the Dante-Arkush treatment for the unmade *Young Teachers*. In *Hollywood Boulevard* it becomes the culmination of the film's sophisticated hi-jinx with suture, the fundamental operation of film language, which invisibly shapes the classical form of serial killer cinema and is X-rayed by the revolting modernism of slashers.

Hollywood Boulevard begins with an accidental death: the stunt girl for Miracle Pictures star Mary McQueen (Mary Woronov) dies in a sky-diving accident and is replaced by naïve newbie Candy Wednesday (Candice Rialson). This triggers the chain of murders: seeing her double die and fearing that she'll be replaced by the newcomer, Mary starts killing her co-stars so she can have the spotlight to herself. Like a surprising number of cinematic serial homicides (cf. *The Leopard Man* [1943]), her crime spree is triggered by an arbitrary event (there was no reason for Mary to kill some faceless stunt girl), which Dante represents with a cartoon image: a Wile E. Coyote-style hole in the ground with a vaguely anthropomorphic shape that traumatizes Mary because she sees her own absence in it.

Logically enough, the hieroglyphic hole was made by a non-existent person: one of the sky-divers from *Night Call Nurses* (1972). The same logic of "found-footage" assemblage governs the murder series, punctuated by the Bava-esque nocturnal shenanigans of a pair of black-gloved hands: Bobbi (Rita George) is attacked by a cobra from *Night of the Cobra* (1972); Jill (Tara Strohmeier) is apparently shot by a prison guard from *Savage!* (1973) ("Art, reality – where does one end and the other begin?" ponders Eric the director, played by Paul Bartel); Mary and Candy are almost incinerated in a car explosion from *Death Race 2000* (1975), during which Candy dons Keith Carradine's black leather get-up at one point to match the old footage; and Bobbi – who has herself only recently escaped from a roller derby sequence in *Unholy Rollers* (1972) – is stalked through the midnight streets of the western set by Mary wearing Carradine's Frankenstein costume. (Bobbi thinks it's Mary until she sees the knife.)

The next day the headlines scream: "SLASHER STRIKES IN HOLLYWOOD – Motiveless Murder." Unaware that the camera at the movie ranch has been switched on, Mary is exposed when she pulls her mask off after stabbing Bobbi. And when she attacks Candy with an ax at the foot of the Hollywood Sign, forgetting that she just sawed through one of the mooring cables, she is crushed by the 'Y,' which looks as it topples toward the camera like the foreshortened Y of the pre-Columbian hole that catalyzes the murder series and structures the film. It may be held together with spit and baling wire, like the Sign itself, but the prototype is finished.

As mainstream critics were surprised to discover when *Scream* (1996) introduced the genre to a wider audience, slashers are frequently mysteries littered with red herrings. (A sinister peeking-through-the-reeds shot while the topless actresses discuss cinema as voyeurism turns out to be the ubiquitous horndog Scotty, played by the director of *Night Call Nurses*, Jonathan Kaplan.) In *Hollywood Boulevard*, the big red herring is Candy's boyfriend, the writer Pat Hobby (Jeffrey Kramer), who arouses her suspicions by locking himself in a shed to plot a screenplay based on the murders. Discovering his research – pictures of the girls in the murder series – Candy jumps to the wrong conclusion and flees into the claws of the insane murderess. Stupid? Perhaps. Meaningless? Perhaps not. Candy misreads the series of photographs (a *giallo* symbol for vision, true and false, unfolding in a series), but the spectator sees through her mistake by reading an image correctly.

When Mary hears over the phone that Candy "knows who the killer is" (Candy thinks it's Pat) and suddenly starts looking shifty, she is backed by a poster for *Untamed Mistress* (1956) with her name pasted in. The shot eliminates the big image of the heroine getting raped by a gorilla to focus on the title, which frames Mary as a dangerous animal ("Powerful! Daring!") in her own right. But drive-in spectators could read the first *vide* on the lower left, "SEE Gorilla fight man for a luscious woman whose only weapon is love!" – and perhaps did, out loud, sitting in their cars – aided by a smaller image of that lustful combat. "I don't know," Mary

Hollywood Boulevard

says earlier, distractedly waving away the producer when he seeks her approval for an extra in a tweaked gorilla costume with whom she will apparently be making *Untamed Mistress* for the fifth time. "I'm too nuts."

AT THE DRIVE-IN

The directors of *Hollywood Boulevard* made a film to showcase three years of New World Pictures from 1972 to 1975, and the little film they made to mesh with the excerpts was a slasher. Setting aside the inevitable pun on "cutting," the film is self-reflexive from start to finish like Truffaut's *La Nuit américaine* (*Day for Night*), released by Roger Corman's New World in 1974, without being narcissistic (like the Truffaut). Instead the *Day for Night*-like interview segment on the western set veers into a reflection on the relationship between the audience and the image when Mary laments that her last two films for Miracle Pictures led to the legalization of abortion and "the decriminalization of marijuana in 13 states."

The question of the image is raised as soon as Candy returns to Hollywood from the Philippines and attends the drive-in premiere of *Machete Babes of Mora Tau* – a comic sequence that interrupts the slasher story while reflecting on the conditions of possibility for the form

Hollywood Boulevard is turning into before our eyes:

– A soft drink ad (a real commercial previously appropriated by Dante and company for *The Movie Orgy*) makes Candy thirsty, so she proceeds to get drunk;

– In keeping with the marquee in front of the drive-in promising "Sᴇx," everything on the screen is sexualized, even the pizza and meatballs "waiting for you" at the refreshment stand;

Dementia 13
(1963)

– Horrified by her rape scene, Candy makes her drunken way to the projection booth and tells the projectionist to "take it off";

– He starts raping her and is joined by an angry Republican father who has come to the booth to demand the same thing;

– When Candy's friends go looking for her, they elicit scary responses from solitary spectators in their cars: sex and violence, the commodities on display.

Played for laughs, the sequence still measures the gap between Joe Dante's youthful communal experience of Saturday matinees and the drive-ins serviced by New World, where people are subjected to sexual shocks and act on them in the privacy of their cars: a new relation to the image that would continue to make slashers possible long after all the drive-ins had closed.

"That isn't the real me!" says Candy, angry and outraged like her own giant image firing a machine gun on the screen. "This isn't what I dreamed of in Indiana!" she laments, like the Republican father, whose wife and teenage son just want to see the rape scene. "This is worse than television!" says the shocked dad. *Hollywood Boulevard* is haunted by images of solitude when a character is suddenly alone in the image, framed to look tiny in a very wide shot in descending darkness, menaced by the camera eye. In these dark grace notes the film becomes a slasher as well as an indictment of New World Pictures, which is making this one.

Of course it's not news that *Hollywood Boulevard* is a satire of New World and Roger Corman that plays every conceivable variation on the word "exploitation." Dante didn't dream up cinematic "re-cycling" by himself. In fact, ten years after *Hollywood Boulevard*, Corman re-cycled Dante's masked slasher as a vampire from outer space in a remake of his own *Not of This Earth* directed by Jim Wynorski.

Corman is also one of the fathers of the slasher, not because of his Poe films, but because of *Bucket of Blood* (1959), the five-day black-and-white wonder starring Dick Miller as busboy-turned-sculptor Walter Paisley, who recycles corpses covered with cement as ghastly statues to earn the approval of the beatniks he waits on at the local coffeehouse. A doomed artist-figure like Vincent Price in the Poe films, whose art, like theirs, is in the service of death, Walter Paisley is a critique of Corman by Corman more severe than anything in the good-natured *Hollywood Boulevard*. *Bucket of Blood* recycles from Price's *House of Wax* an image of André Bazin's theory that film is akin to mummification. Originally called *The Living Dead* before being marketed as a comedy, it features death sculptures as shocking as anything in the Poe cycle, which kicked off a year later.

When Miller takes the Paisley name for the second time in *Hollywood Boulevard*, playing Candy's agent, the character seems more comfortable in his skin, having scuttled his artistic ambitions and embraced Hollywood as exploitation. He represents Roger Corman as P. T. Barnum, with a circus full of animal clients (no stabbed cats) and a dollar sign on his lapel. (Miracle Pictures mogul "P. G." is a creep who smokes: always a badge of evil in a Dante film.) But Walter's name reminds us of his past role ("I used to do some acting…") as a "death artist," one of many titles Corman gave the TV movie remake of *Bucket* which he produced in the '90s with Anthony Michael Hall as Walter.

BLOOD BROTHERS

The triple feature Candy and her friends take in at the drive-in is a miniature pre-history of New World Pictures stretching back to the AIP days, when the first generation of Corman directors were learning at the master's feet. "Zombie in the Attic" is scenes from *The Terror* (1963) with Miller and Boris Karloff that were filmed by Corman before handing the project off to Francis Coppola et al, and "Moonmen from Mars" is the extraterrestrial sex scene Coppola filmed to boost the monster quotient in *Nebo Zovet* (1959), a Russian science fiction film released by AIP in 1962 as *Battle Beyond the Sun*. The Coppola references situate the second New World generation, represented by third-billed *Machete Babes of Mora Tau*, with respect to the leader of the first generation, whose own Philippine war movie was about to start shooting even as *Hollywood Boulevard* was being made.

But Coppola's Corman-produced proto-slasher, *Dementia 13* (1963), is notably absent. A *Psycho* ripoff (by way of *The Girl Who Knew Too Much* and Seth Holt's *Taste of Fear / Scream of Fear* [1961], among others), it was made the same year as *The Terror* and had also fallen into public domain. Coppola and Corman (still rattled by the way Coppola had blown the entire remaining *Terror* budget on the scenes in the

Jaws (1975)

witch's hut) clashed when the producer sensibly insisted on the need for another ax murder (which ended up being filmed by Jack Hill) and had Monte Hellman shoot a fake doctor's examination of the spectator's sanity à la William Castle (the schlockmeister whose revenues may have inspired *Psycho*, after which he remained more or less in the forefront of exploitation filmmakers who nursed the embryonic genre through the sixties). Yet Dante, who says he first became aware of Coppola when he saw *Dementia 13*, evokes the maker of the *Godfather* Saga with images he created for Corman of alien monsters that look like sex organs "getting it on," as Candy observes. "Not well," says Walter.

Walter's comment about these precocious images filmed by the most conspicuous satirical target among the first generation of Corman graduates might be coming from the director who was going to take the lead, without publicist or possessory credits, among the second generation, but it's being said by the film's benign Corman figure because Corman is the only producer who ever got away with telling Francis Coppola that his film was "unreleasable" and ordering additional scenes and a narration done by other hands. In Coppola's filmography Corman figures as the Imp of Heterogeneity (*The Terror* and *Dementia 13*, made the same year), and he is obviously the patron imp of Coppola's recent low-budget trilogy (*Youth Without Youth*, *Tetro* and *'Twixt*, the last of which went direct to video in the US), but in 1976 Francis Ford Coppola was the big brother who had made good and needed to be reminded of where he came from, quite literally: the vagina horribilis stabbing with one of its knife-like talons a headless creature with eyes on stalks for arms, then eating and/or fucking its insides, is the *Origine du monde* (1866) of the Raging Bulls generation and their younger brothers and sisters as well, who would bear witness to dislocations in the audiovisual universe circa 1960 in different ways.

Dementia 13 is a cut above as *Psycho* ripoffs go, but the drive-in sequence puts it in its place as a structuring absence – by showing instead in the most literal way, as filmed by Coppola himself, the drive that is being entertained in the big underwater scene of his debut feature. It was inspired by a dream Coppola had about a blonde beauty swimming in her underwear before getting slashed à la the *Psycho* shower scene when she climbs out of the water. The metaphorical choice – letting Coppola's Boschian evocation of the embattled scopic drive stand in for the missing wet-underwear shots of Mary Mitchell – could very well be Dante's (that penile eye returns in *Small Soldiers*): show Big Brother being immature by portraying sexuality as interspecies slasher porn. "I think it's kind of… disgusting," says Walter. But Walter is an idealized version of Roger, and by assuming his condemnation of Big Brother's ocular priapism, Dante is rejecting Coppola as his aesthetic godfather and identifying with the perpetually underrated visionary who schooled them both… even though deep down Younger Brother is still ashamed, after all these years, of the wet tee-shirt audition he was obliged to conduct for *Hollywood Boulevard*.

These rivalries continue to be more fraternal than Oedipal to this day, like the brother relationships in *The Hole* and *Tetro* (both 2009), where an eye in a hole and the ax from *Dementia 13* make prominent appearances. *Gremlins* and *Gremlins 2: The New Batch* do not pose an existential threat to *The Godfather* and *The Godfather Part II*, but they do propose a more ele-

gant way to skin a cat. If images are going to be "just images" now – a premise the creator of *One from the Heart* (1982) could hardly argue with – then let's see what's going on *inside them*.

JUST AN IMAGE

A piece of *The Movie Orgy* pops up to orient us in the sequence after the drive-in, where the actresses who survived *Machete Babes* are absorbing the fifties by living in a time-capsule built by the ebullient P. G. A small audience has assembled to view a commercial for Intestinex, the Oral Enema: a black-and-white "X-ray-style" animation of clogged plumbing being cleaned out by "the greatest medical discovery since the Salk vaccine." Candy, who was turned on at the drive-in by the oral imagery in the Concession Break featurette (which sickened Pat), is disgusted by the anality of all that plumbing and slips away (or rather, down and out) in the dark, only to be replaced by Pat rising into her seat. As usual the asshole (P. G.) is in charge.

The pictured plumbing recalls the gypsy dance of freeways they navigated to get to the drive-in and the celluloid spaghetti *Machete Babes* turned into during the scuffle in the projection booth, with a toilet prominently positioned in the shot to receive Rapist Dad when Walter karate-chops him. In the midst of this "behind-the-scenes" madness, the last man standing – after Jack Hill or Cirio Santiago or Jonathan Demme has burned down the jungle-prison set during the big battle scene in the Philippines – throws up his arms in apocalyptic despair, then burns up in the gate, like the last shot of Monte Hellman's *Two Lane Black-top* (1971).

Blink and you'd miss that one-second image, which nonetheless has the cool impact of the silent footage, replayed more than once, of Glen Mannering, the unfortunate hero of *The Amazing Colossal Man* (1957), being half inciner-ated by an A-bomb test. It also reminds us, more recently, of Sandra Knight's melting death's-head at the end of "Zombie in the Attic," which is paid off quickly and cheaply with the repetitious shots of meatballs covered with slime that await us at the Concession Stand. (What other "concessions" will we be asked to make?) But at the end of the drive-in sequence, when a nameless soldier throws up his arms somewhere in the Philippines or Viet-nam or the San Gabriel Mountains and burns up in the gate, his shock at his own evanes-cence is imprinted on our recollection of a me-mento mori (the melting corpse) that was also filmed by Monte Hellman, the Big Brother who had never made a film for a major except *Two Lane Blacktop*. Nine times out of ten these kinds of rhyming riffs are only visible to the editor, and *Hollywood Boulevard*, a film made by not one editor but two, is full of them because all its images are "just images," available for every kind of metastasis inside the film's body.

THE SLASHER CINEMA OF JOE DANTE

The important difference is that while Coppola and Dante both made films about serial killers for Corman as their first features, Coppola tried to make something that could still pass muster as a classical film, while Dante and Arkush made something more like a Futurist painting of a film. *Hollywood Boulevard* is a slasher-in-process that is at the same time a critique of the genre and the modernism it spearheaded: a new kind of film that looks under the skin of appearances into the theater of Freudian drives and their vicissitudes (the pun on "drive-in" is virtually obligatory), where all the components of the cinematic signifying chain are figured directly rather than being disguised by a realis-tic narrative.

Because the cinematic signifying chain can be evoked by the shabbiest series of capital of-fenses, serial carnage became the artery, so to

Piranha

speak, of the new form, with the scopic drive identified by Freud's successor Jacques Lacan as the "walking point,"[2] usually in the form of the "prowling camera" codified in 1978 in *Halloween*. And now Joe Dante, having found the kind of film he wanted to make in *Hollywood Boulevard*, even if he didn't want to put a name to it, made his first "real" slasher in 1978, too.

Piranha is not, as is sometimes said, a parody of *Jaws* – it's a cheap rip-off of *Jaws* that Dante pulls off with a straight face against mean odds, and a highly effective entry in the "Nature Gone Wild" slasher cavalcade harking back at least to *The Birds* (1963), which *Piranha* recalls as much as it does *Jaws*. Corman was a prophet here as well with his follow-up to *Bucket of Blood*, *The Little Shop of Horrors*, and identifying with Corman has enabled Dante to escape the Spielberg Trap: it's a genre where "closure" isn't hard to come by.

Pascal Bonitzer has described *Jaws* as a film composed of bodies that are all "sacks," whose insides arouse the curiosity of the scientist played by Richard Dreyfuss. "It wasn't a mo-

torboat that did this," he tells the Mayor after examining the first remains. "And it wasn't Jack the Ripper." But of course Jack the Ripper was obsessed with the insides of bodies too, and so are slashers.

Piranha reverses the givens of *Jaws*: the piranha are inland and mustn't get to the sea. This permits Dante to begin with what slasher expert Carol Clover calls "The Terrible Place," descended from the Bates Mansion in *Psycho*. Versions of The Terrible Place are a constant of

2 Lacan used the image of the soldier who goes out ahead of an infantry squadron entering unfamiliar terrain to illustrate his idea.

87

Dante's slashers: the isolated Poe-like house in "It's a Good Life" (Dante's episode in the 1983 *Twilight Zone* movie); the Colony in *The Howling* (1981); the Klopek House in *The 'Burbs* (1989); and Johnny Splatter's house in *Splatter* are textbook examples. The Terrible Place in *Hollywood Boulevard* was the empty western town with an illuminated dressing table waiting for Bobbi's last performance. In *Piranha* it's an abandoned research facility where you don't ignore the "No Trespassing" sign and go swimming.

The danger is that the swarm will reach the sea, passing through a system of gateways along a river. That itinerary becomes a murder series – an artery, if you will – that keeps the film's blood flowing. When the hero shows the authorities on a map how the swarm can bypass the Sawmill Dam to get to Lost River Lake where the water carnival is, stopping along the way to slash the children at Camp Jackson to bloody ribbons, we realize that the film itself is a body, and that the characters are inside it, as we are.

Dante's slashers travel like viruses through the bloodstreams of their movies: the piranha, the lycanthropes, the gremlins, the Klopeks, and the extraterrestrial virus of *The Screwfly Solution* (2006), which turns every man on Earth into a slasher who will slaughter any woman that arouses him until the human species becomes extinct, like the screwflies of the title.

Slashers – the genre and its protagonists – are shape-shifters. Eddie Quist in *The Howling* is a classic serial killer, which Dante says served as a generic red herring for getting audiences into a movie about werewolves, one of the mythical identities that have been assigned to serial killers in the past. And the Hitchcockian serial killer suspenser, "Quiet, Please" (a 2001 segment for the TV series *Night Visions*), disguises itself until the payoff as a remake of *Wabbit Twouble* (1941).

Trivial images (ads, cartoons, educational films) are another kind of virus contaminating the body of the film, like the found footage in *Hollywood Boulevard*; or the virtual hierarchy of the ten-minute segments composing *Splatter*, the Internet series where Dante, reunited with Roger Corman, inaugurated a new era of spectatorial interaction with the image. (The series title refers to the lowliest realms of slasher cinema, carved out by Herschell Gordon Lewis and George Romero before Dante [but not Corman] was making films.) In Joe Dante's hands, the slasher is a form of experimental cinema.

Piranha

The Howling:
Polaroid reference photos
from the special effects
creation process

Dušan Rebolj

Dante's Agents

In his career, Joe Dante has never taken a screenwriting credit. With the exception of the story credit for *Rock 'n' Roll High School* (1979) which he shared with the film's director, Allan Arkush, he has never formally assumed ownership of the dialogue, initial story development or conceptual basis for any project he has been involved in. The stories he is telling, and the ways in which he tells them, don't necessarily display interconnectedness and a thematic cohesion that would constitute a *project* in the strict auteurist sense of the word. Nevertheless, certain motifs and points of view are threaded throughout his body of work and come across as unmistakably his own. Together, or rather in succession, his films resonate with each other to form a clearly individual worldview of which the basic recurring pattern, the one that expresses itself more forcefully than virtually all others, seems to be self-reflexivity – both in terms of Dante's characters and their frequent self-reflection, and in terms of the films' own engagement with cinema as such.

In the latter respect, *The Movie Orgy* (1966–2009), originally a seven-hour montage of B-movie excerpts, commercials, TV series and industrial films, conceived and edited by Dante and Jon Davison, stands as an ideal specimen – a work of pure reflection, not only on cinema and mass media in general, but on the act of editing itself. Introducing *The Movie Orgy* at the 2012 St. Louis International Film Festival, Dante assured the audience that "none of it amounts to a hill of beans," and that "the program was designed to be walked out on."[1] Yet on another occasion he did acknowledge that "there were several features that were intertwined, so there was a story that went through the whole thing."[2]

Whatever the case, *The Movie Orgy*, a mammoth sequence of resurrected footage, functions as a snapshot of the cinematic and cultural landscape at and prior to the time of its making, as well as a testament to the power of the moving image, within or without narrative bounds, to provoke an experience in the viewer. Furthermore, according to Dante, viewers may find "a lot of things that over the years in my movies I have lifted from *The Movie Orgy*. Sometimes it's actual footage, sometimes just stealing ideas and lines of dialogue. It's sort of the unlocked key to my work."[3]

---

1 The video is available at http://youtu.be/iSP9uqyxFKQ.

2 Rob Christopher, "Joe Dante Presents The Mother Of All Supercuts," *Chicagoist*, July 26, 2012. Available at http://chicagoist.com/2012/07/26/ joe_dante_presents_the_mother_of_al.php

3 Joe Dante at the St. Louis International Film Festival

The Movie Orgy

Gremlins

After *The Movie Orgy*, Dante's progression from mash-ups of existing footage to the more conventional narrative film form was gradual. After two years of cutting trailers for Roger Corman's New World Pictures, he was assigned to co-direct *Hollywood Boulevard* (1976) with Arkush when Jon Davison, also employed at New World, bet Corman that Dante and Arkush could make the company's cheapest film to date.[4] The bet stipulated that they would be allowed to use New World's vast library of stock footage. Thus was born *Hollywood Boulevard*, a film woven around action sequences from earlier Corman productions. Dante's directorial debut was self-referential in that it mirrored its own production background – it was a story about independent filmmaking. And by sheer economic necessity it partly retained the reproductive aspect of *The Movie Orgy*.

One way or another, cinema finds its way into Dante's work. Most explicitly through action taking place in a movie theater, as in the finales of *Gremlins* (1984) and *Matinee* (1993). Or through countless movie posters, billboards and TV sets broadcasting their references somewhere in the background. Or names, as in *The Howling*, whose character nomenclature is essentially an homage to the creators of werewolf cinema. And lastly scripted in-jokes, for example the epic Daffy Duck-Bugs Bunny rivalry, which starts in the title sequence of *Gremlins 2: The New Batch* (1990) – "fifty years of you hogging the spotlight is enough," says disgruntled Daffy to Bugs – and escalates in *Looney Tunes: Back in Action* (2003). In practically every film, and in terms as certain as a screenwriting credit would have been, Dante points to the fact that it is indeed a film, and to himself as its creator.

4 Roger Corman with Jim Jerome, *How I Made a Hundred Movies in Hollywood and Never Lost a Dime*, New York: Da Capo Press, 1998, p. 197

5 Incidentally, Big Sur is where Roger Corman, prior to making *The Trip* (1967), took LSD to acquaint himself with the film's subject matter.

TRANSFORMING AGENTS

Self-reflection, however, is also one of the signature traits of Dante's characters: in his outlook on human nature, which deserves particular attention, humans have the capacity to act as willful, moral agents, and occasionally these actions take on an explicitly political significance. One particularly clear example is *The Howling*, where dilemmas of human agency and shifts between human and nonhuman states take center stage.

John Sayles, at the time a Corman regular who had also penned Dante's *Piranha* (1978), expanded the scope of Gary Brandner's pulp horror novel and added satirical barbs aimed at New Age spiritualism, particularly the '60s Human Potential Movement and the Esalen Institute, the organisation's Big Sur think-tank.[5] It is to an Esalen-like therapeutic retreat in northern California that the film's protagonist, TV reporter Karen White, is sent by her therapist Dr. George Waggner (named after the director of the classic 1941 *The Wolf Man*). The Colony, as it soon emerges, is not only a secluded place in the woods where patients "channel their energies" and connect with the elements, but a den of werewolves which will terrorize the film's heroine. In the film's dramatic confrontation, Dr. Waggner attempts to persuade Karen to accept the "gift" of werewolfery (and thus rejoin her husband, who has already shifted shape), but is overruled by his lycanthropic constituents who resent his attempts to bring them into the human mainstream. "You can't tame what's meant to be wild," one of them opines, "It ain't natural." Karen is bitten but escapes to give her final TV appearance: a speech about "the struggle between what is kind and peaceful in our natures, and what is cruel and violent." "For some of us," she tells her audience, "that choice has been taken away." To illustrate the point, she assumes her wolf form and is ultimately killed by her co-worker Chris, the film's surviving human hero.

In *The Howling*, lycanthropy is conceived as an irreversible slip across the human/inhuman divide. The condition is seen both by Karen and the reactionary inhabitants of the Colony as a definitive and defining state of existence. As far as Waggner's reluctant disciples are concerned, "it ain't natural" for a werewolf to attempt a civilized relationship with its traditional source of sustenance. Karen, on the other hand, sees in her werewolfery a loss of the distinctly human ability to be "kind and peaceful." The only character in *The Howling* who seems to think there is a way to bridge the gap between the two states of existence is Waggner. Put differently, Waggner's therapy is based on the assumption that werewolves, as well as people, can achieve coexistence by adjusting their respective present conditions; by acting as autonomous, willful subjects. And indeed, the success of Waggner's therapy would be the only way for the story not to end in mutual conflict and Karen's planned suicide-by-proxy. But his therapy *doesn't* succeed. As Waggner is dying, we get a glimpse of the screenwriter's and, possibly, the director's position on the matter. "Thank God," the doctor mutters, letting us know that even though he may have detested his lycanthropic urges, keeping them at bay was a constant, agonizing struggle. If the drive to enlighten could not even be sustained by its initiator, how can enlightenment ever be expected from those completely in the dark? Still, Wagner's gratitude for a merciful death, as much as Karen's self-sacrifice, when they both could have enjoyed pleasurable, healthy, immortal, albeit immoral, lives as werewolves, speaks to the presence of some moral kernel: a source of goodness which imbues them with a belief that certain kinds of life – particularly life at the expense of other lives – are not worth living.

LIBERATED AGENTS

The nature of the transformations in Dante's *The Howling* and the significance of its residual human moral kernel can be contrasted with the case of David Cronenberg – a contemporaneous body of work in which the existence of any moral kernel is denied time and again, and which is – as it might seem redundant to point out – largely preoccupied with themes of transformation and transcendence of the human state of existence. Arguably, most protagonists of Cronenberg's body horror films end up as borderline, or as something other than, human. And while their transformations look horrifying and disgusting, they do present an opportunity. In *Videodrome* (1983), Max Renn is transformed by the Videodrome signal into a human VCR, a modular receptacle for external programming, thus becoming the embodiment of the Orwellian thesis that there is no healthy human core, no innate morality or strength of character, to safeguard us from the onslaught of dominant ideology. On the other hand, if there is indeed no stable ground for human subjectivity to make a stand against an invading ideological force, there will consequently be nothing to prevent the newly established dominance from disintegrating as well. In this sense Cronenbergian transformations are essentially

The Howling

neutral processes, which merely reflect the on-going personal and social delineation of what it means to be normal, human, alive: they imply rebirth no less than death, liberation no less than enslavement.

Where might this attitude place Dante in relation to Cronenberg? At first glance, *The Howling* concludes in much the same way as Cronenberg's *The Fly* (1986): the protagonists in both – Karen, transformed into a werewolf; Seth Brundle, a new biological entity named Brundlefly – are unwilling to live with the result of their respective transmutations, and opt for a mercy killing. But Karen's and Brundlefly's decisions to die actually spring from opposite situations with regard to subjectivity and agency. For as much as Brundle is defined by flesh, what emerges from the teleportation pod is no longer Brundle, but the Cronenbergian "New Flesh", set to depart for new worlds, and to drag behind it the unwilling, but ultimately impotent consciousness. When *The Fly*'s third-stage hybrid – Brundlefly combined with the teleportation pod – finally consents to die, it is motivated not by any morally concerned remnant of Seth Brundle, but by the unbearable pain of its existence. It *is* consciousness; it is *a kind* of subject; but it is also a subject determined by the endless permutations of flesh. It chooses death be-cause life is no longer a sustainable option. *The Howling*'s Waggner and Karen, on the other hand, welcome the extinction of the living, unencumbered and monstrous flesh as a reaffirmation of their moral subjectivity.

It is somewhat counterintuitive, however, to say that the transformations of *The Fly* are a lighter, happier prospect than those in *The Howling*. If Cronenbergian transformations are in themselves indeed neutral, they are so only as long as we are willing to forgo our attachment to what currently constitutes our humanity and society. They might offer a chance at liberation – but only if we are ready to concede that our present condition may be one of captivity. Dante and Sayles, on the other hand, present the human condition as essentially liberated. In *The Howling*, both humans and were-wolves are capable of acting as moral subjects, as Karen's sacrifice and Dr. Waggner's gratitude for being killed attest. But only humans stand to gain anything from choosing kindness and morality. Moral life as a werewolf is either an eternal struggle with one's killing urges, or a prelude to suicide. In opposition to the Cronenbergian universe, transgressing the borders of humanity in Dante's *The Howling* offers no chance at reinvention, except as a beastly murderer or a martyr.

The Hole

PROHIBITED AGENTS

The idea that there is a terrible price to pay for tinkering with the human condition, or any other natural condition, is what drives a number of Dante's films. In *The Hole* (2009), brothers Dane and Lucas discover a padlocked trapdoor in the basement of the house to which they have recently moved with their mother. Acting on impulse, they open the trapdoor and find the seemingly bottomless titular hole underneath. They probe it with a few ingenious empirical methods to no avail. The hole gradually reveals itself to be an amplifier of individual fears, and the story progresses to a satisfying, as well as sequel-friendly, conclusion.

A trapdoor held in place by six sturdy padlocks is an explicit visual rendering of what human society understands as *prohibition*. Its concealment – the trapdoor is hidden under a rug topped with an armchair – extends an invitation as much as it sounds a warning. The film's typical Western middle-class youngsters – engaged in sibling rivalry, immersed in high tech gadgetry, subsisting on junk food, and left to their own devices while their single mother works – violate the prohibition using pragmatic, meddlesome means, and in the process unleash hell. The example is all the more poignant, and the metaphor all the more distilled, because what exemplifies the prohibition, and the dangers inherent in violating it, is basically a blank space: a locked hatch, extending into a bottomless void. Here, in a nutshell, is what Dante's horror films are about.

In *Piranha*, pragmatic tinkering with genetics produces a strain of mutant killer fish which proceed to terrorize and slaughter summer vacationers. It is a cautionary tale against violating the natural order of things, in which the first victims seal their fate by ignoring a "No Trespassing" sign ("A little lawbreaking will do you good," says one of them). As dictated by the cultural clichés of its era, *Piranha*'s trespasser characters have an unmistakable, though belated "hippie" aspect to them, which connects their transgressions and eventual demise to those of *The Howling*'s esoteric community. Dr. Waggner's attempts at psychological therapy and reeducation of the werewolves is a clear reference to the New Age precept that there is virtually no limit to what sentient beings can do; which, as we have seen, is doomed to fail because "it ain't natural."

Of course, the best known of all prohibitions issued in Joe Dante's films are those concerning a Mogwai being exposed to bright light, coming into contact with water, and being fed after midnight. As Dante acknowledges in his commentary to *Gremlins 2: The New Batch*, these rules are arbitrary, but that is precisely the point. There is some confusion as to whether these rules imply an unfathomable natural order or a metaphysical, supernatural one, since all of them appear to extract the Mogwai from the perceived way of things.[6] In either case, Gizmo the Mogwai is a deceptively adorable cousin of the Hole. It is an object of no practical value beyond the fascination it generates. It exists in the natural world as a monad of sorts: its character cannot be pragmatically moderated or negotiated with, and any transgression against the prohibitions it embodies, nonsensical as they may appear, can only spell disaster.[7]

ERRING AGENTS

In both *Gremlins* films, Gizmo's cycle of multiplication and transformation is launched by human error; the first time by a clumsy boy who knocks over a jar filled with water, the second by a careless plumber repairing a drinking fountain. But the first installment, based on a darker, more violent spec script by Chris Columbus, makes this point much earlier on. Gizmo is introduced to American society when "he" is sold by a Chinese boy to Randall Peltzer, a bungling inventor, who in turn gives the "pet" to his son Billy as a Christmas present. The boy does so against the wishes of his grandfather Mr. Wing, a curio shop owner who refuses to sell Gizmo. "With Mogwai comes much responsibility," he cautions, meaning,

6 There are varying amounts of water in all living beings, yet it is allowed for a Mogwai to eat – and thus come in contact with – meat and vegetables before midnight; not to mention the fact that a Mogwai, being alive, must partly consist of water itself. And, as the smartass technician notes in *Gremlins 2*, it is always midnight *somewhere*.

7 Moments later, the technician is attacked by the very thing that he has observed makes no sense.

8 This may seem laughable in view of today's global economic situation, where China has surpassed the West in its industrial mastery of matter. On the other hand, Mr. Wing seems to represent an ancient, Daoist perspective, favouring respectful coexistence with the universe rather than its intrusive reshaping.

Gremlins

"you can't even make a toothbrush work, so why should I entrust you with a magical creature?"

Both films are replete with examples of innovations that don't work, particularly *The New Batch*, set in a "smart building" and essentially conceived as a series of gags that frequently comment on some facet of our obsession with technology, the endless bending of matter to fit our desires, derailed and spinning out of all proportion. With such recklessness the task of caring for a Mogwai is fundamentally incompatible with Western culture, a point accentuated by giving Gizmo Chinese caretakers.[8] When Mr. Wing accuses the Peltzers of doing with Gizmo "what your society has done with all of nature's gifts," it seems we've just had *Gremlins* deciphered in terms of a broad geopolitical satire.

Our society's failure in taking responsibility for all of "nature's gifts," the idea of cultural or societal mistakes taking on a life of their own, is embodied in the life-cycle of the gremlins themselves. After Gizmo multiplies into several Mogwai – a consequence of human error alone – the malicious offspring will do everything it can to feed after midnight, form slimy cocoons, and complete its metamorphosis into gremlins. These, again, will do their best to get wet and spawn even more creatures. The motifs of contamination, infection, infestation, and other uncontrollable phenomena are completely in line with how we imagine, and what we fear about, chemical and biological disasters.

Even more obviously, what gremlins do when they set out on their rampage is monstrous and grotesque because it is a cartoonish exaggeration of human behavior. In one of *Gremlins'* highlight sequences, Chloe is forced to tend bar while gremlins indulge in binge drinking, exhibitionism, playing videogames, cross-dressing, gambling, gun play, and the destruction of the bar's inventory. This infernal version of a tired human cliché – drunks harassing the waitress – amounts to role-playing: the creatures are, in essence, playing at being human. In the sequel this is famously spelled out by the "Brain Gremlin" who has, through experimenting with genetic matter, acquired the trait of eloquence (and an upper-class accent): "What we want is, I think, what everyone wants… Civilization… The niceties, the fine points. Diplomacy, compassion, standards, manners, tradition. That's what we're reaching toward." And like every diplomatic, compassionate civilization with its standards, manners and tradition, both batches of gremlins maim and kill mostly with technological means. Few of their victims actually get bitten or clawed: most are eliminated with things like snowploughs, electric stair climbers, dental tools and kitchen utensils. It seems the crimes they commit are human because their very existence is of human commission.

Still, what hope Dante affords in encountering the prohibited, in keeping it from being violated, seems to reside in the fragile and fallible human agency. Like Karen and Dr. Waggner, Bill and Chloe in *Gremlins* are ethical agents struggling against all odds to put the proverbial genie back in the bottle. In Dante's cinema, the regions that should be most avoided, as well as the faculties by which to avoid them, both reside within humans themselves. As Jim Kalla ruminates during the carnage in the closing shots of *The Second Civil War*, "we are an unfinished piece of art; part tragedy, part comedy, part joy, part farce, a work in progress. But for the moment, we're still painting and writing in blood."

BLOODY AGENTS

In at least two of his works, Dante has treated the theme of human bloody-mindedness in the context of intersexual relations. Consider the example of Karen's husband Bill in *The Howling*, a vegetarian and health club owner who's been harboring doubts about his manhood. Married to a successful and prominent woman, Bill is routinely subjected to compliments about his wife's bravery, and at one point, since she hasn't taken his surname, to being referred to as "Mr. White" by a TV station employee. This mistake obviously stems from a patriarchal perspective – the assumption that "White" is Bill's rather than Karen's surname. But Bill corrects him instantly – and with a degree of annoyance that certainly betrays what *he* associates with being called "White", i.e. the subversion of his traditional role as a husband. The last blow to his self-image comes when Karen, following the attack, stops responding to his sexual advances. He is only capable of regaining his masculine self once he has turned into a werewolf and had sex with Marsha, one of The Colony's

The Screwfly Solution (2006)

she-wolves. Traditional concepts of manhood are only aligned with his state of being when he becomes a naturally conditioned killer.

Dante goes even further in depicting maleness as a murderous trait in his second *Masters of Horror* episode, the adaptation of Alice Sheldon's short story *The Screwfly Solution* (2006). The title refers to a technique used to eradicate the parasitic screw-worm flies – releasing a large numbers of sterilized male specimens into the wild, thereby breaking the species' reproductive cycle. In the story, a similar eradication measure is used on humans by aliens who want to conquer Earth. The difference is that the method doesn't sterilize human males; rather, it blurs the boundaries between their sexual desire and violent impulses, causing them to murder women. The story plays with certain slippery notions of manhood – for instance, that every male is constantly plagued by his sexual drives and violent urges, and is therefore a rapist (or a murderer) in waiting, or that men can only relate to women to the extent that

they want to have sex with them. *The Screwfly Solution* makes for Dante's darkest work by far: not only because aliens succeed in wiping out humanity, but because humanity itself is unable to retain any capacity for moral action.

RISEN AGENTS

Homecoming (2005), Dante's first contribution to *Masters of Horror*, is a venture in the opposite direction. Here, the capacity for moral action extends beyond the boundaries of the human lifespan, and triumphs over the flesh that makes such short work of it in *The Screwfly Solution*. Even more so than *The Second Civil War*, which took its cues from the lingering separatism in certain segments of American politics and culture (brought to attention by incidents such as the Waco siege and the Oklahoma City bombing), *Homecoming* is Dante's direct reaction to the headlines of the day and as such one of his most explicitly political films (even if most of his works entertain ideas with implications for political life). Similarly to *The Second*

Civil War, it is based on a "what if" scenario, but whereas the former is a far-fetched speculation, *Homecoming* is essentially an allegory; most of its thematic elements can be linked to contemporaneous events and their protagonists. The hypothetical premise of the film has soldiers – killed in an unspecified, ongoing war – rising from their graves with one purpose only: to vote the current administration out of office. Their resurrection is a direct response to talk show speculation by a government spin doctor that if a bereaved mother's son were to come back to life, "he would tell us all how important this struggle is… for the safety and security of all Americans." Such co-opting of the dead into the second Iraq War agenda was one of the more glaring instances of the Bush administration's propagandist rhetoric. The point of contention is not necessarily that it didn't confer on the fallen their due dignity – military service is not compulsory in the U.S. today and anyone enlisting had to be, or should have been, aware of the possibility that they would be deployed to war for less than justifiable reasons. It was contentious because it was unverifiable. The dead can neither confirm nor deny how they feel about the circumstances of their deaths.

The question posed by *Homecoming* is thus "What if they could?" Yet in order to answer this question, *Homecoming* must resort to the very rhetoric it is attempting to subvert; it essentially states that if the dead were to come to life they would oppose the administration's wars, whereas the administration has used the same unverifiable premise to claim the opposite. This impasse in the film's hypothesis weakens its subversive potency somewhat. Arguably, its line of argument, and the metaphor that supports it, would have been more effective if the story only progressed to the point where the first zombie soldier turns in his vote. The episode does succeed, however, in glorifying human moral agency, thus adding a paradoxical twist to the zombie genre. The risen soldiers of *Homecoming* are the opposite of the stereotypically mindless, flesh-devouring zombies populating the genre. The metaphorical usefulness of the run-of-the-mill zombie is that it is, in itself, a rather boring, blank-slate creature. It is a readymade receptacle for any number of meanings one would care to ascribe to it. Dante gives zombies volition and a message, and in turn delivers another affirmation of hope – no less inherent to the human condition than its horror and destructiveness.

Homecoming (2005)

J. Hoberman

The *Gremlins* Franchise:
Standing Spielberg on His Head

"Everyone kept saying: This is *E.T.* with teeth. Which, I think, is something Steven would like to do – get that side of his *E.T.* personality out – except he doesn't really want to do it himself." – Joe Dante, *Film Comment* (June 1984)[1]

Or, as David Chute put it with a nod to *Forbidden Planet* in the *Film Comment* cover-story that heralded the coming of *Gremlins*, the eponymous creatures in Joe Dante's movie were the "monsters from *E.T.*'s id."

Sugar laced with strychnine, *Gremlins* revels in the horror that lurks beneath the surface of the cute; it reveals the creature from the bland lagoon. Our first view of the film's collective, eponymous monster is heralded by the saccharine sound of Johnny Mathis crooning "Do You Hear What I Hear?" The movie's climactic *Walpurgisnacht* is set, for maximum desecration, on the holiest night of the Christian calendar and in the innocuous Warner Bros. "small town" which, among many other things, was invaded by Soviet troops in the 1962 public service film *Red Nightmare* – part Frank Capra's Bedford Falls, part Ronald Reagan's "Morning in America," all Hollywood.

"The ideas of the ruling class are in every epoch the ruling ideas," Marx and Engels opined. Is it a paradox that *Gremlins* – opening salvo in the Summer of 1984 (1984!), the year that, in addition to the John Milius *Red Nightmare* remake *Red Dawn*, brought (on the very same day) the magic of *Ghostbusters*, the scarcely less wondrous American triumph in the a-Soviet "We're Number One!" Los Angeles Olympics, the release of Bruce Springsteen's head-banging anthem "Born in the U.S.A.," the second coming of Indiana Jones, a Camp David screening of *Bedtime for Bonzo*, and the euphoric re-election year frenzy of Reaganmania – was widely understood as the simultaneous triumph of Spielbergism and its antithesis, and that this double apprehension was instantaneous?

"I make the illogical logical." So claims Rand Peltzer (Hoyt Axton), the feckless inventor-salesman-dad, a Bizarro World Thomas Edison, who, following his nose into a Chinatown novelty store, discovers the original cute and cuddly Keane-eyed Mogwai, soon to be known as Gizmo. Really the Peltzer motto is meant to be read in reverse. If anything, his time-saving

---

1 On the other hand, when interviewed for *Time* magazine by *Film Comment*'s editor Richard Corliss, Dante cautiously maintained that "If I thought [*Gremlins*] was close to *E.T.*, I probably wouldn't have become associated with it."

Gremlins

inventions turn straightforward notions into utter nonsense just as Joe Dante, *mutatis mutandis*, may be considered the gremlin that put the kibosh on the (not yet named Dream-Works) Spielberg machine.

It's all so easy: just add water. Is there a rational reason, even in the storybook world that *Gremlins* creates, why Gizmo – a furry, pet-able pet far more lovable than the reptilian E.T., presented by Rand to his too-old-for-toys son Billy (Zach Galligan) for Christmas – should, if carelessly sprinkled with ordinary H_2O, erupt in icky pustules that hatch altogether less adorable versions of the Mogwai and that these fur-balls, if allowed to feed after midnight, turn into hilariously mean, scarifying black leather creatures from the pit of hell? Or, with respect to the studio that produced the movie, perhaps *Gremlins* was spawned by the unit nicknamed Termite Terrace – a Warner Bros. cartoon run amok?

Dante creates an ambiance of cozy, all-American wholesomeness purely for the fun of staging an adolescent or – appropriate to the post-*E.T.* world – an infantile desecration. *Gremlins'* key image has one of its loathsome monsters blowing its snout on the living room drapes. There's something primal going on. Even during the movie's blatantly innocent first third, Dante uses an exploding juice squeezer to stage an excremental attack on Mom's spotless kitchen; later, Mom herself (Frances Lee McCain) is compelled to employ assorted kitchen appliances as instruments of (extremely messy) pest-control.

No less than *Red Dawn* or *Ghostbusters*, *Gremlins* is a nightmare of enemy invasion. The xenophobic notion of the infernal critters as foreigners is articulated throughout the movie (mainly by a guy obsessed with the decline of the U.S. automobile industry), but the gremlins' gleeful destruction is against interpretation and beyond good and evil. They begin their reign of terror by stringing up the Peltzer family dog, then, after doing battle with Mom, go on to torment the town's resident "Miss Gulch" (with yuletide carols no less), and take over a local bar, where the younger Peltzer's chaste girlfriend (Phoebe Cates) is inexplicably employed, trashing, flashing, and otherwise staging the nastiest puppet show in the history of Hollywood before adjourning to the Kingston Falls bijou, where they first destroy the projection booth and then treat themselves to a special screening of *Snow White and the Seven Dwarfs* (1937), happily singing along with "Heigh-Ho."

This bravura bit of double animation allows Dante to hold up a less than flattering mirror to

Gremlins

his audience (identified by reviewer Scott Rosenberg in the *Boston Phoenix* as "American youth sotted and crazed from a steady diet of exhausting Spielberg and Lucas flicks") and even – anticipating the comic highpoint of Quentin Tarantino's *Inglourious Basterds* by a quarter century – blow them sky high. Why not just say it: Gremlins 'R' Us?

As *New York Times* reviewer Vincent Canby realized, Dante's movie was ("unfortunately") at its funniest when being "most nasty." Dabbling in real blood while intimating pain, flashing a chainsaw and stopping in its tracks for Cates's resident ingénue to recount straight-faced a long sick joke about why she hates Christmas (Grandma did not get run over by a reindeer but Dad did get fatally trapped, coming down the chimney), *Gremlins* lurches as uneasily from greeting-card hyperglycemic to disgusto near-splatter, oscillating between horror-comedy and ultra-violence, as its compulsive cross-referencing would suggest. A condensed version of Dante's and Jon Davison's *The Movie Orgy* (1966–2009), *Gremlins* is, at any given moment, merging *The Wizard of Oz* (1939) and *The Thing from Another World* (1951), *E.T.* (1982) and *Invasion of the Body Snatchers* (1956), *It's a Wonderful Life* (1946) and *Forbidden Planet* (1956), *Snow White* and *The Texas Chainsaw Massacre*

(1974), or *Alien* (1979) and "The Sorcerer's Apprentice" sequence from *Fantasia* (1940) – to name only those films Dante explicitly acknowledges.

It's humor in what *MAD* used to call a jugular vein. "I've no idea how children will react to the sight of a Kingston Falls mom, carving knife in hand, decapitating one gremlin and shoving another into the food processor, head first," Canby confessed. "Will they laugh when Billy Peltzer, the film's idealized, intentionally dopey, 20-year-old hero, is threatened by a gremlin with a chainsaw and then stabbed by a gremlin with a spear gun? Will they cheer when Billy blows up the Kingston Falls movie theater, where the gremlins, now resembling an average kiddie matinee crowd, are exuberantly responding to *Snow White and the Seven Dwarfs*?"

Somebody must have cheered, at least at Warners. *Gremlins* surpassed the studio's two previous box office champions, *Superman: The Movie* (1978) and *The Exorcist* (1973), needing only 42 days to gross $100 million.[2]

~

"In the original version of the story, which was incredibly gruesome, the gremlins were more… well, they ate the kid's dog." Joe Dante, *Film Comment* (June 1984)

More than that: in the early drafts of Chris Columbus's script, the gremlins also decapitated the hero's mother and rolled her head downstairs.

If the lethal mischief of *Gremlins'* Main Street-trashing visitation suggests the ten plagues of Egypt as devised by avenging deity Daffy Duck, the movie's back story has something of an Old Testament quality itself. The script had been written during the summer of 1981 – not long after Dante had achieved a measure of underground success for *The Howling* – by recent New York University graduate Columbus, then resentfully holed up in a shabby midtown loft overrun by vermin. Somehow the scenario made its way to Steven Spielberg who, sensing its possibilities as a low-budget, attitudinous, special effects-driven horror flick like *The Howling* (or his current Tobe Hooper-directed project *Poltergeist* [1982]) reached down out of

---

2 Along with *Indiana Jones and the Temple of Doom* (1984), *Gremlins* inspired a reaction against violence in ostensive children's fantasies that led to the creation of a new PG-13 rating. At the same time the movie anticipated the 1985–86 grade school craze for "Garbage Pail Kids," artfully gross-out trading cards that, beloved by eight-year-olds and hated by grade school authorities, trashed Cabbage Patch dolls as *Gremlins* travestied *E. T.*

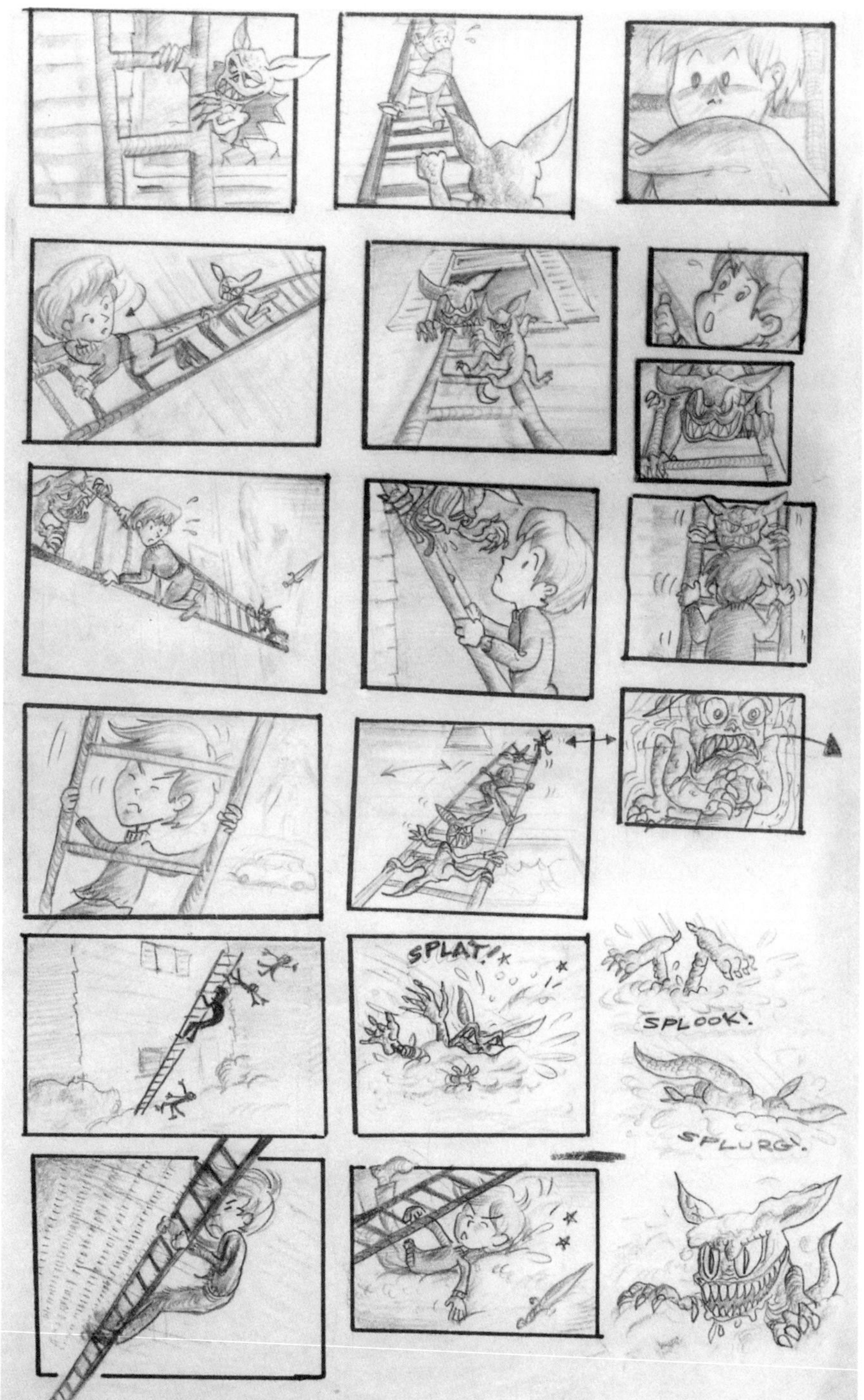

Gremlins storyboard

the blue and anointed the astonished Dante to direct.[3]

"Who is this picture for?" Dante mused in his interview with Chute. "Is it for kids, or is it for grownups, or is it for grownups who wish they were kids?" The same might be said regarding any number of Spielberg films; the difference is that Dante's world view is authentically, knowingly juvenile. Columbus's protagonists were initially young teenagers but, according to Dante, "Steven saw that as 'way too close to *E.T.*'" and instructed Columbus to raise their age levels. "However, the behavior of the lead characters did not really alter that much" – thus adding a discordantly backward quality to their portrayals. They are neither kids, nor teenagers, nor young people but, no less a textual effect than the gremlins, "innocent" creatures fashioned from Flubber.

Gremlins is a movie about, if not for, children of all ages predicated on the venerable and quintessentially Spielbergian fantasy of toys come to life – in this case a small army of two-foot tall latex-covered puppets created by Chris Walas. (The whole gang, including 12 versions of Gizmo, had a price-tag of $1.3 million – slightly less than the cost of the puppets for *E.T.*, a comparably priced production, and slightly more than 10% of the movie's overall budget).

Preoccupied with *Indiana Jones and the Temple of Doom*, much of which was shot on location in Sri Lanka, Spielberg was something of an absentee landlord, albeit one that *Gremlins* evokes throughout. The local movie theater is showing "Watch the Skies" and "A Boy's Life" (the original titles for *Close Encounters of the Third Kind* [1977] and *E.T.*), a billboard advertises a radio personality with a distinct resemblance to Indiana Jones, and a toy shop features an E.T. figure. Gizmo harmonizes with Billy on something very close to the *Close Encounters* communication song. Dante told Spielberg biographer Joseph McBride that his patron was a bemused good sport. "He got the joke right away… But I don't think he was prepared for how wacky *Gremlins* was. I remember sitting with him in a

3 While *The Howling* was shot in under a month, *Gremlins* required half a year. Pre-production took so long that, before Dante even began shooting *Gremlins*, he was drafted into another Spielberg project, namely *Twilight Zone: The Movie* (1983), a tribute to the Boomer-cherished TV series of the early '60s. Dante's segment was adapted from an episode in which a demonic 10-year-old uses telekinetic powers to terrorize his hometown. For Dante, it's the kid's televisual powers – he gives his pintsized *übermensch* an imagination fed exclusively by TV funny animal cartoons. More than a few reviewers, myself included, saw this mini-masterpiece as a satire of the movie's producer that "hilariously undermines Spielberg's junk-food notions of childhood innocence." (*Village Voice*, July 5, 1983)

Dante directing *Gremlins*

Warners screening room, and I saw him in the row behind me hitting his head [again and again] while he was watching the movie."

Despite his misgivings about *Gremlins'* manic misanthropy, Spielberg supported Dante when the studio attempted to excise the Cates character's impassioned, deadpan denunciation of Christmas. According to Dante, Spielberg's "major change" – and consequently *Gremlins'* major concession to Spielbergism – was keeping Gizmo alive throughout the movie long after logic dictates his demise. The decision would reap millions in adorable Mogwai dolls and *Gremlin* ancillary rights even as it contributed to the movie's schizoid self-awareness. "The merchandising thing started after we were well into shooting, so I can't say, conceptually, that it played any large part," Dante told Chute, adding that he was nevertheless appreciative of Rand Peltzer's excited declaration, upon seeing the Mogwai, that "every kid in America will want one of these!"

Gremlins' mise-en-scène is characterized by Spielberg's then-current form of brand name naturalism, with logos for Burger King, Coors, Snickers, and Mobil gas all prominently on display but, thanks to the persistence of Gizmo, the movie would be a magnificent advertisement for itself. As reported by *Variety*, *Gremlins* spawned the greatest promotional blitz in Warners' history – a mix of radio spots, mall banners, store signage and shopping bags designed to produce 100 million "shopper impressions." The audience was primed. Janet Maslin attended an early preview and told the readers of the *New York Times* that on first glimpsing Gizmo, spectators "emitted what sounded like the 'Aaah!' heard round the world."

The hope was that *Gremlins* would rival Fox's *Star Wars* franchise and Universal's *E.T.* as a merchandizing bonanza. In addition to the requisite action figures, story books, paperback novelizations, posters, trading cards, T-shirts, children records, videogames and lunch boxes, there were pajamas, pencil cases, underwear, bed linen, Halloween costumes, greeting cards, air fresheners and gumball dispensers. Scott tissues offered free stickers. So did Ziploc brand Sandwich Bags. Ralston produced a Gremlins Sweetened Cereal ("only one cereal satisfies a Gremlin appetite!").

The water was on the Mogwai. By late July, according to *Variety*, Warners had asked the US International Trade Commission "to take action against 32 manufacturers, importers, and distributors of unlicensed merchandise," mainly based in East Asia. "These counterfeiters," the studio explained, "can produce and ship some 300,000 items a month and have the potential to 'substantially' destroy the market for legitimate *Gremlins* goods in this country." It's suggestive that after Billy successfully blows up the movie theater and destroys the gremlin horde, the gremlin leader remains... hidden in the toy store behind an E.T. doll.

If *Gremlins* is conspicuous by its absence in Andrew Britton's masterful analysis "Blissing Out: The Politics of Reaganite Entertainment," a text (all the more impressive for having been written in the heat of the moment) that devotes considerable space to *Red Dawn*, *Ghostbusters*, and *Indiana Jones and the Temple of Doom*, as well as *E.T.* and even *Poltergeist*, it may be so because

it was so shocking an anomaly. The film alone succeeded in using what Britton called "the ritualized repetitiveness of Reaganite entertainment... with its delirious, self-celebrating self-reference [and] interminable solipsism." [4]

Yet, thanks to Spielberg's last-minute intervention, *Gremlins* also succeeded as a Spielberg blockbuster, allowing the audience to participate in Dante's critique by negating it with the purchase of dollars of worthless paraphernalia. There's a parallel to be found in the way that Springsteen's deeply pessimistic and even despairing "Born in the U.S.A." was embraced and appropriated (and not only by the Reagan campaign) as an upbeat celebration of American patriotism. [5]

~

"I hated Joe Dante's *Gremlins* – a malignant horror-comedy more mean than funny...
but *Gremlins 2: The New Batch* is a sensationally entertaining movie." – David Denby,
New York magazine (June 25, 1990)

Gremlins was a mass of contradictions. Indeed, as was often observed, the movie was as schizoid as its Mogwai mascot.

For Jonathan Rosenbaum, *Gremlins* conjured "a second movie, diametrically opposed to the first, that gleefully assaults everything the first movie holds sacred: Christmas, Norman Rockwell's America, consumer society, and good old-fashioned family entertainment," while David Chute noted that Dante seems to make his movies and their *MAD* magazine parodies at the same time. This built-in travesty may be the reason why *MAD*'s parody "Grimlins," written by Stan Hart and illustrated by Mort Drucker, doesn't quite work.

And yet, "Grimlins" does point to *Gremlins'* critique of American self-delusion: "This is *Stinkton Falls*… a typically American small town!" Bilgy Setzer explains. "Our *drinking water* is *polluted* with *carcinogens!* Our *streets* are *paved* with *radioactive materials!* Our *classrooms* are lined with *asbestos!* And we've got a *toxic waste dump* that's *emptying* into our *basements!* Man, if *that* doesn't make us *typically American*… I don't know WHAT *does!*"

MAD's suggestion that *Gremlins* is *E.T.* with "an extra-added wrinkle" or characterization of Gizmo as *"a midget* YODA… *in drag!"* are not without merit but the notion of Kingston Falls as a Potemkin Village is the key insight of the piece. Hart and Drucker's most pointed joke is found on the side of the microwave oven used to incinerate a gremlin: "AT GENERAL ELECTRIC, REAGAN WAS OUR MOST IMPORTANT PRODUCT."[6]

The spell had been broken and George Bush was 18 months into his presidency when

4 Andrew Britton, "Blissing Out: The Politics of Reaganite Entertainment," *Movie* , no. 31/32 (Winter 1986); also in: *Britton on Film: The Complete Film Criticism of Andrew Britton*, edited by Robin Wood and Barry Grant, Detroit: Wayne State University Press, 2008

5 Produced at Paramount, Dante's next film *Explorers* (1985) – in which a trio of 12-year-olds builds a working space rocket – was, as I wrote then, "an example of Spielbergism without Spielberg" and all the more critical: "Seldom has the adolescent love of sci-fi, comic books, and cybernetics been shown to be so blatantly compensatory. It's a Spielberg Way of Knowledge, but Dante is more self-aware and gadget-oriented than the master: he's naturally alienated. The three explorers suffer from creepy families, are picked on by bullies and embarrassed by teachers, dream of spying on girls …

The film's payoff gleefully travesties the cloying religiosity of Spielberg's extraterrestrial films and even more powerfully, scores the nostalgic cultural solipsism of the Spielberg ideology … Face to face with a hilariously bug-eyed monster, Ben reaches back into his stockpile of old movie clichés, gasping, 'We come in peace.' Imagine his disorientation when the BEM reaches back into his stockpile, segueing from Bugs Bunny to Goofy to Ed Sullivan to W. C. Fields to Little Richard to Humphrey Bogart in a demonic 15-minute spritz complete with 35 years of video transmission." (*Village Voice*, July 23, 1985)

6 General Electric's slogan, during the eight-year period that Ronald Reagan served as the company's spokesman, was "Progress is our most important product."

Gremlins 2: The New Batch was released in June 1990 – the same week that the US Supreme Court declared the law against desecrating the American flag to be unconstitutional. What had once seemed to some to have been malignant and mean was now… fun. The times had changed and the wheel was in spin. (The lengthy *Gremlins 2* shoot began shortly before the Tiananmen Square massacre and ended the month that saw the collapse of the Berlin Wall.)

The headline over Janet Maslin's *New York Times* review read, "They're Back. (But Much Nicer.)" *Gremlins 2* was "only rarely scary or disgusting," she announced. Additionally, it had "much more verve, cleverness and good humor than the film on which it is based." The gremlins themselves seemed "a lot less like horror-film fixtures, and a lot more like mischief-loving children." Heigh-Ho!

Certainly, *Gremlins 2* was more posh than *Gremlins*. According to *Variety*, the negative cost more than doubled that of the original. New York's Chinatown was not a set but actual Chinatown. Still, *Gremlins 2* was structurally identical to the original, requiring the viewer to spend nearly half the movie waiting for all hell to break loose. What had changed? Compared to its progenitor, *Gremlins 2* was just as yucky, equally violent, and even more cynical.

(L'il Gizmo is revealed to be a Rambo fan.) The id-monsters had scarcely reformed – except rather than attack "innocent" Main Street they attacked perfidious Wall Street.

Indeed, id-monsters aside, *Gremlins* had no villain (the villain was us); *Gremlins 2* posited the avaricious Clamp, part Donald Trump developer, part Ted Turner media baron, as its designated (and redeemable) Reagan-era bad guy. Less Gordon Gekko than the sort of glad-handing nerd Gekko might eat for breakfast, Clamp has the mind of a Hollywood agent; snatching Gizmo, he compulsively asks, "Has anybody talked to you about merchandizing?"

Moreover, *Gremlins 2* was too entertaining to effectively travesty the notion of entertainment as Tim Burton did six years later in his most Dantean opus, *Mars Attacks!* (1996). Who could resist what might be the most elaborate set piece in the Dante oeuvre – a screen full of gremlins singing "New York, New York," appearing in Busby Berkeley formations, or dancing the conga? Rather than disrupt anyone's pleasure, Dante's self-reflexive strategies only added to the fun. At one point, TV critic Leonard Maltin is drafted to reiterate his pan of the original *Gremlins*; at another, the film *Gremlins 2* appears to slow down and melt in the projector gate, to be replaced by a bit of gremlin

Gremlins 2:
The New Batch

shadow play and then "Volleyball Holiday." Wrestling star Hulk Hogan rises out of the audience to restore order even as an irate mother berates the theater manager, "This movie is even worse than the last one!"

Clamp is the embodiment of a system. As noted by Michael Wilmington in the *Los Angeles Times*, the Clamp Tower "encapsulates consumer-culture America. It's dotted with drippy-slick little boutiques and yogurt bars, monitored by a crypto-fascist security system." Writing in *The New Yorker*, Terrence Rafferty made the same point and then missed it. "This towering steel-and-glass wedge – a monument to the runaway acquisitiveness of the eighties – and the craven go-getters who work in it offer Dante more comic possibilities than the first film's scrubbed Andy Hardy community, which never existed anywhere but in the movies (and, unfortunately, in the imagination of the actor who was our President at the time)." *Gremlins'* subject was not the system but its ideological apparatus. Jonathan Rosenbaum observed in the *Chicago Reader*, "*Gremlins 2* has no ambiguous attitude about its world and its characters, or any subversive agenda apart from its up-front satire."

1984 had come and gone; the Age of Reagan was over. Assigned to remake his greatest hit, Dante was free yet stymied. *Gremlins*, which incorporated its own auto-critique, had been assimilated, just as Spielberg knew that it would be. (As Marx and Engels put it, "the class which has the means of material production at its disposal, has control at the same time over the means of mental production.") Moreover, as signaled by *The Color Purple* (1985), Spielberg had assumed the mantle of Irving Thalberg and moved on, applying the logic of Spielbergism to historical subjects. Thus, its logo and trademarks regularly spoofed, Warner Bros. stands in for Spielberg or Spielbergism.[7]

Identifying gene-splicing with capitalist expansion, *Gremlins 2* could be read as a precursor to Spielberg's epochal *Jurassic Park* (1993). Still, with no choice other than satirizing the marketplace that had embraced and assimilated his earlier film – and no means to challenge the mentalité that produced it – Dante could do little more than attempt to turn *Gremlins* on its head.

7 The targeting of Ted Turner is prescient; Turner Broadcasting would not merge with Warner Bros. until 1996.

Pages 119–124:
Polaroid reference images from the
creature-making process of *Gremlins*

NEW COPIES OF @GREMLIN FACE MOLDS.

UNFURLING PUPPET

MOGWAI FACE FURRING

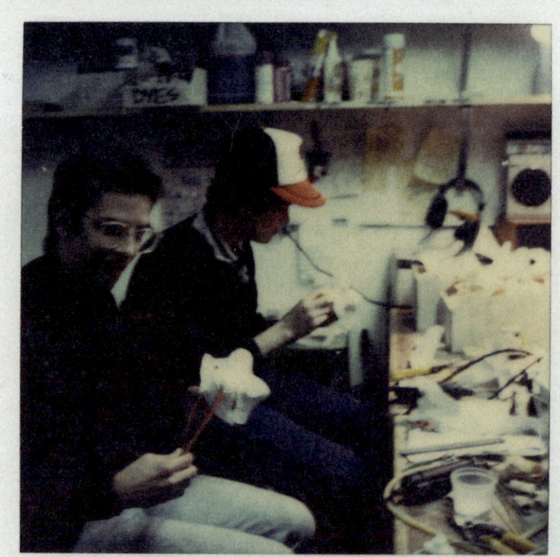

GREMLIN UNDER-SKULLS IN PROGRESS

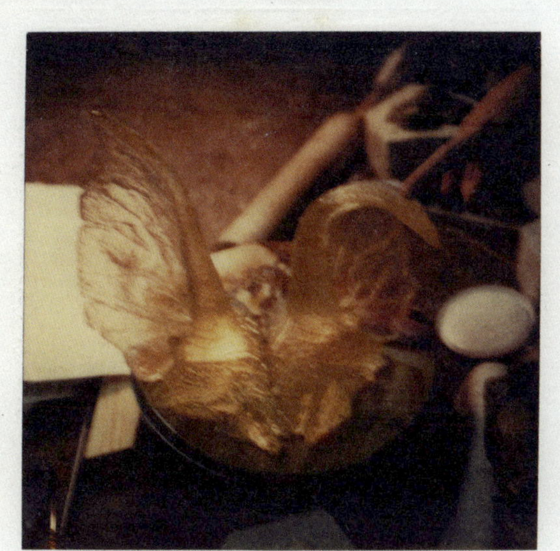

TRANSLUCENT GREMLIN EARS.
(unpainted).

EYELIDS REDONE to STRENGTHEN

"Fuzzy" POSITIVE

SPITTING MOGWAI
MECH. COMPLETE

FULL WHITE RING

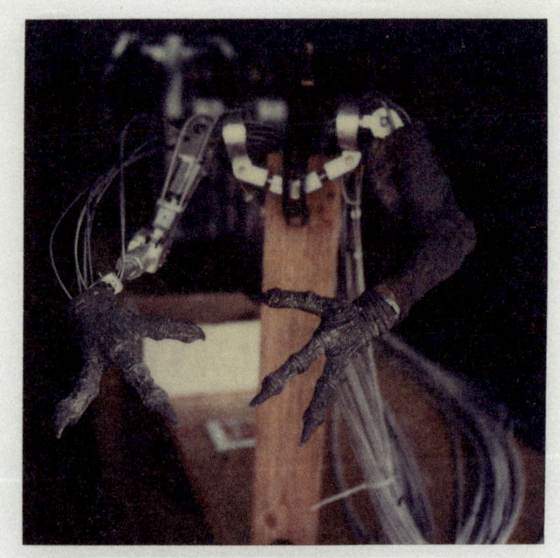

COVERING SUPER ARMS

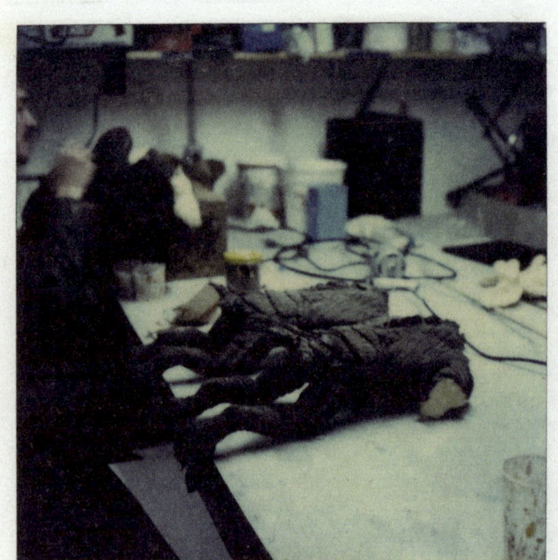

GREMLIN BODY ASSEMBLY LINE

SUPERARM HAND CONTROLS W/ NEW TENSION CONNECTORS.

MARIONETTE WALKER.

COMPLETED GREMLIN FACE MECHS.

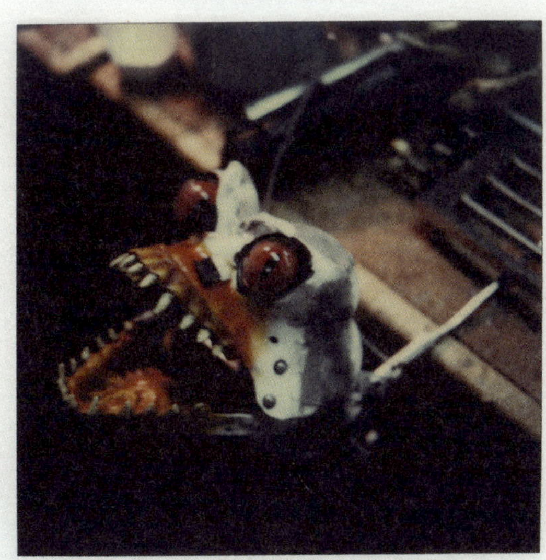

MORE MECHS

OLD REGULAR FACE
REMEMBER?

"DAZED" FACE

Gabe Klinger

Keep Your Eyes Open for the Scary Parts

Matinee, The Second Civil War, and *Small Soldiers*

Joe Dante, starry-eyed Saturday matinee kid turned weathered soldier of the Hollywood trenches, has made a career out of unnerving the corporate establishment. By sheer virtue of wanting to make personal films at a mass audience level, his every production is a battleground of conflicting interests, resulting in hard-won victory and, more often than not, bitter loss. Once upon a time it was possible for a power player like Steven Spielberg to stand up for a fledgling Corman protégée like Dante; now it would seem the industry has fully safeguarded itself from such interventions. Dante's unwritten memoir would surely dash the hopes of any young filmmaker with aspirations to break into the system nowadays and retain any vestige of his or her personal vision (for sufficient proof, venture to the earlier pages of this volume). Still reaping the benefits of having made a $200 million earner (1984's *Gremlins*), the '90s provided Dante with a last chance to play by the rules after the box office under-achievement of *Explorers* (1985), *Innerspace* (1987), *The 'Burbs* (1989), and *Gremlins 2: The New Batch* (1990) helped to whittle away the studios' confidence in him. He managed to get final cut on one theatrical feature (1993's *Matinee*), while losing out to Burger King on his next (1998's *Small Soldiers*), a progression that

was sadly inevitable for a nervy genius whose precisely rendered point of view has consistently triumphed over committee thinking, even as the odds of Hollywood survival stacked in his disfavor. Dante's fallen auteur status – or, more accurately, the studios' lack of investment in Dante's authorship – is neatly summed up in Jonathan Rosenbaum's now-canonical essay pitting Spielberg's *Saving Private Ryan* (1998) against *Small Soldiers*:

"[T]he media profiles accorded these two releases were so radically different that the relevance of Dante's film to Spielberg's went virtually unnoticed. As far as most of the public was concerned, *Small Soldiers* was anything but an auteur film: the name 'Joe Dante,' barely known in the first place among American filmgoers, was given so little emphasis in the film's advance publicity that I failed to notice it myself [...] One way of partially accounting for this confusion was the deceptive nature of the ads – which I was later surprised to discover Dante had approved, perhaps as one way of negotiating and rationalizing his ambiguous alliance with the movie's intricate tie-ins with Burger King and the sale of various war toys. These ads foregrounded the toy soldiers known as the Commando Elite as if they were the movie's unironic heroes rather than its pathetically programmed comic villains, falsely equating the movie's essence with the crassness of Commando Elite's manufacturer in the movie, known as Globotech."[1]

It's conceivable that at one point Dante could have become a prestige filmmaker like Spielberg. Early on, his efficient staging, special effects savvy, editing knowhow, collaborator loyalty, and skillful project management all contributed to his regular employment in the movie industry. But Dante's most valuable asset proved to be his visionary capacity to enlarge the boundaries of genre cinema both in terms of production value and resonant storytelling at the precise moment when Hollywood was attempting to corner the dried up exploitation market. The choice of leaving the grindhouse circuit did not run counter to Dante's own intuition; rather, it was a natural progression for a director whose worldview had grown introspective to the point of fierce disillusionment, a sentiment which the studio system has occasionally afforded him an opportunity to transmit to a vastly wider audience than the one that had been accessible to him before. Dante's disquietude creeps under the surface in the '80s and boils up in the '90s with *Matinee*, his first film in which a real-life political context – the Cuban missile crisis – appears front and center. And while the film's integration of this context into its emotional blueprint likens it, at least superficially, to Spielberg's historical prestige products, a crucial difference may be found in *Matinee*'s careful rejection of patriotism and ambiguity. Dante makes his aim clear from the first minute, when the film's upbeat main titles are replaced with harrowing stock footage of nuclear bomb tests. In the process, he reveals the protective apparatuses in place to shield Americans from catastrophe to be as flimsy as the do-it-yourself nuclear bomb shelter owned by *Matinee*'s stand-in paranoiac (played with typical over-the-top gusto by Dante regular Robert Picardo). The premise invites comparisons to the present, as it should, when the precautionary strategies have failed Americans not once (9/11), not twice (the events surrounding Hurricane Katrina), but thrice (the decade-long occupations of Iraq and Afghanistan that resulted in thousands dead and billions in debt). No doubt bearing in mind the first Iraq invasion, Dante felt that history was beginning to repeat itself. Excluding his TV melodrama

1 Jonathan Rosenbaum, "At War with Cultural Violence: The Critical Reception of *Small Soldiers*," in: *Movie Wars: How Hollywood and the Media Conspire to Limit What Films We Can See*, Chicago: A Cappella, 2000, p. 64–65

Matinee

Runaway Daughters (1994), his '90s features – *Matinee*, *The Second Civil War* (1997), and *Small Soldiers* – can be seen as a loose trilogy in which his growing indignation with U.S. foreign and domestic policy offers a coherent through-line.

~

Interestingly enough, the Cold War practice of air raid drills – that humiliating and wholly inadequate safeguarding measure that asks kids to crouch face down with their hands behind their necks in the school hallway – was still a common practice in 1993 and thus entirely relatable as it's depicted in *Matinee*. Passive military brat Gene (Simon Fenton) abides by the practice, even as he looks on intently to outspoken Sandra (Lisa Jakub), who loudly educates her peers on the gruesome particulars of radiation poisoning (she gets a week of detention for her transgression, remarking to Gene, "They put Gandhi away for a year.") Dante's teenage surrogate is clearly divided between these two characters, the first a quiet but perceptive observer who looks to horror movies for catharsis, the other a proto-'68 radical fully out of her shell and ready to stir the pot. "They're gonna bomb us?" Gene's younger brother Dennis (Jesse Lee) asks, and the older sibling doesn't know whether to take a cue from his teachers and sugarcoat reality or untap Dennis's impressionable eyes to reveal the scary truth about the nuclear age. The latter impulse eventually wins out, albeit in the shape of mutant insects in *MANT!*, the trashy horror-sci-fi film within the film from producer Lawrence Woolsey (John Goodman), a peddler of cheap thrills cut from the William Castle cloth, who takes full advantage of the nuclear zeitgeist in his marketing of a new process he's dubbed "Atomo-Vision." Suffice it to say, *MANT!* doesn't need high production value to capture the town's imagination: Castro, Khrushchev and Kennedy were already doing most of the heavy-lifting.

Evidently, audiences in 1993 didn't feel they needed an affectionate throwback to the days of the low-fi B movie romp. Spielberg's CG dinosaurs were the novelty, and *Matinee* must have looked pretty quaint in comparison. Furthermore, Dante had embedded a sophisticated war critique into the story that required some unpacking, while *Jurassic Park* offered a special effects bonanza that was free from any meaningful subtext. Nevertheless, Dante's Renfield Productions followed the effects trend after *Matinee* by developing a $25 million reboot of *The Mummy* for Universal, but the studio remained unconvinced that it was worth the investment (journeyman director Stephen Sommers would end up attached to the project a short time later). Maneuvering discreetly into TV as his large-scale studio projects continued to gestate, Dante happened upon Martyn Burke's ambitious HBO script for *The Second Civil War*. A biting satire envisioning a future conflict between the federal government and the state of Idaho, it came as a necessary digression, offering Dante an even more forceful political tableau to sink his angry teeth into. HBO's built-in audience seemed like a guarantee for relative freedom, and though he suffered the usual meddling, the result is as trenchant as anything Dante has ever directed.

While the action in *Matinee* is confined to a single Key West town (with off-screen Cuba only 90 miles away!), *The Second Civil War* sees Dante discarding his usual device of having a suburb or small town serve as microcosm for the entire country (*Gremlins*, *Explorers*, *The 'Burbs*), instead depicting three simultaneous spaces that represent opposing power structures: liberal New York City newsroom, centrist White House, and neo-con middle America (Idaho, in this case, though it could have easily been Texas or any other red state). Dante seems to have equal parts affection and disdain for the people who inhabit each of these places, affording a reactionary governor (Beau Bridges) nuance by way of an extra-marital romance with a Latina reporter (Elizabeth Peña), while strategically placing a sage newsman (played with Edward Murrow-like resignation by James Earl Jones) at the redemptive center of an overly sensationalistic media enterprise. The only character in *The Second Civil War* that gets the short end of the stick is Phil Hartman's clueless Commander in Chief, although considering the film's non-fictive equivalent, the impulse to caricature is entirely justified. Working with his greatest ensemble, Dante lends each of these roles and each intertwined subplot ample latitude, a decision that compli-

The Second Civil War

ments the film's clever straddling of satirical embellishments and plausible drama. The most impressive juggling act of Dante's career, *The Second Civil War* can't help but feel prescient keeping in mind CNN's demotion and Fox News ascension, escalating border tensions between the U.S. and Mexico, recent National Security Agency scandals, and the mounting influence of gun nut sub-cultures with every new school shooting. Given the country's separatist tendencies, it isn't surprising that in his subsequent film, *Small Soldiers*, Dante chose once again to confine the war element to U.S. soil.

It's perhaps useful to point out that Dante has only dabbled in the war genre peripherally as a means to open up a larger discussion about "everyday cultural violence" (to borrow again from Rosenbaum's discussion of *Small Soldiers*). Fusing combat picture with fantasy, the film's social critique works in spite of the studio and its merchandizing affiliates' intentions to sanitize it. Whether the filmmaker liked it or not (one could safely venture in guessing *not*), Burger King's packaging of war toys in partnership with Universal Studios even had the effect of emboldening Dante's position. Less productive was the conflation (supported by most North American critics) of Dante's agenda with that of the studio. Roger Ebert didn't give the film's young adult audience the benefit of the doubt when he wrote: "What bothered me most about *Small Soldiers* is that it didn't tell me where to stand – what attitude to adopt. In movies for adults, I like that quality. But here is a movie being sold to kids [...] When Barbie clones are being sliced and diced by a lawn mower, are they going to understand the satirical purpose?"[2]

Ebert's presumption may be productively countered by critic Dave Hickey's formulation that "what we want to see and what we want to see represented" are altogether distinguishable properties. For Hickey, "the blazing spectacle of lawn-mowered cats, exploding puppies, talking ducks, and plummeting coyotes" (referring to the vast array of violent cartoons available to kids in the '50s, when both the author and Dante grew up), were clearly representations, and the parade of "ebullient, articulate, indestructible animals" simultaneously "acknowledged and alleviated" his and other kids' anxieties about adult responsibilities.[3] What reinforces this point in *Small Soldiers* is Dante's

2 Roger Ebert, "*Small Soldiers*," *Chicago Sun-Times*, July 10, 1998

3 Dave Hickey, "Pontormo's Rainbow," in *Air Guitar: Essays on Art and Democracy*, Los Angeles: Art Issues Press, 1997, p. 48

Small Soldiers

decision to anoint his adolescent characters with a sense of responsibility lacking in their grown-up counterparts. Denis Leary's brazen Globotech CEO and Jay Mohr's do-whatever-it-takes careerist are presented in stark contrast to 15-year-old Alan Abarnathy (Gregory Smith), whose introspection ultimately leads him to consider those around him. Failing a larger commentary, Dante remains optimistic in his belief that kids are smarter in their reading of pop culture artifacts than the adults who make decisions for them will ever be, a view not shared by many American tastemakers.

"You think grown-ups have it all figured out?" Woolsey asks Gene near the end of *Matinee*, "That's just a hustle, kid. Grown-ups are making it up as they go along, just like you." The Token's rendition of "The Lion Sleeps Tonight," a favorite of American G.I.s during the Vietnam War, is played over *Matinee's* final moments as we see Woolsey taking off to the Cleveland premiere of *MANT!* (nuclear crisis averted, the American people can still look forward to being traumatized by "Atomo-Vision"). A Sikorsky helicopter flies over the Florida reefs while Gene and Sandra lightheartedly frolic below (in a make-believe sequel, longhaired Gene and beret-sporting Sandra would be burning draft cards). The helicopter announces the return of the missing father and forebodes the war to come; meanwhile, in the globalized present-day of *Small Soldiers*, Denis Leary's high-powered executive descends in a helicopter to attend… a business meeting. The film's commentary on the war machinery as an emblem of consumerism in Dick Cheney's America is hammered home when Phil Hartman's goofball dad blankly observes, while watching *To Hell and Back* (1955) on his new big-screen TV, "I think World War II was my favorite war." In an even more pungent moment, action figure Chip Hazard (voiced by Tommy Lee Jones, doing his best Patton emulation) blasts The Spice Girls' "Wannabe," that brainless marketeer's concoction that was as ubiquitous in the late '90s as "The Lion Sleeps Tonight" was in the early '60s, as a means of psychological warfare – the reference to the U.S. Marines' use of the same technique on Manuel Noriega in the '80s is not lost. Turning the gag on itself, Wendy Schaal's sloshed mom suddenly comes around to exclaim, "I love this song!"

While Paul Verhoeven's acerbic war satire *Starship Troopers*, released the year before *Small Soldiers*, operated in the adult-oriented action movie register of *Independence Day* (1994), Dante's film was unfortunately linked to the merchandizing behemoth that was *Toy Story* (1996). Asked to curb the violence when Universal partnered with Burger King so that the latter could sling Chip Hazard dolls, Dante was left with little recourse but to surrender. The director's ball and chain remained *Gremlins*, a film with a subversive design aimed at discerning adult viewers that nevertheless played successfully to kids. Verhoeven, a ferocious satirist not unlike Dante, had never cornered himself into the adolescent niche, whereas Dante remained beholden to it, at least at the studio level. *The Second Civil War*, free from such concerns, offered a startling respite for the filmmaker. Typical of HBO production, the film is

foul-mouthed and peppered with sexual innuendo – qualities that are deemed appropriate for late-night cable audiences and the European theatrical market, where it enjoyed a brief run. But apart from these superficial differences, what sets *The Second Civil War* apart from Dante's other films is the filmmaker's righteousness in depicting a divided U.S. This position gains metaphorical fortitude in the image of Jasper Johns' multi-dimensional *Three Flags*, which hangs behind news producer Mel Burgess's (Dan Hedaya) desk. Johns' implicitly political flag paintings were partly inspired by the McCarthy hearings, in which the American flag repeatedly appeared on television, and Eisenhower's signing of an amendment to add "under God" to the pledge of allegiance on Flag Day. The superimposed U.S. flags in Johns' painting may be broadly seen to allude to the three divided Americas (right, centrist and left) depicted by Dante. The interpretation doesn't seem that far off when one considers that Phil Hartman's President apes Eisenhower's Little Rock intervention from 1957 – the same year as Johns' painting – as his own model for federal action. Dante, whose production design frequently invites historical inferences, offers some of his most surprisingly erudite ideas here. In other, more characteristically blunt

Small Soldiers

moments, such as when a group of immigrant White House speechwriters whose ethnicities are exaggerated for maximum irony fabricate an Eisenhower speech for the President to deliver to the nation, no visual metaphor is required.

The legacy of Eisenhower, as summed up in his famous 1961 sign-off speech to the American people (better known as the "Military-Industrial Complex Speech"),[4] is autobiographically imbued in every aspect of *Matinee*. In view of the United States' recent wars, Eisenhower's optimistic premise provokes retrospective wincing from Dante, who must have already felt weary of the rhetoric about the great empire by 1968, when he and Jon Davison edited Nixon's Checker's speech – a clumsy sermon that contributed to the demonization of the Communist Other – into *The Movie Orgy*. As the first political speech of many to appear in Dante's cinema (Eisenhower, Kennedy, Reagan, and Bush Sr. and Jr. have all made their cameos), it set up the sardonic tone for what was to come. *Matinee* is a film in which the characters are still enacting Eisenhower's legacy; by the time *Small Soldiers* rolls around, that memory has been eviscerated by the Vietnam and Gulf wars. The Military Industrial Complex, now in cahoots with toy manufac-

turers, has programmed war into every mundane aspect of existence, Dante seems to be arguing, to the point of browbeating the culture into a state of complete and utter passivity on the subject. Perhaps this lends some reason to Dante's attempts to stay inside the studio system, where he can reach and put forth questions to the common denominator, as a subversive force to be reckoned with. Dante's '90s films were UFOs, failing to dent the administration's body armor, but important to those who saw them as a necessary riposte to the numbing war spectacle represented by contemporary examples such as *Forrest Gump* (1994), *Independence Day* and *Saving Private Ryan*.

One radical and necessary corrective to such Hollywood Endings is the outcome promised in the title of *The Second Civil War*, which comes to play in the film's concluding ten min-

---

4 Of particular resonance to *Matinee* is the second paragraph: "We now stand ten years past the midpoint of a century that has witnessed four major wars among great nations. Three of these involved our own country. Despite these holocausts America is today the strongest, the most influential and most productive nation in the world. Understandably proud of this pre-eminence, we yet realize that America's leadership and prestige depend, not merely upon our unmatched material progress, riches and military strength, but on how we use our power in the interests of world peace and human betterment."

The Second Civil War

utes. Trading Eisenhower for Lincoln, the President hastily declares war on Idaho after receiving intel that's revealed as faulty only a little later. Fearing a public relations scandal, the federal government chooses to bury the misunderstanding and persist in waging combat. Both *The Second Civil War* and *Saving Private Ryan* end on the image of a fluttering American flag, one image tinted with contradiction, the other a heart-warming salute to the nation's fallen heroes. To paraphrase newsman Jim Kalla's final voiceover in *The Second Civil War*, Joe Dante's art is messy as hell where Spielberg's is a well-ordered deception.

~

"Keep your eyes open" are Lawrence Woolsey's parting words to Gene and Sandra. "Keep your eyes open for what?" asks Sandra. "The scary parts," Gene retorts. Earlier in *Matinee*, Woolsey adapts Plato's Cave Allegory to help Gene understand why he makes horror movies. "People who go like this [masking his eyes] at the scary parts, they're not getting the whole benefit. You gotta keep your eyes open… a zillion years ago, a guy is living in a cave. He goes out one day – bam! – he gets chased by a mammoth. Now he's scared to death, but he gets away. And when it's all over with, he feels great… He goes home, back to the cave. The first thing he does, he does a drawing of the mammoth. And he thinks, 'People are coming to see this. Let's make it good. Let's make the teeth real long and the eyes real mean.' Boom! The first monster movie. That's probably why I still do it. Make the teeth as big as you want, then you kill it off, everything's okay, the lights come up." With his "war trilogy," one wonders if Dante, in the '90s, still shares Woolsey's belief in a cinema that only fleetingly creates scares – or if he wants to open his viewers' eyes to the continuity of fear as it remains unbroken and cast upon the world.

Matinee

Christoph Huber

Eat at Joe's

*(A Scientific Study of Corporate Identity)**

Joe Dante directing *Looney Tunes: Back in Action* (2003) should have been a match made in heaven. But in reality, the production seems to have been the opposite of the film it comes closest to in Dante's body of work, *Gremlins 2: The New Batch* (1992), which has been described by Dante as "the most unnecessary of all sequels," and for that very reason the film on which he enjoyed the most creative freedom (as long as the successful critters returned as a marketable quantity just in time to fill the summer slot). The making of *Looney Tunes: Back in Action* was hampered by constant studio interference, and the complaints leveled at Dante must have felt like the real-life-tragedy equivalent of an amusing gag he had staged in *Explorers* (1985). In this unlikely adventure of space-faring teenagers, the much-desired "first contact" turns into a disturbing letdown: instead of discovering the secrets of the universe, the young adventurers stumble upon couch-potato aliens addicted to the maelstrom of round-the-clock human television programming, the most ardent of the alien fans confounding the terrestrial visitors with a bizarre stand-up-routine backed by a psychedelic nightmare of channel-surfing. Earlier, the alien blurts out Bugs Bunny's immortal catchphrase "What's up, doc?" as a greeting, to which the earth kid incredulously replies: "What?" In a production meeting on *Looney Tunes*, Dante was asked the similarly inconceivable question of whether or not Bugs *has* to deliver his signature line. The old staple of self-conscious Looney Tunes cartoon wit – breaking the fourth wall – was also repeatedly challenged.

Both *Gremlins 2* and *Looney Tunes* were financial disappointments upon their release by the same studio, Warner Bros., both open (and end) with Looney Tunes cartoon animation, and both can be considered among Joe Dante's most personal triumphs. The two films also discard straightforward narrative for a series of digressions – a Dante specialty, undoubtedly influenced by his love for *MAD* magazine and its gag-filled panels, not least in the movie parodies drawn by Mort Drucker (who delighted Dante with his take on the first *Gremlins* film in 1984). A former cartoonist and rabid cinephile, Dante clearly cherishes Looney Tunes, as attested by numerous tributes throughout his career. There is even an obvious lineage via Frank Tashlin, who rose from cartoonist to animator to director at Termite Terrace, as the holy headquarters of Warner's animation depart-

---

* Strictly adhering to the rules laid down by Peter Lorre's mad scientist

Joe Dante on the set
Looney Tunes: Back in Action

ment came to be known. The genius loci of Termite production was preserved in Tashlin's later live-action pop satires, whose cartoon-influenced vein Dante has been expanding on ("total filmmaker" Jerry Lewis is the crucial link in-between).

Even if *Looney Tunes: Back in Action* may be occasionally compromised by corporate interference, it emerges as a connoisseur's love letter and a true-to-the-spirit invitation to discover the anarchic Looney Tunes universe: an ecstatically enjoyable experience, especially for the aficionados – as opposed to the unworthy commercial pap that preceded it (the big screen live action-animation hybrid *Space Jam* [1996], thoroughly franchised to the point of harmlessness, and among the many films spoofed in passing in Dante's superior not-quite-sequel). In typical Dante fashion, whatever negligible limitations are still noticeable, they are transcended by throwing themselves into the satirical equation. At times, the film appears as a satirical exposé of its own genesis, not unlike Dante's first professional work as (co-)director, *Hollywood Boulevard* (1976), whose opening includes a real-life reenactment of a cartoon sight gag (the human-shaped hole in the ground after a parachuting accident at a film shoot). Dante's great theme is the allure and violence of pop culture, both literally and as an intrusive, paradoxically liberating and destructive force in the modern world – and *Looney Tunes: Back in Action* is the culmination of his ongoing commentary about its increasing capitalist corporatization. The original Looney Tunes were among the greatest achievements of Hollywood's golden era for their satiric subversion of the cinematic customs and possibilities of the studio system. Working with much less freedom, Dante's films are the closest equivalent we have to the old cartoons in today's era of postmodern, blockbuster-oriented production.

Similar to the old days, a film by Joe Dante is never announced as "a Joe Dante film." Rather, it is part of a recognizable universe he has fashioned by deliberately and consciously maintaining longstanding collaborations with team members all the way down from producer Michael Finnell (although his non-involvement in *Looney Tunes: Back in Action* represents a point of departure, while other contributors, like the animation director Eric Goldberg, never worked with Dante before or since). Many members of the "Dante family" appear in the film, including regulars Robert Picardo, Kevin McCarthy and "lucky charm" Dick Miller, as well as semi-regulars like Roger Corman, Mary Woronov, and the Dan and Don Stanton twins.

Looney Tunes: Back in Action

Indeed, Dante's *Looney Tunes* fully bears out his signature. With his healthy sense of humor and attention to detail, he demonstrates a personal sensibility that is at work at all times. It would seem silly not to acknowledge the self-awareness of someone who directs an episode of *Amazing Stories* in 1986 titled "Boo!", follows it up with a *CSI: NY* Halloween episode again called "Boo" 21 years later, and tops that with a *Hawaii Five-0* Halloween contribution in 2011 that sneaks a neon-written "Boo" into its "Ghostbusters"-scored, chock-full of Jack-o'-lanterns establishing montage. Speaking of montage: despite the iconoclastic pleasures of his inimitable tableaux, Dante (who started out in the film business as an editor) has made montage the overriding principle in the riotous, near-apocalyptic carnival that is his cinema: contradictory juxtapositions are *the* main weapon in his satiric arsenal.

In this world of paradoxical signals, identity manifests itself as a highly fluid construct, often ascribed from outside and constantly beleaguered by the pressures of a society in thrall to the horrible, glorious detritus of encroaching, ever-expanding pop culture. Its heroes – no matter how inspiring, including the anarchic Tunes characters – have increasingly become disdainful products, used to forcefully colonize

the collective imagination for profit. But profit can surpass mere financial accumulation, as Dante's enriching work attests to. *Looney Tunes: Back in Action* concludes an increasingly embattled trilogy of sharp criticism coming straight from the heart of (and with generous means from) the entertainment assets of a rampant business model it satirizes to the point of clear recognition. The shopping mall world welcomed (with a twist) in *Gremlins 2* appears again – this time with a vengeance – in the homes of the characters in *Small Soldiers* (1998), a less pronounced representative of Dante's tableau tactic. The military-technology-powered assault of toy violence ("Don't call it violence," Denis Leary's sniping CEO insists, "call it action: kids love action!") also represents a step towards the total corporatization envisioned with absurdist abandon in *Looney Tunes: Back in Action*. There, the chairman of the beloved ACME corporation schemes to get the "Blue Monkey" diamond so he can transform all humankind (except himself) into an army of monkey workers that will churn out worthless merchandise and buy it once he has turned them back to humans. "AC-ME! AC-ME! AC-ME!," chants the board of directors, after the CEO proclaims that their corporate identity "will tower over the equator." Humans are considered useful only when they're acting as consumers: couched in the midst of Dante's essentially good-natured humor is his most radical statement on the inhuman excess of capitalism. This critique doesn't appear out of thin air – after all, in both *Gremlins 2* and *Small Soldiers*, the evil businessmen got away.

Then again, John Glover's "evil" media mogul in *Gremlins 2* was more like a spoiled child whose worst sin may have been colorizing old black and white movies (then a pet project of Ted Turner – on whom Glover was partially modeled – and a pet peeve of Dante, who was an outspoken adversary of the practice), and in *Small Soldiers*, the CEO's ruthlessness is a perfect fit for the ranting persona Denis Leary had forged as a stand-up comedian: there is a wicked wit on display even in his most cynical lines and actions. It is characteristic of Dante to prefer his villains edgy and his designated heroes soft – a thought-provoking premise, even though the point couldn't be clearer when it turns out that the toy line of Leary's "Globotech" goes by the family-friendly name of "Heartland." In having this conglomerate disseminate military research to the suburban idyll via kids toys, Dante takes things a step further than in his previous subversive contributions to '80s Spielbergiana, *Gremlins,*

Joe Dante in a publicity photo for *Looney Tunes: Back in Action*

Explorers, and especially *The 'Burbs* (1989), a film in which humans *are* the aliens, fueling xenophobic paranoia in the community. Driving home the point of total commercialization in the media age, Leary demands toys "that actually can do what they do in commercials." The culpability of media (and movies, by extension including Dante's, despite their unruly opposition) in the cycle of dumbed-down pop invasion is a key theme running through all of Dante's films, while the "corporatization trilogy" shows he's especially adept at comically unmasking the barbarity behind the whitewashing phrases of managerial and PR speak. (The mall in *Gremlins 2* knows no blackouts, just "brownouts," as if that would make it nicer.) Reaching its apex in *Looney Tunes: Back in Action*, the doublespeak is either patently ridiculous or absurdly funny in its obliterating directness, as when Daffy Duck is physically fired by Warner Bros., but not as a brand: "We own the name!" Even the evil CEO is a grandiose joke, like his world-conquering plans (or are they?): heroically played by Steve Martin as a human toon, he is inevitably upstaged by the "real" tunes, including the Tasmanian Devil, whom he introduces in a way that's applicable to the entire conspiracy: "our most vicious operative," but "also really stupid."

Dante's potent, counterintuitive approach to genre-bending consists of carving horror out of comedy rather than the other way round, a trait he shares with his favorite Looney Tunes director Chuck Jones, who probed gruesome, even existential fears through funny setups (*The Ducksters*, his merciless 1950 take on TV culture, is proto-Dantean to the extreme) and animated the Bugs and Daffy sequences for *Gremlins 2*. With *Looney Tunes: Back in Action*, Dante's strategy is so refined that the horror can easily be overlooked. The film's world is unreal in every sense, from its mixing of techniques to Daffy saving the day, which adds the final glimmer of delusional fantasy or impossible utopia. Martin's tooned-out character is a culmination of the toonish acting scattered through the Danteverse (even in the uncommonly Hawksian *Innerspace* [1987], there's not only a *wabbit*, but Martin Short, who resorts to animated spasms in moments of crisis); equally prominent is the takeover of the entire (filmic) universe by cartoon terror – the very subject of Dante's earlier contribution to *Twilight Zone: The Movie* (1983). But in *Looney Tunes*, this terror is like an amiable extension of its Las Vegas episode, a gaudy theme park condensation, as exemplified by the parodic imagining of Paris, scored to irresistible Lelouch-la-la-la, with red balloons drifting between Eiffel Tower, faux Louvre and Jerry Lewis posters. By the showdown, the line between human and cartoon presence has been thoroughly erased – and

why not? After all, the characters are basically the property of one company or another, with ACME being only pro forma more villainous than Warner Bros. itself (both managerial boards are filled with gusto by "Dante family" members). As Dick Miller pointed out in the fashion of a true paranoiac in *Small Soldiers*, there is only one giant corporation: no matter which logo it bears, it is the harbinger of imminent destruction, a notion that's cherished throughout *Looney Tunes: Back in Action*.

That said, I also would like to thank the corporation for the endless joy that *Looney Tunes: Back in Action* has given me on many viewings. The most touching among its many highlights is the extended Louvre sequence, in which Elmer Fudd chases Daffy and Bugs through famous paintings by Munch, Toulouse-Lautrec, Dalí and others, the animation changing accordingly with hilarious results. This sequence finally gives Looney Tunes their proper place in the history of art.

Looney Tunes: Back in Action
Joe Dante directing Steve Martin

Violeta Kovacsics

Season 1: Joe Dante and Serial Repetition

"Repetition and recollection are the same movement, just in opposite directions, because what is recollected has already been and is thus repeated backwards, whereas genuine repetition is recollected forwards. Repetition, if it is possible, thus makes a person happy, while recollection makes him unhappy."
Søren Kierkegaard[1]

"Foreverware," the pilot episode of *Eerie, Indiana* (1991–92), arguably Joe Dante's most personal serial work,[2] deals precisely with Kierkegaardian themes of time, the possibility of eternity, and with repetition that never reaches an end. Marshall Teller, the series' teenage protagonist, moves with his family from New Jersey to a small town called Eerie (pop. 16,661). As he soon realizes, something is amiss in the town; in episode after episode he encounters increasingly bizarre, disturbing and fantastic events. The first case involves Foreverware, a Tupperware-like line of containers that keep produce fresh for an indefinite period of time. Astonishingly, Foreverware is also used to preserve people, who appear to stop aging. Yet what appears like a dream come true (the promise of eternal life) turns into a nightmare. "You don't know what it's like to be in seventh grade for thirty years, it's a living hell,"

complains a neighborhood kid who, along with his twin brother, has been sealed in the plastic containers for years. The possibility of repetition as something approaching eternity, the repetition which according to Kierkegaard "makes a person happy," is here perverted into something slightly terrifying and expressed as a contradiction: the twins and their mother, who are preserved in Foreverware, are eternally condemned to repeat the same choices, mistakes, grades, lives, but are, simultaneously, incapable of "recollecting forward." Stuck at a particular age, these characters are not allowed to advance; only at the end of the episode will they be freed and permitted to age again, thus also allowing true Kierkegaardian repetition to finally be set in motion as they resume their suburban lives.

Cinema has always aspired to eternity; faces, lines of dialogue and stories from cinema's history survive the passage of time. Barthes wrote

---

1 Søren Kierkegaard, "Repetition: An Essay in Experimental Psychology," *Repetition and Philosophical Crumbs,* Oxford: Oxford University Press, 2009, p. 3

2 Dante directed the series' pilot ("Foreverware") and four episodes: "The Retainer", "The Losers", "Heart on a Chain" and "The Hole in the Head Gang." *Eerie, Indiana* was developed and produced for NBC by José Rivera and Karl Schaefer with significant input from Dante, who is credited as "creative consultant."

Eerie, Indiana
(1991–92)

about Garbo's eternal face in *Queen Christina* (1933), a film that challenges perceived notions of the passage of time. Similarly, Ida Lupino, playing an actress in decline in "The Sixteen-Millimeter Shrine," a *Twilight Zone* (1959–64) episode directed by Mitchell Leisen, doesn't want to leave her home projection room, where she constantly re-watches past movies she has acted in. An idea crystallizes: as time leaves its tracks on her, the actress enters cinema as a place where she can always remain young. This astounding episode combines the pleasures of the serial, the repetition of a model, with the melancholic weight of memories. It also combines the general premise of the series (the hypothesis of alternative dimensions) with Leisen's particular obsessions (women characters and genre hybridization through mixing of melodrama and fantasy).

In the case of Joe Dante, authorship – and by extension, the issue of how it can engage with the repetitive structures of the TV series format – is visible in at least ten serial works he has directed: all of his *Eerie, Indiana* episodes; the two *Masters of Horror* entries (2005 and 2006); an episode for the '80s revival run of *The Twilight Zone* (1985), as well as the more famous film segment for the eponymous theatrical feature (1983) produced by Steven Spielberg; and, fi-nally, two episodes for *Amazing Stories* (1986), another Spielberg vehicle, which was largely inspired by *The Twilight Zone* concept.

EPISODE 1

First, there is a series of disorienting and progressively more terrifying travels through time. Second, pensioners in a retirement home yearn for childhood and its carefree games. Third, a child assumes command of his family, as if he were an adult. These are the plots of the first three *Twilight Zone: The Movie* segments, directed by John Landis, Steven Spielberg and Dante, respectively (I will leave out the fourth segment, directed by George Miller, since it is significantly different). Each of the three stories is essentially concerned with temporal displacement: (1) a man leaves a bar where he has just given a racist speech and then finds himself transported to Nazi Germany, the Ku Klux Klan American South, and the Vietnam War; (2) a group of retirees return to infancy but soon realize that they shouldn't have defied the natural order of life; (3) a boy challenges adult hierarchy to hold his family under a reign of terror, feasting on hamburgers and cartoons for days on end. As it appears, Spielberg's and Dante's segments are ultimately two aspects of a similar premise: Spielberg denies his elders a return to youth, while Dante denies his boy a progression to adulthood. As in the pilot to *Eerie, Indiana*, the logic of time is challenged, but ultimately a more stable temporality is restored.

The film's segments are loosely based on or refer to episodes from the original *Twilight Zone* TV series, inadvertently suggesting a strange temporal "dimension" that, as the show's first season proclaims, is "as vast as space and as timeless as infinity." Keeping in mind the ideas of time explored in *Twilight Zone: The Movie*, one might think that this temporal displacement *is* the so-called "fifth dimension"– the "dimension of imagination" – lying somewhere between the present and the past, between maturity and adolescence. It presents itself as a crack or a slip in time.

EPISODE 2

The imaginary of the Landis segment is writ large in its author's signature style: Nazi-occupied France, war-torn Vietnam, the slave-owning southern states – all of these look no different than the Great Britain of *An American Werewolf in London* (1981). Landscapes are obscured and shrouded in mist, spaces appear open yet lack detail in a way reminiscent of the B movies enjoyed by Landis. Similarly, Spielberg's seg-

ment leaves no doubt about its paternity: a sentimental morality tale shot in deep focus so that its community is clearly defined. And the Dante segment? Television is everywhere. The cartoon universe, one of Dante's perennial obsessions, is imposed on human characters, and once again we find ourselves participating in a kind of movie orgy. Consider the tone, too, which shifts effortlessly between horror and comedy, just as it would one year later in *Gremlins* (1984).

The three directors explore, each in their own signature manner, the contours of different temporal dimensions. But while Dante's segment contains many of his trademark qualities, one still has to ask: does this signature work in only one direction? Case in point: Dante's touch permeates the segment, but then the original series itself must have left its mark on his imagination. The *Twilight Zone* cosmos is a constant presence in his other serial works: not only *Amazing Stories*, which essentially follows the same template of packing fantastical premises into self-contained episodes with no aim of continuity, but also *Eerie, Indiana*, a series that Dante was deeply involved in and which operates within a similar realm (although one with continuity in characters and locations), as well as both *Gremlins* films, each setting off from the interstitial zone of a fairy-tale Chinatown at twilight.

EPISODE 3

Serial work constantly defies the basis of *auteur* politics: the principle according to which authorship belongs only and exclusively to the director. Nowadays, in what is generally considered a new golden age for episodic television, accomplished feature filmmakers are delighted by the opportunity to work on TV shows. An interesting question is whether a director's point of view is conditioned by a predetermined structure and concept (as determined by series creators and show runners) or whether a series has the possibility to change when a certain director comes on board. Consider a few contemporary examples: Lodge Kerrigan directed an episode of *Homeland* (2011–), in which one could recognize his poetic and self-reflexive touches, but the episode itself doesn't seem out of place in the context of the series as a whole. Quentin Tarantino and David Cronenberg guest starred in *Alias* (2001–06), and even though authorship of this series can be clearly attributed to J.J. Abrams, both filmmakers turned in roles that seemed to be oriented towards their own individual obsessions – or, at least, their established *"auteur* logos" in the

cinephile world. Tarantino was involved in an episode that mixed action with humor, had self-referential gags and long, orchestrated takes – all characteristics of his style. Cronenberg appeared as a mad doctor, a scientist who studies the dark side of the human mind – long before he directed *A Dangerous Method* (2011), but paying tribute to similar roles he had played in earlier films, such as Clive Barker's *Nightbreed* (1990).

There is also the inverse case of series creators working in cinema. J.J. Abrams has made two *Star Trek* films (2009, 2013), both of which introduced elements of serial continuity in aesthetic and narrative terms. On the other hand, he also directed *Mission: Impossible III* (2006), the third installment in a film franchise that sheds its skin with each new director. Brian De Palma was concerned with the duplicity of images, John Woo with plasticity of action, J.J. Abrams with narrative construction and mixing the intimate sphere (everyday family life) with adventure, while Brad Bird introduces comedy as the vanishing point of the *Mission: Impossible* universe. The constraints of the serial structure recede to the background, while individual authorship assumes a more prominent role.

The Landis-directed prologue of *Twilight Zone: The Movie* shows its main characters hum-

*Twilight Zone:
The Movie*

ming theme songs of TV series, among them Leonard Freeman's original *Hawaii Five-O* (1968–80) and *The Twilight Zone* itself. In Dante's part, the boy treats his family as if they were cartoons: he possesses the power to erase parts of their bodies (their mouths) and make them explode. Everything seems possible in the segment's imaginative dimension, but like the Landis prologue it frames these possibilities in terms of pop culture. A similar celebration of popular culture and its power to constantly refer to itself can be found in *Amazon Women on the Moon* (1987), the orgiastic film directed by John Landis, Dante, Carl Gottlieb, Peter Horton, and Robert K. Weiss (rather than taking on an episodic structure, the film consists of individual sketches embedded within a central narrative, which are attributed to individual directors only in the end credits). The accumulation of sketches and various inserts, which mimics the non-consequential experience of watching TV, expresses the idea that popular culture, as well as any of its genres, is in itself built on constant repetition and variation.

EPISODE 4

In his essay, "Le Point de vue de la guerre," Harun Farocki writes: "Operative war images from the 1991 Gulf War, which didn't show any people, were more than just propaganda, despite the rigid censorship meant to hush up the 200,000 deaths of the war. They came from the spirit of a war utopia, which takes no account of people, which puts up with them only as approved, or perhaps even unapproved, victims. A military spokesman in 1991 said, when asked about the victims on the Iraqi side: 'We don't do body counts.' This can be translated as: 'We are not the gravediggers. This dirty work has to be done by other people.'"[3] I remembered Farocki's words when I saw *Homecoming* (2005), Dante's first *Masters of Horror* episode, for the second time. Here, Dante shows us precisely what Farocki has identified as missing from "operative war images": the corpses. In Dante's "point of view of the war," dead bodies are able to express themselves. *Homecoming* is also a universe removed from action spectacles in which cities are destroyed, things constantly blow up, and yet the audience never gets to see a corpse. The fallen soldiers rise from their graves to vote, to do a "body count" on themselves, ex-

3 Harun Farocki, "Le Point de vue de la guerre," *Trafic*, no. 50 (2004), p. 451 [English translation in Georges Didi-Huberman, "How to Open Your Eyes," in Antje Ehmann, Kodwo Eshun, Nora M. Alter, and Harun Farocki, *Against What? Against Whom?*, London: Koenig Books, 2009, p. 47]

Homecoming

ercising their democratic powers and thus attempting to disempower those responsible for the unjust war.

"If I had a wish, I would wish for your son to come back," says the main character of *Homecoming* to the mother of a dead soldier. Dante shoots this scene with the protagonist in the foreground, while behind him a blurred television screen shows the soldier's mother. This is television as a politician's tool, as a public platform of considerable power, but also as the medium that transmits the fateful words which carry the plot forward. Television speaks about the power of desire, a premise that is quite typical of *The Twilight Zone:* be careful what you wish for (or what you happen to say on TV), because it can turn into reality. The politics of its era – Cold War realities such as the Red Scare witch-hunts – always hovered in the background of *The Twilight Zone.* In the very first episode, "Where is Everybody?" (1959), a military experiment makes its soldier protagonist delirious. I like to imagine Dante as a devo-

tee of this episode: it deals with the military in a way that prefigures both *Homecoming* and *The Second Civil War* (1997).

The most powerful scene in *Homecoming* takes place in the hangar where corpses of soldiers arise from coffins. In a high-angle shot, Dante shows a body wrapped in the American flag, a horrifying vision of patriotism turned upside down. The realms of the political, of the imaginary, and of genre cinema are never far apart: the graves of soldiers, killed in past wars, bear names like Jacques Tourneur and George A. Romero, filmmakers who have created the cinema of the undead as a political allegory.

EPISODE 5

While *Homecoming* is the work of an *auteur* in each and every respect, this claim cannot be easily extended to the two episodes Dante has directed for the rebooted *Hawaii Five-0* (2010–) series. The second of these, "Olelo Pa'a" (2013), takes place in the divided Koreas, where one of the heroes – a member of the Hawaii special police force – is trying to retrieve the corpse of a former army comrade. This episode could very well be entitled "Homecoming" too, as it concludes with the coffin of the fallen soldier being lowered to the ground back in his homeland. But while the plots of *Homecoming* and "Olelo Pa'a" have a lot in common – war, dead soldiers returning home, patriotic ceremonies – their respective tones and statements could not be further apart. The critical stance of *Homecoming* depends on irony and the inherent absurdity of war; "Olelo Pa'a" is quite the opposite, as the soldier can rest in peace after he has been avenged by his fellow countryman. His war is waged as a vendetta, for personal reasons, as one of the characters explains. We can see how both works mirror and negate each other: in *Homecoming*, the rebellious zombie soldier, wrapped in the flag, rises from death to seek justice and political change; in "Olelo Pa'a," justice has been served as the fallen soldier is laid to rest, wrapped in sentimental patriotism and the glory of military ritual, which speak not of change but to repetition.

EPISODE 6

The essence of the new *Hawaii Five-0* is traceable through both episodes directed by Dante: the first, "Ka Iwi Kapu" (2011), is a lightweight Halloween tale with a criminal plot unfolding in the background; the second, "Olelo Pa'a," contains a tragic foundation that is made explicit through constant flashbacks. Tragedy always has its origins in the past, as a trauma or, in this case, a foundational crime: the death of a comrade, which motivates the protagonist. With this episode the series becomes much darker; one senses that Dante is more comfortable with the lighthearted atmosphere of "Ka Iwi Kapu" than with the J.J. Abrams-style tragedy of "Olelo Pa'a." The former starts in a playful way – through the eye of a video camera that two characters use to search for a mysterious creature in the forest. The scene speaks of Dante's taste for that which cannot be seen, but is suggested. The harmless plot of the episode frees him to work with such aesthetic preoccupations.

Another difference between the two episodes concerns space: "Ka Iwi Kapu" is set in Hawaii, a colorful backdrop for the exploits of the special police force protagonists; "Olelo Pa'a" switches between Hawaii and both South and North Korea ("enemy territory"). These geographic shifts signify the importance of the series' idea of space as a symptom of stability. The break in continuity (in relation to both space and characters) is a break with the very essence

Hawaii Five-0
"Olelo Pa'a"

of serial work, its repetition and routine. If we feel comfortable with spaces that appear over and over again – Hawaii, or the fictional town of Eerie, Indiana – then the Koreas are a perfect place to introduce discomfort. This sense of dislocation and instability belongs less to Dante than to the series' creators Alex Kurtzman and Roberto Orci, whose scripts for *Alias* are perfect examples of repetition and rupture, of continuity and traumatic change.

EPISODE 7

As in *Twin Peaks* (1990–91), the opening credits of *Eerie, Indiana* display a road sign with the town's name and population. The similarities don't end there. Both series are dark portraits of a small place that seems quiet and peaceful, revealing the idea that routine in itself can become an infernal device. The seemingly idyllic Eerie – which Dante named after the horror comics magazine that ran from 1966 to 1983 – is the perfected American dream, hiding unspeakable horrors. The series turns the open multi-verse of *The Twilight Zone* into a closed community, which has both fantastical and comical aspects, as Dante's communities often do in their enjoyment of nature (*Piranha*), celebration of Christmas (*Gremlins*), or survival of the combined thrills of the Cuban missile crisis and "Atomo Vision" (*Matinee*). Communities are places to defend, places where stability can be retained, even when they conceal something perverse. *Eerie, Indiana* is the culmination of Dante's serial work: it distills the *Twilight Zone* premise into a formula in which sinister threats are conquered by a communal space which reasserts its power over and over again.

EPISODE 8

Inhabitants of Dante's communities often seek acceptance from those around them, even if the latter are mostly eccentrics – as in the case of *Eerie, Indiana*. In the pilot, Marshall desires that his mother would not change into the "perfect mom." On the other hand, the twins' mother has to do everything perfectly to maintain an idyllic relationship with her children. The moral of the tale is that we should not seek perfection: it's impossible to conform to all the "rules" of a community. The same holds for *Gremlins*, *The 'Burbs* (1989), and "The Shadow Man" (1985), Dante's episode for the 1980s *Twilight Zone* series, which is essentially a short story about the importance of school popularity. "Boo!" (1986), one of Dante's *Amazing Stories* contributions, is also concerned with maintaining a strange kind of status quo: a couple of old ghosts who occupy a typical American family home appear far less weird than the couple that invades their house.

EPISODE 9

"Focus on the only thing that doesn't lie: evidence," says Gil Grissom in the first episode of *CSI: Crime Scene Investigation* (2000–). *CSI* has always dealt with evidence and with the empirical; the show's policemen are essentially presented as scientists. It is interesting to consider how Dante, a filmmaker who has usually worked with the powers of the imaginary, could fit into this highly materialist universe. In his episode for *CSI: NY* (2007), Halloween once again serves as the alibi. And, again, the episode shifts between the empirical and the fantastical. In "Ka Iwi Kapu" forensic analysis collided with Hawaiian superstitions; in the *CSI: NY* episode the procedural intertwines with a zombie

story. The episode also contains two classical horror attributes: haunted houses and the living dead. Dante's interests are clearly drawn out, creating tensions with the idiosyncrasies of the series, as in the scenes when a character tries to scientifically explain the existence of zombies. Once again, the imaginary has to be tied to empirical grounds. However, many of Dante's characters who attempt scientific analysis end up badly: the science teacher in *Gremlins* is killed; Clamp's scientists in the sequel who try to dissect Gizmo learn nothing; the doctor manipulating fish on government orders is one of the first victims in *Piranha*, etc. Dante's scientists are a breed apart: they are unsuccessful idealists or well-meaning inventors of failed gadgets (and often teenage characters' parents, as in both *Gremlins* films and *Eerie, Indiana*).

As Xavier Pérez and Jordi Balló note, all the off-shoots of the *CSI* franchise (*Las Vegas, Miami, NY*) deal with death as a vital part of everyday life: "the coexistence with death is turned into a life activity […] in what appears to be a typical series about professionals, death plays not the marginal, but main role."[4] When

4 Xavier Pérez and Jordi Balló, *Yo ya he estado aquí. Ficciones de la repetición*, Barcelona: Anagrama, 2005, p. 149

Joe Dante on the *Eerie, Indiana* set

one of the detectives in "Ka Iwi Kapu" discovers that an apartment where a crime took place is available to rent, he takes advantage of the circumstance by bargaining down. For the police officer, coexisting with death is a matter of experience. What is exceptional becomes routine; what is magic is turned into evidence. However, Dante's *CSI: NY* episode concludes with a self-referential gag that opens the door to fantasy. "They're caught between the living and the dead," says the policeman while looking at the murder victims. With this invocation of the zombie imaginary, Dante casts a shadow of doubt onto the series' closed empiricist universe, opening worlds of possibility.

EPISODE 10

"The Shadow Man" presents us with a villain who is nothing more than a shadow, as if to emphasize the general importance of shadows for Dante's mise-en-scène. In *Piranha*, carnivorous fish are often only teeth and shadows. *Gremlins'* best scene is a brilliant achievement of suggestion: in the school laboratory, the science teacher gets killed by a gremlin only after he has crossed the film projector's beam and cast a shadow on the screen. In *Homecoming*, Dante uses silhouette to suggest a zombie decapitating a man. (The unshadowy exception is *The Screwfly Solution*, which contains the goriest moment of Dante's cinema: the stabbing of a woman.) In *Eerie, Indiana*, a further example of horror through suggestion can be found, inspired by a tale from Oscar Wilde's *The Happy Prince:* the short glimpse at the grave of an adolescent who died and had his heart transplanted. Such affection for off-screen space, shadows, details, popular culture, genres and their hybrid nature, irony, and moods that straddle humor and melancholy runs through the entirety of Dante's work, proving again and again that the very foundation of film authorship lies in repetition.

Mark Cotta Vaz

From Rubber to Digital

Special Effects in Joe Dante's Cinema from The Howling *to* Small Soldiers

With the exception of Ray Harryhausen, there weren't a lot of names associated with special effects when Joe Dante was growing up. "Those of us who knew *King Kong* (1933) were familiar with Willis O'Brien," Dante recalled. "There were good effects people we learned of as we got older, like John Fulton at Universal in the '30s. But Ray was the name in special effects and the reason you would go see the picture. *It Came From Beneath the Sea* (1955) was pretty monumental. In the '50s we weren't used to spectacle, at least in science fiction, and here was Ray doing this seamless material where it looked like giant squid tentacles were knocking down buildings."[1] Finding himself working in the realm of special effects many years later, Dante's professional conditions were decidedly more adverse than Harryhausen's. Making *Hollywood Boulevard* (1976) and *Piranha* (1978) for Roger Corman, his budgets didn't allow for the same level of elaborate invention. It wasn't until *The Howling* (1981), his third film and the first produced by a major studio, that he had the support to try something more ambitious.

Rick Baker, an effects guru who was beginning his career at the time and had been similarly influenced by Harryhausen, was enlisted to design the human-to-werewolf transformation needed for *The Howling*. Previously, a werewolf-type metamorphosis required an actor to keep still through a series of dissolves featuring a progression of makeup. The actor might even fall out of view and then rise back up fully transformed. "There hadn't been a werewolf movie in some time," Dante said. "And we didn't want to do [the transformation] the way it had always been done. So we came up with the concept of changing a person into a wolf in one shot. The line in the script was: 'Eddie stands in front of a door and turns into a werewolf.' That's the equivalent of 'A thousand horsemen come over the hill.' Easy to write, hard to do."

As it turned out, director John Landis had been discussing just such a breakthrough effect with Baker for his own werewolf film, the long-gestating *An American Werewolf in London* (1981). Baker had already been experimenting by punching hairs through a piece of rubber to simulate facial hairs rapidly growing through skin in real time, but couldn't pull enough hairs through multiple angles of a face. Instead, he developed changeable prosthetic body parts that could have movements made through

1 All quotes in the article are transcribed from the author's personal correspondence over e-mail and phone which took place from May 9 to June 24, 2013.

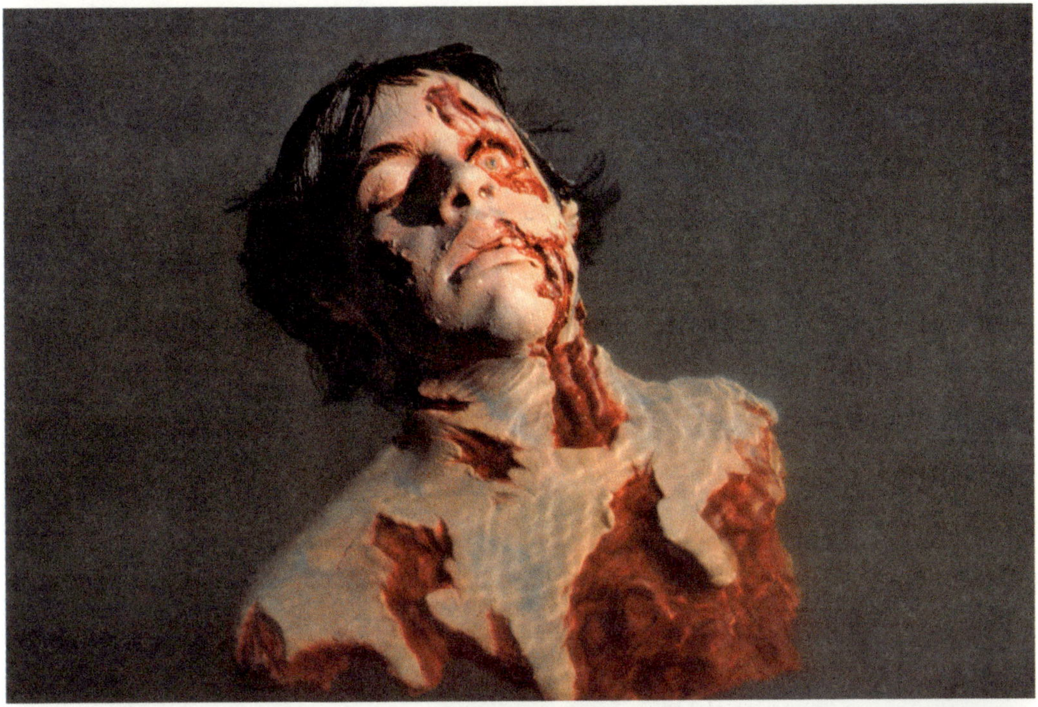

Piranha

The Howling

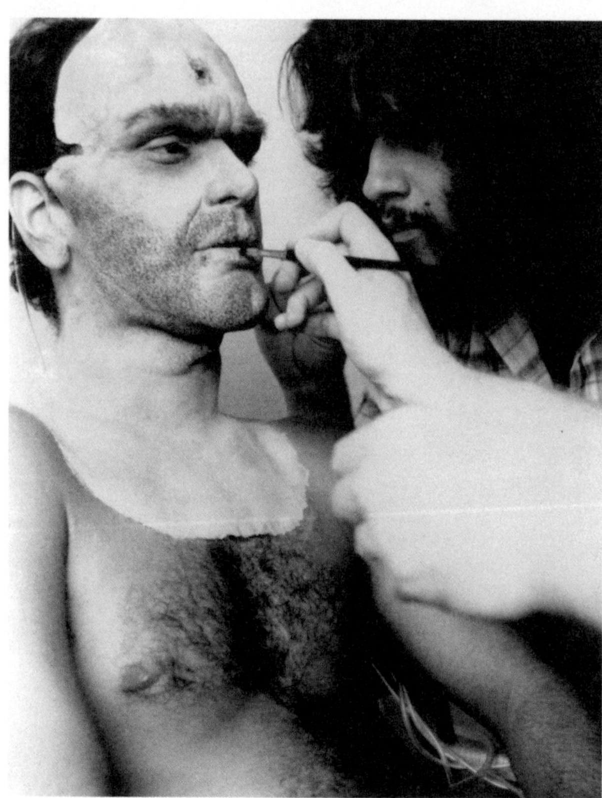

The Howling: Rick Baker mask creation

makeup effects consultant. Although both werewolf movies would be released in 1981, *The Howling* was already in production and would be the first into theaters. Famed comics artist Bernie Wrightson had done drawings of a biped werewolf that caught the fancy of *The Howling* camp, while Landis was adamant that his werewolf be four-legged. *The Howling* would also have traditional horror movie lighting by cinematographer John Hora, with shadows helping to hide certain details, while the transformation in *American Werewolf* would take place in a fully lit room. There was also a stylistic difference. "Rob tends to go over the top, while I wanted my transformation to be logical in an anatomical way," said Baker. Dante admits they never really knew if they were getting the right effects, and their fear seemed justified when they saw dailies. "We'd always envisioned smooth transitions, but instead things were popping and gearing. Then, all of a sudden it was, 'If we put a bone crack [sound effect] on that it will look like his bones are actually breaking,' which became more interesting. So that whole sequence made a turnaround in the editing room."

For Dante's next feature, *Gremlins* (1984), the effects creation would be both more elaborate and leave less uncertainty about the final result.

cable controls and air pressure. Almost a decade after Baker's werewolf talk with Landis, Dante and producer Michael Finnell called Baker about *The Howling* thinking that *American Werewolf* would never happen. Baker agreed to use his transformation ideas on *The Howling* before Landis called him again to announce that he had secured financing for his project.

At that time, Baker worked out of his workshop at his parents' house in North Hollywood, and had taken on Rob Bottin as a protégé. Although Bottin was young and green, Baker felt he could do *The Howling*. To ease Dante and Finnell's concerns, Baker agreed to serve as a

The Mogwai and gremlin characters in the Chris Columbus script would be brought to life by Chris Walas, a creature consultant at Industrial Light & Magic (ILM) who had been working on the big budget *Return of the Jedi* (1983) for George Lucas. Walas left before the end of the *Gremlins* production to form his own company, Chris Walas, Inc. Ethan Wiley, a UCLA film school graduate whose first professional experience was working on *Jedi*, would eventually join Walas's team. "A script rolled in from Chris' old pal, Joe Dante," Wiley said. "They had worked together on *Piranha*, so *Gremlins* was Chris' first big break on his own. It was going to be a fairly low budget movie. An effects movie back then was $35–40 million, but the budget for *Gremlins* was like $11 million. So we had to come up with a lot of gremlins on a tight budget. Chris hired a lot of young people like me who were willing to work long hours and extra weekends to get all the craziness done."

Walas's department created the two different creatures: the furry and cuddly Mogwai, and the nasty gremlins. The gremlins were generally hand puppets enhanced with cable control features, what Wiley describes as "a very sophisticated Muppet." The Mogwai, who was named Gizmo, kept getting smaller as Dante and Spielberg gave their input – with the reasoning that smaller equals cute – until it got so small it couldn't fit on a puppeteers' hand. The Mogwai became a cable controlled rod puppet filled with mechanics for blinking eyes, wiggling ears, functional arms, and other movements.

Although the gremlins would all look alike, Wiley suggested a distinctive design for the main villain, Stripe: a furry Mohawk down its reptilian spine that Walas liked and approved. "We worked on different designs and rigs because they had to do special behaviors," Wiley added. "There was the gremlin that gets ground up in a blender, one that explodes in a microwave, one that rides a tricycle. Some had metal armatures, certain things we would marionette with a monofilament line, we had a sophisticated robotic gremlin that was an amazing piece of engineering, and basic 'dummy gremlins' for background action. We had a disco gremlin with rods coming out the feet so it could be moved like it was dancing – for a shot where it break dances, we used a drill so it could spin." After their preparations, Walas brought the Mogwai and gremlins to Southern California in a trailer truck that served as a movable workshop, parking it on the stages so it would always be close at hand. During principal photography, new gremlin ideas were encouraged. A large sheet of butcher paper was put up so the crew could write down potential gags.

Working closely with Walas's team was the special effects department supervised by Robert MacDonald, Sr., an old pro whose credits include *Ryan's Daughter* (1970), *The Outlaw Josey Wales* (1976), and *Superman* (1978). His son, MacDonald, Jr., helped take care of the shop and his father's company, but it was Sr. who was "the brains," recalled *Gremlins* effects man Richard Stutsman, who describes himself as one of the "worker bees" creating sight gags. Stutsman had come into the film business after college, when he was looking for work and a friend and off-road racing partner, Matt Sweeney, brought him to Universal Studios, which still had a special effects shop. "MacDonald, Sr., was a cantankerous old codger, but a mechanical genius," Stutsman said. "Give him the right materials and he could build the Eiffel Tower horizontally, and he'd tell you all about the structural physics of the steel while he was doing it. He helped rig the flying monkeys on *The Wizard of Oz* (1939)."

Richard Ratliff, a former plumbing contractor with a mechanical background who had been working for MacDonald, Sr., described the workflow with the effects departments on *Gremlins*. "We executed whatever Bob and Joe Dante decided in meetings with producers and the art department. Sometimes we got storyboards or drawings from the art department to build a particular prop or a machine that had to do something. It was a lot of experimenting, too – take off and have fun. You'd build something and Bob or the art department would have a look. You'd perfect what they wanted and they'd show it to the director and [he would say] yes or no. [If no] you'd go back and work on it a little more." Ratliff ran one of the crews that showed the effect of gremlins multiplying in water. "We prepped the swimming pool [at the Warner Bros. ranch] with an air compressor and air hoses to get it bubbling and then we pumped liquid nitrogen into the water to get a steam effect to come off. We also installed a grid of electrical sockets to put in big flash bulbs below the water's surface. When the multiplication sequence was coming it would be bubbling and steaming and the flash bulbs would be going off, giving the effect that a lot was happening under water."

It was an arduous, challenging production, Ratliff observed. "It was kind of early in the business for me, and all new to me, but I knew this was one of the first films that had attempted

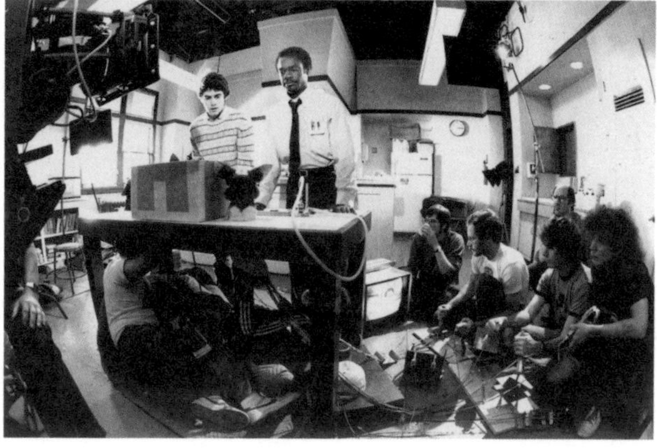

so many puppets, with all the mechanics and remote control they had, as opposed to stop motion. It was a big endeavour making all these creatures look as real as they did." Ratliff and his crew often moved ahead of the filming unit to get the next set ready. The story was set in wintertime, so their major focus was usually dressing out sets with fake snow. The effect included white powdery gypsum brought in by the truckload and spread using the flocking drums typically employed to add fake snow to Christmas trees. There was polyester bunting that could be stapled to rooftops to give the illusion of snow accumulated on ledges and eaves. There was painstaking detailing, such as cutting polyester material to fit a given surface and applying it with spray adhesive."

A major challenge was that the puppet animation work, including wires and cable controls, had to be out of camera view. "The whole set was built up on stilts, and there were puppeteers literally living under the sets," Dante said. "We had to figure out ways to work through carpets and doors and sofas and all kinds of stuff. These setups included video monitors with a flipped picture, like looking in a mirror, to see what they were doing." Wiley, although not a trained puppeteer, found himself with his hand up many a gremlin. "I had done some comedy and improv acting, and I found out I had a knack for puppeteering. You'd have your hand up inside the creature operating the mouth, the body language and movement. We did video tests and rehearsed before we got to the set. Hidden underneath the stage would be eighteen operators and maybe fourteen cables for one puppet. The operators had little guns we manufactured that they could hold to pull the different cables to make eyebrows go up and down, ears move, noses sniffle or wiggle, to control the bladders to [simulate] breathing. You'd work in weird, uncomfortable positions for hours, so physical stamina was an issue."

For a scene of nearly fifty gremlins taking over a movie theater showing *Snow White and the Seven Dwarfs* (1937), it was "all hands on deck," Stutsman recalls, with special effects guys, grips and stagehands and any available crew helping animate the raucous scene. "It was a ground floor set, so we all crawled down between the theater seats. We'd move our puppets and be tossing popcorn and cups around, and when the dwarfs start singing 'Heigh-Ho, Heigh-Ho, it's off to work we go,' we were all waving back and forth to the music." Stutsman's *Gremlins* work included a mailbox rigged as an "envelope shooter" that used cylinders of air to blow out envelopes – if someone slid a letter into the slot, it shot back out, as if by the mischievous gremlin ostensibly hidden inside. Another gag had the mother of the boy make coffee that was supposed to ooze into her cup as brown goo. "The goo squirter was basically a pod full of brown goo, with air pressure on top and a suction tube off the bottom so the air could push the liquid up the top and out a hose," Stutsman explained. "But the pressure pod was running low and air got into the tube. As we did the take, a big gulp of air blew out and sprayed her and everything around her.

Everybody got a laugh out of that, and they ended up using that take in the movie."

In another shot, a gremlin falls into a blender and gets sliced and diced, its guts spraying all over the kitchen. MacDonald's team worked out everything from the green goo, testing with clear gels to get the right consistency, to building mechanics for the prop blender. "We built the apparatus that would spray green cellulose food coloring for the blood," Ratliff explained. "The prop blender was a bowl-type affair that sat on top of the counter, where we cut a hole. We ended up with a piston we could draw down into a tube that was about two or three inches in diameter. We poured the gremlin blood into the tube and filled it up, with the piston at the bottom. We energized it with air and that would bring the liquid to the top of the tube, where we had a series of air jets that worked sequentially, in a circular motion, to blow the stuff around the room at different angles – as if blades were spinning and splattering this stuff around. As we were forcing the liquid up and swinging it around, the puppet could be pulled down through a hole, it sort of disappeared as if it was being chewed up by the blender." The blender gag was "one of the fun ones," Wiley recalled. "I was in a giant bucket underneath the set in my bathing suit and a rain

Explorers production still

poncho because when that gag went off I got completely covered in green goo."

Sunlight will kill a gremlin, so when Stripe gets hit by light Walas' unit had a test phase to determine the chemicals needed to melt the puppet, the frame rates to make it look real as it bubbled down, and the proper expansion and deflation of the bladder within the puppet. Other shots featured a radio controlled Gizmo, stop motion, animated shadows as gremlins crowded into the movie theater, and detached heads and other body parts for detailed close-ups. After filming wrapped, a second unit spent three to four weeks doing nothing but gremlin shots. "We used every technique in the book," Wiley said. "Joe was strong about what he wanted and had a lot to choose from in the editing room. He had experience as an editor and shot like an editor. You had to have options in the editing room for something as crazy and freewheeling as *Gremlins*."

Dante's next film was *Explorers*, and for the visual effects, including a glowing force field that makes the spaceship fly, the studio contracted Industrial Light & Magic (ILM). The production period, and the film's release in 1985, were pivotal years at ILM and even set the course for the future of effects-driven filmmaking. *Young Sherlock Holmes* (1985) featured the first computer graphics character in a feature film, a painted knight who bursts from his perch in a stained glass window. The effect had been led by a new computer division George Lucas had organized, and included the first digitally manipulated matte painting, with ILM matte department artist Chris Evans painting stained glass elements directly onto the computer. It was a radical, historic departure from the oil and brush technique traditionally used to realize environments too difficult, or impossible, to build or find. 1985 was also the year Steve Jobs bought Lucas' computer division and made it a standalone computer animation studio called Pixar.

"It was a very dynamic and interesting time because new technologies were coming up that had really never been thought of before," explained Craig Barron, who was then working in ILM's matte department. "Traditional visual effects had gotten to their limits, so the technology was being enhanced with new optics, better optical printers, better photographic stocks, computers controlling [the movement of] cameras… All these things added great value to traditional effects. *Explorers* represented a high point of photochemical visual effects and the traditional way of making movies." Barron eventually left ILM with matte artist Michael Pangrazio to form Matte World, a visual effects house dedicated to matte shots. *Explorers* provided an opportunity to develop "invisible effects" that had to seamlessly fit into real world environments, a technique Barron would specialize in with his own company. "A lot of films we worked on in the ILM matte department were very fanciful. *Explorers* was science fiction, but set in suburbia. The boys fly their spacecraft through the town at night, but it wasn't practical to light an entire neighborhood. It had to be fabricated, but undetectable as effects work. So, part of a house was lit and filmed for the live action, and we created the neighborhood through matte painting techniques."

Ultimately, the spaceship was composited photochemically in ILM's optical printing department. ILM had pioneered motion control, by which eighty-foot stage cameras were computer programmed for repeatable movements, allowing for the creation of intricate composite elements. For Bruce Nicholson, ILM's visual effects supervisor on *Explorers*, opticals was the final stop where a composite shot came together. But that would change in the not too distant future. "*Explorers* was starting to point the way [to a new way of making movies]," said Bruce Walters, who ran ILM's animation department and headed animation work on *Explorers*. "I don't think that was because of Joe Dante, it was just the way it was. We had the tools and the right people. Actually, what we did on *Explorers* inspired me to set up a new effects camera department." The animation tool used by Walters' department on *Explorers* was an Oxberry animation stand with an Oxberry camera, the kind of classic downshooter used to film cel animation. Prior to *Explorers*, Walters' department added motors and an IBM 286 computer with the latest motion control software. (The computer had a black and white monitor, no mouse, a teletype keyboard, and a dot matrix read-out.) The computerized motors on the rock solid table controlled all axes of movement, and could be raised or lowered six feet on rails of solid steel

Explorers

pipes. Walters and his crew called it "the Ox." For the force field that makes the spacecraft fly, Walters made animation cel artwork that resembled the highlights on a glass ball. The art, no bigger than a quarter, would ultimately be composited with the live action element, or "background plate."

The live action was first projected down on the stand to plot out the match move for the animation. With the computer setting the coordinates, and after black and white tests, they then shot the animation element. "The Ox" didn't even have to shoot a frame at a time, as with traditional cel animation. The computer could film every eight or sixteen frames, with the camera operator correcting or smoothing out the move if needed. Although Walters says they could have done the composite, it was sent off to ILM's optical department for the final shot. "*Explorers* was the film where things were changing from big stage cameras to smaller cameras. We could shoot miniatures and models, but also do lighting effects or motion track things. Traditional motion control was programmed by hand and could repeat, but our moves could be created in the computer. We could select key points and move through them, adjust, edit, and mathematically change a move. We could move the force field around, and motion track it to objects shot on stage, or eyelines of people who were supposed to be watching this spacecraft. We could track anything, lining up something to exactly match the original photography. This was a big change in motion control."

Rick Baker sums up another turning point in the making of special effects: films got bigger. Baker, who re-joined Dante for *Gremlins 2: The New Batch* (1990), recalls that on *American Werewolf* he had a six-person crew, whereas on *Gremlins 2* he had at least fifty people. The volume of work dictated that specialization was the most efficient way to go. "On *The Howling* and *American Werewolf* we did everything: sculpt and mold, cast rubber in it, paint it. But things got more departmentalized as people began to specialize in things they were good at. It was just the way the business kind of evolved." Producer Michael Finnell had contacted Baker about the sequel, but Baker felt Chris Walas had already set the tone and design on the original film. The Mogwai and gremlins all basically looked the same, so Baker said he would be interested in *Gremlins 2* if he could re-design the characters. "I wanted to make Gizmo look more real, I wanted to make individual characters. I thought it would be cool to make the gremlins like Warner Bros.' cartoon characters. I wanted to make one called Daffy, who was kind of a screwball, I wanted to do a big dumb one and a little mean one. I ended up doing a painting of what I thought Gizmo should look like and showed it to Joe at the Universal backlot where he was filming *The 'Burbs*. He liked it and agreed to let me do that. I also wanted to contribute ideas and gags and they agreed to all that. So I took the job and started making hundreds of gremlins."

Movies were on the cusp of the digital age, but *Gremlins 2* still had to use physical puppets, build special sets, and hide puppeteers. "We had a lot of raised sets with puppeteers underneath sticking their arms through holes, and had to frame bits out," Baker noted. "Digital compositing didn't exist, you couldn't do wire removal. I wish the digital revolution had happened when we were doing *Gremlins 2*. We could have done so much more. I do stuff with rubber and people always try to pit the rubber guys against the digital guys. To me, it's any way you can achieve an effect. There are definitely limitations when you have an arm shoved up a puppet that you have to hide." Baker did use the computer as a design tool on *Gremlins 2*. On previous films he would do a concept painting, but that prompted vexing questions – should he leave it alone, or should

he risk screwing it up by continuing to paint and hopefully get closer to the idea in his head? Later he learned there were computer programs that could save and edit and cut and paste images, just as a word processors did with words. "I got Photoshop 1.0 around 1988. I realized that on a computer I could save something, or save multiple versions of something, cut and paste... I could do things on a computer that weren't possible with paint and brush. I fell in love with what I call No Fear painting."

Baker used his computer to produce hard copy images for a couple of shots on *Gremlins 2*. For a scene where Gizmo makes a series of Xerox images of his face, Baker used Photoshop to image process Gizmo head shot photos, then printed them to use as the photocopies. For a dentist's office, he created a gremlin X-ray image. The *Gremlins 2* crew included Barron and Pangrazio's Matte World. A key shot involved tricking the light-allergic gremlins into thinking it's nighttime, and lured out into the sunlight that will melt them, by a gigantic painted backdrop of a moon and stars that is lowered outside the building's windows. Barron recalls that Matte World's wide shot involved a large silk backing about thirty feet wide, but scaled to look two hundred feet wide.

The matte team then used a building filmed in New York, and added miniature cranes lowering a miniature painted backing, along with a matte painting of surrounding buildings. Barron heard that when Steven Spielberg saw the movie, he thought the shot was real and wondered how they got permissions, and overcame the daunting logistics of shooting the scene in New York.

"It was complicated to do some of the things in *Gremlins 2*, but Joe was very knowledgeable about effects," Barron noted. "Joe made sure the live action he was photographing, which was the foundation we were building on, was done well so we could do our best work. There was a lot of careful preparation and execution. Back then, if you didn't do it right the first time, quite often the shot would fail. Joe was very aware of that and gave us the value of his time."

In 1993, Dante released *Matinee*, a film that plays extensive homage to old-fashioned B movie effects, which are embedded into the story. Ironically, it was the same year that audiences became awestruck by the digital dinosaurs ILM had created for Spielberg's *Jurassic Park* (1993). Bruce Walters recalls that within six months everything at ILM changed: the opticals department shut down and camera rooms no longer had cameras in them. "All that stuff was gone, cut up, scrapped. I found camera parts sitting out in the rain. And these great, renowned, stage guys and model builders were working on computers. There's this thing about computers, whether you're making a movie or music or figuring out spread sheets – it's the same machine. You sit in a chair, move a mouse, you type. You still transmit thoughts into art, but there's nothing you can touch, no physical models, no smell of paint from the matte department, and no special sounds."

Joe Dante recalls the digital age as sneaking up on people, likening it to the frog in boiling water that is enjoying the hot bath and doesn't realize it's being scalded to death. It all came home to Dante on his *Small Soldiers* (1998). Mechanical effects wizard Stan Winston and his studio, who had built the full-scale animatronic dinosaurs in *Jurassic Park*, would create sophisticated physical puppets, with ILM adding computer generated puppets as needed. "The majority of scenes were going to be done with puppets, but during the shooting of the movie it became apparent that it was more efficacious to just shoot the plate and let ILM put the [CG] puppet in, rather than work the puppets on stage," Dante explained. "When I did *Gremlins*, you had to frame shots so puppeteers were hid-

Lawrence Woolsey's
MANT! in *Matinee*

den, but now you could matte the puppeteer out. Virtually anything you could think of could now be presented if you spent enough time and money to make it look right." Stefen Fangmeier, ILM's visual effects supervisor on *Small Soldiers*, recalls a shift from the puppets to CG work, although not as radical as happened on *Jurassic Park*, where plans to complement Winston's mechanical dinosaurs with a lot of traditional stop motion animation were discarded. ILM had since created other CG characters, including the ghosts for *Casper* (a 1995 film for which Fangmeier was digital character co-supervisor), and Draco, the dragon of *Dragonheart* (1996). "I think Joe was comfortable dealing with CGI," Fangmeier said. "The film wasn't necessarily ground-breaking. It was more about the challenge of matching and getting the animation style of what the [Winston] puppeteers were doing."

Many veteran filmmakers have welcomed digital filmmaking, but decry the loss of other technical and creative approaches. "I love the technology," Baker declared. "What I don't like is that people seem to think it's the answer for everything. There are so many things I still think we can do with rubber these days, and do better, that they won't even attempt. The digital revolution has also made for sloppy filmmaking. On *Gremlins 2* we storyboarded everything, we had meetings early on, we had to know what we had to build and what was required, and then it took a while to build it. Now, they don't want to spend that time. Instead of making decisions in advance, they'll just put it off. There is a 'fix-it-in-post' attitude now." Dante affirmed: "I don't think filmmaking will ever be quite the same as what I got to experience. It's an art that had really reached its zenith at that moment. It's been a remarkable sea change, and I think we've lost our innocence along the way."

Michael Almereyda with Jim Robison

Dante Among the Mind-Benders

I met Joe Dante at the Torino Film Festival in 2003, when *Looney Tunes: Back in Action* received its riotous Italian premiere. Joe and I were introduced days later during a tour of the Giandujotto chocolate "laboratorio" – a factory, properly speaking, where we enjoyed a stop-start conversation while plucking samples of the famous local *tonda gentile delle langhe* hazelnut off a swiftly-moving conveyor belt.

This, at any rate, is the salient detail that survives in my unreliable memory. It's amazing how little I remember of the events leading up to my first dinner, about a month later, at the Dante residence, a modest non-mansion at the becalmed end-point of Cahuenga Boulevard. Joe shared kitchen duties with his future wife and producer, the magnificent Elizabeth Stanley, who had also been on hand in Torino. I vividly recall Joe midway through the meal, removing his cape, loosening his ascot, and delivering a dramatic reading of his latest project, "The Man with Kaleidoscope Eyes," a screenplay by Charlie Largent and Tim Lucas chronicling the psychedelic adventures of Roger Corman as he set about directing his 1967 "youthquake" picture, *The Trip*.

Joe acted out all the roles, employing elaborate accents and vocal inflections, but at his urging I had soaked up so much red wine that I couldn't altogether keep track of the story or even count, with precision, the number of cats that jumped on and off the table during the performance.

All the same, I suggested that the material "had great potential." Fueled by the wine, I may have imagined that, like Ray Milland in Corman's *X: The Man with the X-Ray Eyes* (1963), I could see into and *through* the screenplay, to register at its core a glittering, double-exposed world of bottomless possibility.

Joe took my remarks as a shameless self-invitation to apply a few brush strokes to the Lucas/Largent canvas, to deliver what professionals call "a polish." And – again, my memory slides past a few blurry particulars – Joe, with Elizabeth's encouragement, took a gamble. I soon found myself working with my old friend James Robison to provide my new friends with an enhanced version of the script.

Jim is an extraordinary novelist and short-story writer who has collaborated with me on unproduced scripts of astonishing high quality. When I asked him for help recollecting the rest of the story, he supplied the following fleet and lucid paragraphs:

You showed me a script – the Largent/Lucas deal – and I thought it was mostly terrific but, having lived

The Trip (1967)

through the times in the place, I had some "what if" ideas. Joe and I are almost exactly the same age – one month apart – and his readings, taste and enthusiasms square with mine. When you asked if I'd like to help with a polish the answer was of course yes.

The script Joe was starting with seemed a comic and primary-colors homage to Corman, Hopper, Fonda and American International Pictures (though AIP moguls Arkoff and James H. Nicholson came off as thugs). We wanted to save some of that spirit and all the energy and enthusiasm, but maybe add our own inklings about the colossal changes underway at the time – being wrought, or about to be, by new directors (Bogdanovich, Coppola, Scorsese) through the most unlikely studio, AIP, because of Roger Corman. All symbolized by the reality-altering compound LSD. As if movies were getting a dose of a new reality and all those Fright Night Chiller Drive-In double feature films with their hapless characters who would mutate into creatures of the Primal Id were coming true, coming to life on the streets of America, in war years and a time of revolutions, small and large. We saw Roger not just as an avuncular and unlikely or unwitting agent of cultural adjustments, working cheap, but as the force behind a sea change of consciousness, of how we see ourselves, a Prospero who decided to dabble a bit with a new potion for this one movie.

Just as Joe would push boundaries and clip margins between/among comedy, horror and domestic realism to find literary depth in genres seen as stuff for teens only, we thought The Trip transcended, or wanted to, its exploitation expectations.

You hunted down the original Jack Nicholson screenplay and channeled notes and interview snippets after talking to Nicholson's life-long friend Harry Gittes and Corman associate Frances Doel, Peter Fonda and lots of others, and I wrote very rough drafts, sort of from a ground's eye view. We both rediscovered The Wild Angels (1966) and we both understood that while the late Chuck Griffith's Opus Magnum of a Trip script was probably wonderful, young Jack Nicholson's much shorter version, worked up under the sway of Antonioni and his very low-key, hushed, start-in-the-middle methods, was wonderfuller.

Joe seems to work best on a wide canvas taking broad strokes and, in a manner that seems akin to Roy Lichtenstein and his gloriously gaudy and irresistible pop masterworks, Joe is devoutly unpretentious and seems a crowd-pleaser who offers a fantastic show available equally to kids and connoisseurs. But there are layers of irony and craftsmanship in both artists that are deceptively complex. In a sense, our script, while about Roger Corman and crucial days of change in American cinema and life, aspired to address its potential director as well. The substance behind the spectacle. The hard work of observation and record keeping. Joe told me in a jokey email that Hellzapoppin' (1941) informed his aesthetic to an almost embarrassing degree, and I could see that. A film about films and anarchy and lunacy and lust so Harpo-innocent as to seem silly rather than smutty and a happy sense that anything could happen in the next ten seconds. The standard narrative-event-and-consequence and three- or five-act structure gleefully destroyed and the wall of light between observer and film shattered every few beats.

In the way that LSD temporarily destroys narrative, time, even a sense of predictable consequence, I think its anarchic impact on our senses mirrors Joe's spirit of sunny and upbeat destruction. Matinee, remember, is set during a real-life end-of-the-world crisis and his Looney Tunes escape into the pigments of masterworks at the Louvre. In my day, and his, people called such strategies "trippy."

Joe recognized early in his career, or simply knew in his bones, that American life has a gravitational pull toward cartoon reality – by which I mean a reality that is frenetic, elastic, simplified and loud, endlessly violent and relentlessly cute, subject to mayhem but resistant to the pain and finality of death. Most of Joe's movies reflect this condition, this aspiration, in ways that are explicit, hyperbolic, and accurate. This hadn't quite occurred to me until Joe, reviewing our zealous overhaul of the original kaleidoscopic script, confided his opinion that we had, perhaps, over-polished the work of our predecessors. I recall him blinking in the Hollywood sun, looking up from the leaves glittering at the bottom of his drained swimming pool and saying, in that Wellesian rumble of a voice, with an affectionate furrow in his brow, "We can't make an *earnest* movie about Roger Corman."

And, of course, he was correct. Jim and I stepped back, and Joe re-enlisted Largent and Lucas to restore the blunt cartoon contours of many scenes, although I discovered, on reading the current draft, that much of our version remains intact. At any rate, ten years down the road, Jim and I remain grateful for the opportunity to add our smudgy fingerprints to a Joe Dante project, and we're delighted by rumors that "The Man with Kaleidoscope Eyes" may soon be financed and filmed. There is, after all, a good chance that everyone currently associated with the project will be dead in about 40 years. Here's hoping that Joe picks up the pace and makes his movie before we, one and all, drift or plunge into that particular out-of-body experience.

Joe Dante 1976 [1], with John Carradine [2],
The Howling [3–5], *Gremlins* [6–8]

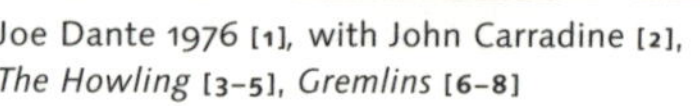

Explorers [1–2], *Amazing Stories* [3],
Innerspace [4–7], *The 'Burbs* [8]

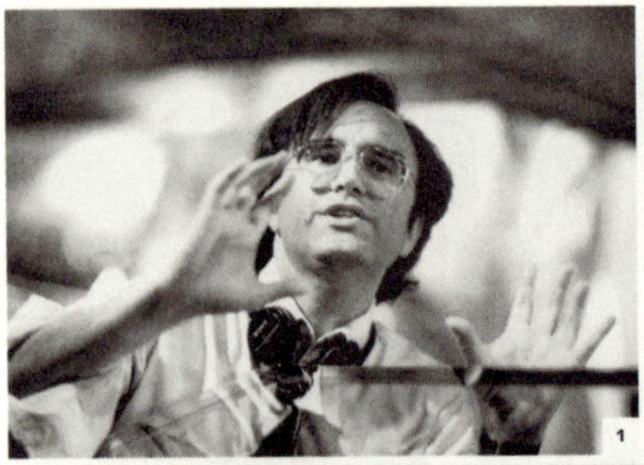
1

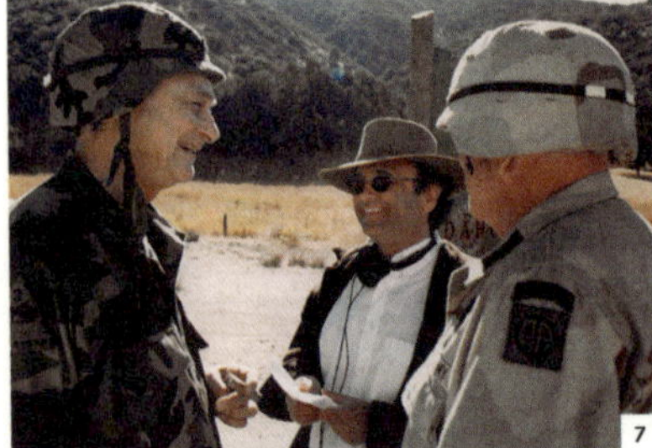

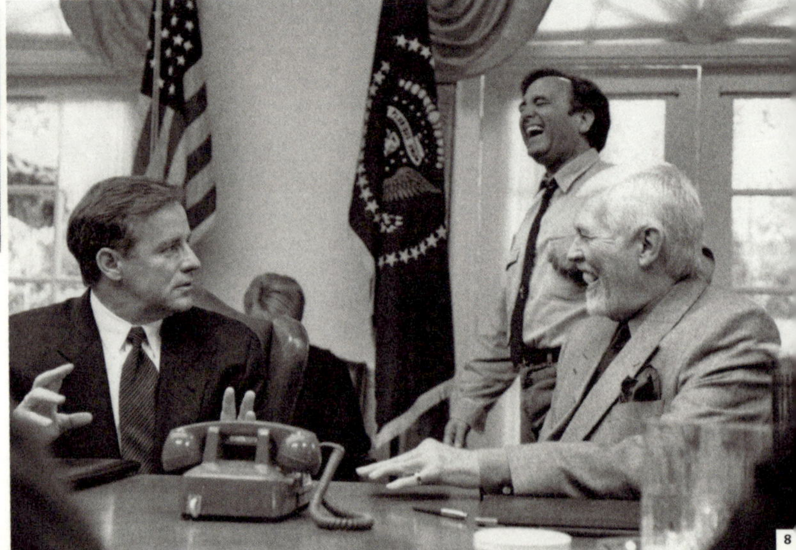

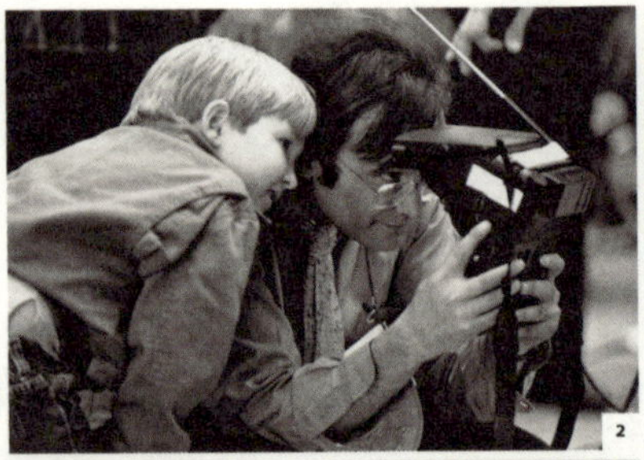
2

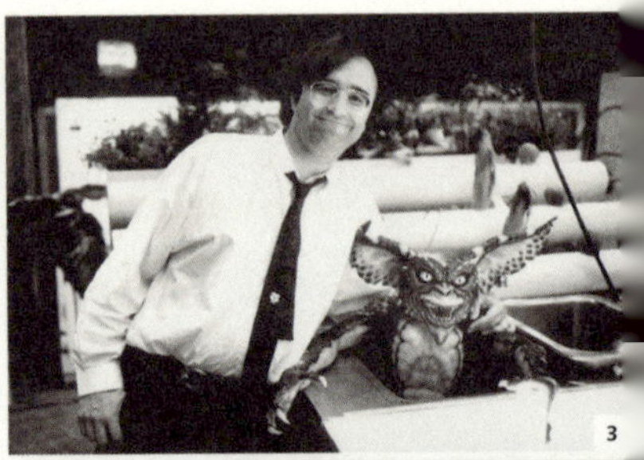
3

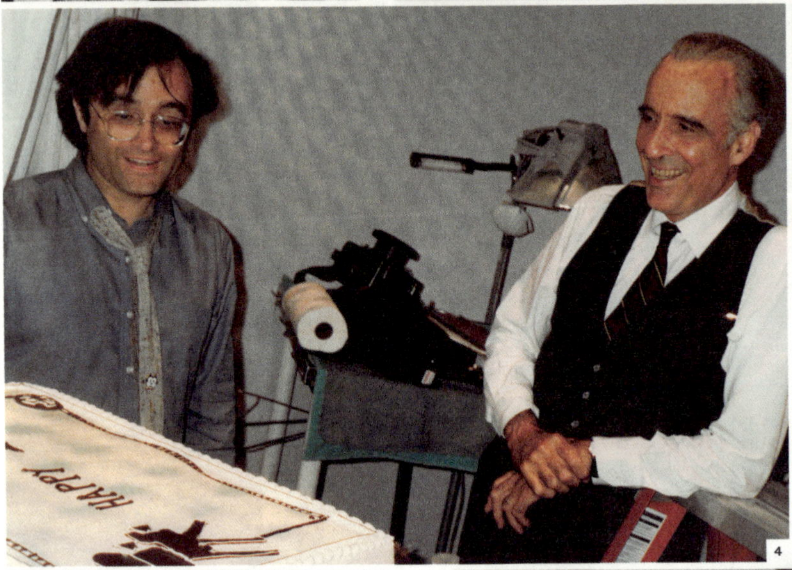

4

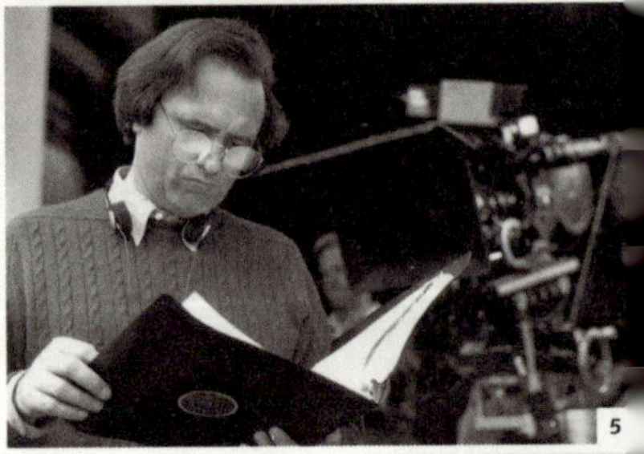
5

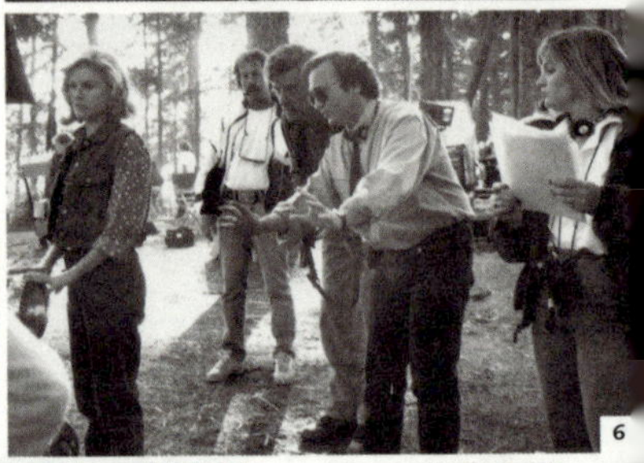
6

7

8

Gremlins 2: The New Batch [1–4], *Runaway Daughters* [5–6], *The Second Civil War* [7–8]

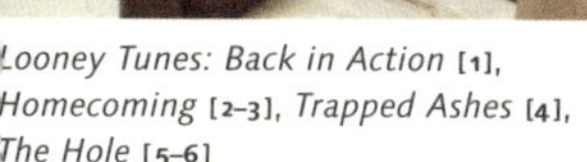

Looney Tunes: Back in Action [1],
Homecoming [2–3], Trapped Ashes [4],
The Hole [5–6]

A Dante, Esq. Chronology

1912 Charles "Chuck" Jones born, Spokane, Washington (September 21).

1916 Forrest J Ackerman born, Los Angeles, California (November 24).

1926 Roger Corman born, Los Angeles, California (April 5). Forrest J Ackerman buys the first issue of *Amazing Stories* (October).

1928 Dick Miller born, Bronx, New York (Christmas Day!).

1946 Joe Dante, Jr. born, Morristown, New Jersey (November 28). Steven Spielberg born, Cincinnati, Ohio (December 18).

1950 (or thereabouts): The impressionable young Joe gets his first taste of television – not surprisingly, his earliest memories are of *Captain Video* and *Learn to Draw with Jon Gnagy* – before his parents' first TV set goes on the blink. Too late… the damage is done.

1952 A lifetime of movie-going commences when Joe's Aunt Natalie and Aunt Betty take him to see *Snow White and the Seven Dwarfs* at the Community Theater in Morristown.

1953 Already a Saturday matinee regular, Joe decides (for a change) to stick around after the cartoons are over; consequently, he sees *It Came From Outer Space*, learns that "outer space is *big!*" and decides he wants more of the same.

1954 Joe buys his first issue (#11) of *Tales Calculated to Drive You MAD* at Silverman's Cigar Store, arousing his concerned parents' evil-comic-book fears, which are quelled by his doting Uncle Bill, who assures them that "it's all right – it's satire!" Joe contracts polio and spends the better part of a year in the hospital, licking the dreaded disease; he misses third grade (and multiplication tables), but compensates by reading every issue of *Classics Illustrated* (including the really gory ones, later suppressed) with a pad of paper by his side.

1955 Restored to health, Joe resumes riding his bike to the movies. He remembers "lots and lots of Westerns" during this period, possibly even including Roger Corman's *Apache Woman*, in which Dick Miller makes his film debut playing both a cowboy *and* an Indian.

1956 Further Adventures of Little Joe at the Movies: apparently mesmerized, he sits through a double-bill of *Abbott and Costello Meet the*

Mummy and *World Without End* twice, prompting his worried parents to call the police; he sees *Forbidden Planet*, and thinks it would be cool to meet Robby the Robot someday; he insists that his father take him to see *Tarantula!*, but is too frightened to remain in the theater.

1957 "Shock Theatre," a TV package of Universal horror classics, makes its debut on New York's WABC-TV Channel 7, giving young Dante his first look at *Frankenstein, Dracula, The Invisible Man, Werewolf of London*, etc. – basically getting him primed for…

1958 Annus Monsteribis: Joe discovers the first issue of *Famous Monsters of Filmland*; he must subsequently buy it many more times, to replace copies confiscated and torn up by teachers and camp counselors. He also directs his own play, "The Mad Doctor of Transylvania Square," in front of his 7ᵗʰ-grade English class.

1959 The budding scholar and critic writes the first of innumerable letters to Forrest J Ackerman, editor of *Famous Monsters of Filmland*, in a desperate bid to see his name in print; also encounters alternate monster magazine, *Journal of Frankenstein*, and is impressed by scholarly tone of material pirated from *Sight and Sound*.

1960 The young showman founds Scribbly International Pictures, for the benefit of his little brother, Ross; the year's product – on paper, for the "shoebox theater" – includes *The Spider!*, *Fort Death*, and the "Spook Quartet" (*The Spook; The Return of the Spook; The Spook Strikes Back; The Spook Meets the Spider*). The first of these is now tragically lost.

1961 Another banner year for Scribbly International, as resident auteur Anonymous Sam turns out *Shock, Scream of Fear, Return to Mystery Planet* (re-issued 1964 as *Planet of the Dead*), and *7 Cities of Gold* – the last-named production miraculously failing to provoke a plagiarism suit by Walt Disney Studios.

1962 Persistence pays off, as Joe's umpteenth letter to Forrest J Ackerman is published in issue #18 of *Famous Monsters of Filmland*, under the title "Dante's Inferno." Having finally crashed the pages of *Famous Monsters*, he soon begins contributing material (starting with his stills collection) to its chief rival, the New Jersey-based *Castle of Frankenstein*.

1963 Nothing much happens, apparently, but to answer the obvious question: it was after school, he was in Mr. Fox's (the art teacher's)

classroom, and the news of Kennedy's assassi-
nation was piped in over the intercom.

1964 "Joe Dante Jr." is first (or *finally*) listed on *Castle of Frankenstein*'s masthead as a Contributing Editor; despite this, he is granted a diploma from Parsippany (N.J.) High School and permitted to enter the Philadelphia College of Art, where he is promptly informed that, his ambition to be a professional cartoonist notwithstanding, "cartooning is not an Art."

1965 Joe decides instead to study film, which apparently *is* an Art: he watches films, thinks about films, talks about films, and learns how to run a 16mm projector, a skill which will soon come in very handy. Concurrently, he dedicates himself to the editorial stewardship of the "Frankenstein TV Movieguide" feature in *Castle of Frankenstein*, which commences its march through the alphabet in issue #6 (*Abbott and Costello Go to Mars* through *Attack of the Puppet People*). In Philadelphia, Jon Davison knocks on his door and introduces himself; in Chicago, the revived *Batman* serial is a big hit, and heads East.

1966 This year sees the debut (and almost immediate demise) of his column "Infernal Dante" in *Castle of Frankenstein*, issues #8 and #9. *Batman* comes to Philadelphia and a light bulb goes on over Dante's head; he stages a "Camp Movie Night," which eventually evolves into *The Movie Orgy*.

1967 Dante makes several student films at PCA – *Thank God It's Only a Motion Picture*, *Thriller* and *Where Are You?* – not one of which is more memorable than its title. Also starts charging money for people to see *The Movie Orgy*, and decides he likes money OK, if only to buy more films with.

1968 College graduate Dante lands a job reviewing films (among more odious chores) for the Philadelphia-based trade publication *Film Bulletin*, and proceeds to amuse himself for five years writing incisive, often scathing reviews of pictures that nobody else gives a shit about.

1969 Dante's name first appears as "Managing Editor" of *Film Bulletin*; "Frankenstein TV Movieguide" takes the whole year (two issues of *Castle of Frankenstein*) to get through the letter "L," then takes a two-issue hiatus while gearing up for "M."

1970 *Film Bulletin* job continues; *The Movie Orgy* plays the Fillmore East in New York City and secures corporate sponsorship from the Schlitz Brewing Company, giving Dante a vital source of income and a travel allowance to college campuses across the country.

1973 Dante receives his first fake screen credit, courtesy Jon Davison, as "dialogue director" on New World's March release, *Fly Me* ("See Stewardesses Battle Kung Fu Killers!"), which leads directly to reviewing more films for *Film Bulletin*. When summertime rolls around, Davison entices Dante to Los Angeles by telling him that he can play with film that's "over twice as wide" as the stuff in *The Movie Orgy*. Dante takes the bait, tentatively, comes West for a while, and "cuts" his first New World trailer, for *The Student Teachers*, in appropriate Southern California Zen-style: as a non-union man he's not permitted to actually touch the film. After the L. A. interlude, he returns to Philadelphia and *Film Bulletin*, where he now reviews films made by people he's actually met.

1974 When a second fake screen credit (editor on Steve Carver's *The Arena*) still fails to ignite Dante's career, Davison has an even better idea. He convinces Roger Corman that having an in-house trailer department at New World will bring some aesthetic unity to the company's advertising product, and, by the way, will save a few bucks as well. Dante moves to L. A., goes to work at New World, and is soon teamed with a fellow New Jersey native, the much taller Allan Arkush. They assume the awesome responsibility of cutting trailers and TV spots that will make New World's films look better than they really are; to this end, they develop and refine the "exploding helicopter" method for raising the excitement level of any given trailer. This technique works well for the films of Cirio Santiago, but is of limited use for those of Bergman and Fellini, which occasionally pop up on New World's distribution schedule.

1975 Trailers, trailers, trailers: *TNT Jackson*, *Death Race 2000*, *Tidal Wave* (possibly the single most deceptive trailer in New World history), etc. And then… Jon Davison makes a bet with Roger Corman, and Dante and Arkush get to make a film: *Hollywood Boulevard*, with a plot cribbed from *The Death Kiss* (1933) and additional footage cribbed from the New World library. On September 19, New World Pictures issues check #3671 to Dante, for the first $88.85 of the grand total of $500 he will receive for co-directing the picture. At one point during the ten-day shoot, intrepid young production assistant Mike Finnell earns Dante's enduring friendship via his repeated retrieval of a wooden prop hand grenade from a swamp. Dante also uses the film to settle various childhood debts by giving cameo roles to Forry Ackerman, Robby the Robot, and Godzilla (billed as "Godzina" to avoid the fire-breathing wrath of Toho Studios). Meanwhile, back East, *Castle of Frankenstein* puts out its final issue, ringing the curtain down on "Frankenstein TV Movieguide" after the letter "R," which leaves Dante's insights into *Teenage Zombies* and Corman's *War of the Satellites* tragically unpublished. (Thankfully for posterity, he had previously reviewed *Voodoo Heartbeat* for *Film Bulletin*.)

1976 *Hollywood Boulevard* escapes (so the joke goes) to public view, and achieves a booking on its namesake street double-billed with *Countdown at Kusini*. The film single-handedly revitalizes the careers of Walter Paisley *and* Dick Miller, and wins favor from Corman. As a reward for their efforts, Corman magnanimously allows Dante and Arkush to keep their jobs in the trailer department. Sensing their untapped potential as thespians (or as a payback for their casting him as Erich Von Leppe in *Hollywood Boulevard*), Paul Bartel casts the duo as geeky grease monkeys in his film *Cannonball*; when even Walter Paisley declines to accept them as clients, however, they must return again to the exploding helicopter. They earn another brief respite from their cutting-room chores in November, when (with Davison) they are invited to pontificate on the making of *Hollywood Boulevard* for a "film analysis forum" at the Art Center College of Design in Pasadena, thus officially anointing it as a "cult" movie.

1977 A year after its initial release, *Hollywood Boulevard* finally gets its premiere engagement in New York: a two-day "run" on 42nd Street, doubled with *Cover Girl Models* (source of the "exploding helicopter" shot). Back in L. A., Dante and Arkush are passed over for Supporting Actor Oscar nominations for their performances in *Cannonball* and determine to break out of the trailer department (again). In spite of his utter lack of technical knowledge about cars, Dante (like Ray Bradbury, a lifelong non-driver) is tapped to edit *Grand Theft Auto* for fledgling director Ron Howard; he also enhances his reputation as New World's "Mr. Fix-It" by cutting a newly-shot, upbeat ending for *I Never Promised You a Rose Garden* (1977). In time, Corman comes up with a pair of directorial assignments and makes Dante and Arkush choose between them: Arkush gets *Rock 'n' Roll High School* because he really, really wants to do it; Dante gets *Piranha* because it's the other choice. Stuck with "a bad idea and a rotten script," Dante gets his first chance to work with John Sayles, a real writer who years later will be given a bunch of money just for being a genius; together they fashion a script for *Piranha* that won't embarrass them, and which has some bite to it.

1978 After two weeks in an L.A. swimming pool shooting rubber fish, and three weeks in Texas shooting people pretending to be eaten by rubber fish, and more weeks back in L.A. cutting film, Dante develops an ear infection and creates a film that he's pretty sure is "the worst in history," despite the presence of Barbara Steele. Audiences in Detroit, Pittsburgh, Europe and just about everywhere else think otherwise, and to everyone's astonishment *Piranha* soon becomes the highest-grossing New World film ever. Dante gets noticed, in that peculiar Hollywood way, by being considered for every water-beast-on-the-rampage project in town ("my aquatic period," he terms it); the biggest fish and payroll ($50,000) are offered by Dino de Laurentiis, for whom the young *metteur-en-l'eau* agrees to develop *Orca 2*. Toil on this thankless task is briefly interrupted the week before Christmas, when Mike Finnell drags him out of bed to finish directing *Rock 'n' Roll High School* after Allan Arkush collapses on the set. This endears Finnell to Dante even more than the hand-grenade thing.

1979 Dante talks de Laurentiis out of making *Orca 2* ("for which the movie-going public owes me a debt of gratitude"), then immediately moves on to the next fishy project, the National Lampoon horror-picture-comedy-spoof *Jaws 3, People 0*, at Universal. This takes up months and months of his time before sinking out of sight. As it sinks, Mike Finnell throws Dante a life preserver and pulls him aboard a project he's preparing for producer Daniel Blatt: a werewolf movie, of all things, to be called *The Howling*. Dante, who definitely knows something about werewolves, eagerly signs on (after extracting a promise from Finnell that there will be no underwater photography involved) and begins working with writer Terence Winkless on developing a plausible story about the subject of people turning into wolves.

1980 Following months of work on *The Howling*, several rather hairy script problems remain, and Dante again calls on John Sayles to fix them. The film is shot in May and June and a little bit in August and a tiny little bit more in October. Eventually it's done and doesn't turn out bad at all: Corman and Ackerman have great cameos; Walter Paisley runs a bookstore that conveniently also sells silver bullets ("we came dangerously close to having our characters go to Clayton [The Lone Ranger] Moore's house for the bullets," Dante recalls); Bob Picardo does the first of his many turns for Dante by turning into a *really scary* werewolf; and the movie's even got John Carradine in it. At a particularly low point during the shooting, the following exchange takes place between the young director and the venerable thespian: "Well, John, I guess this won't be the best movie you've ever been in." "No, son, it won't. But it won't be the worst one, either."

1981 *The Howling* is successfully released in France in January, and is deemed worthy of U.S. release in March. People take notice: Pauline Kael (in *The New Yorker*) and Steven Spielberg, for instance. (Spielberg had noticed *Piranha*, too, of course, but convinced Universal not to sue Corman over it.) Dante and Finnell, meanwhile, are unable to decide which of them gets to retain their luxurious office suite, so neither one moves out, and to stave off boredom they think about making more movies together. One project, *The Philadelphia Experiment*, looks for a time like it might eventually become a movie; and sure enough, eventually, it does, but it's made by other people.

1982 April showers bring May flowers, and *Gremlins* in the mail: a script by that name arrives from Steven Spielberg's office, and Dante thinks it must be a mistaken delivery. (And who's to say, really, that it might not have been meant for Zucker-Abrahams-Zucker, for whom he's just completed two episodes of *Police Squad!?*) But no mistake, it seems, so Dante, now a full-fledged member of the Directors Guild of America (thanks to the *PS!* gig), "takes a meeting," in best Hollywood style, with the creator of *Jaws* – without which, lest we forget, there might never have been a *Piranha* – and, by so doing, finds that he has entered a gravitational field of considerable strength. He agrees to have a go at *Gremlins*, and before you know it, Dante has another job, remaking an old TV show as one of the segments of Spielberg's and John Landis's *Twilight Zone* movie. When the studio and the producers go underground in the aftermath of the exploding helicopter (no joke this time), Dante is given free rein to create what becomes the strangest, yet most widely-admired, segment of that star-crossed film.

1983 In January, *Gremlins* writer Chris Columbus completes the sixth draft of his engaging yet troublesome script. Finished script or no, casting begins in February; among the actors who read and are rejected for the part of "Billy" are Tom Hanks, Emilio Estevez, Michael J. Fox, Dana Carvey, and Kevin Bacon; Hanks, undeterred, comes back three weeks later and reads for "Gerald," with no more success. Somewhere in here, Steven Spielberg complicates matters with the comment "What if Gizmo *doesn't* turn into a gremlin?" In March, a "revised seventh draft" of the script is turned in by Columbus. In April, there is a pre-production screening of *The Birds* ("We are particularly interested in the 'town destruction' sequence as it relates to our project," says a memo from Mike Finnell) and an eighth and so-called "final" draft of the script. Shooting of *Gremlins* begins at the end of April and continues until the beginning of November, leading Dante to comment later that "people were born, grew up and were cast in the film" during shooting.

1984 The hassles of production are succeeded by the hassles of post-production, as Dante alternates between supervision of "Multiple Creature Looping" and battling with Warner Bros. executives over the film's level of mayhem and such details as what is referred to in a studio memo as "Phoebe's now truly famous speech." (One executive admits that he's "not sure whether to laugh or apologize for having the impulse to laugh"; but Spielberg stands up for Dante, and the speech stays in.) *Gremlins* is released in June, and quickly becomes something like a phenomenon. Its box-office returns are substantial ($100 million in just six weeks, setting a company record – for a company that didn't even like the movie very much), and so are the accompanying sales of *Gremlins* toys, books, dolls, video games, children's sleepwear, breakfast cereal, etc. Dante, searching the fine print of his contract for the sub-paragraph detailing his share of merchandising revenues, comes up empty. He is, however, anointed as a genuine American *auteur* by a featured profile/interview which appears in the June issue of *Film Comment* (under the imaginative title "Dante's Inferno"), and *Gremlins* itself receives the high honor of being parodied (as "Grimlins") in the September issue of *MAD*. Taking advantage of the dazed-by-success director, Paramount's Jeffrey Katzenberg badgers him unmercifully to direct a script called "Explorers." Dante agrees, not suspecting that in just a few short months Paramount's Katzenberg will become Disney's Katzenberg, leaving *Explorers* to the mercy of a new studio administration. As the year draws to a close, sales of Santa Claus suits plummet 38 %, a blow from which the American Christmas industry takes years to recover.

1985 *Explorers* is completed but not really finished (or maybe it's the other way around), is unwisely rushed into release by Paramount as their big summer movie, and promptly sinks without a trace. Tired of being pushed around by the Big Bad Studio, Dante and Finnell officially join forces in September and start their own company, Renfield Productions. They enter into a two-year development deal with Warner Bros., and set up offices on their Burbank lot to make it more convenient for that studio to continue browbeating Dante to do a *Gremlins* sequel (an effort which began in earnest approximately 22 minutes after the release of the first film). Exhausted and depressed by the whole experience of *Explorers*, however, Dante chooses to retreat into a variety of small, low-pressure projects: two episodes for the TV

186

anthology series *Amazing Stories* (another Spielberg project) and one for the revived version of *The Twilight Zone*, plus a gaggle of comic skits for John Landis's *Amazon Women on the Moon*. Meanwhile, Joe and Mike discover that the main advantage of having your own company is that it entitles you to one indispensable employee – in their case, it's Betty Moos (pronounced Moss). Inherited from Jon Davison to help out on *Explorers*, she spends the next couple of decades as the company's resident assistant/associate/filekeeper/office Mom.

1986 Ready for a feature film "comeback," Dante turns to *Innerspace*, first proposed to him in 1983, but now appealingly re-imagined as a Martin-and-Lewis fantasy/comedy. Martin, Lewis, Abbott and Costello all being unavailable, he makes the film with Dennis Quaid and Martin Short. The production takes up the better part of 1986, with shooting completed in time for Christmas. This is also the year in which the colorization controversy erupts, and Dante is proud to become one of the 18 signatories to the DGA public letter protesting the practice; later, he helps with the writing of John Huston's videotaped statement objecting to the colorization of *The Maltese Falcon* (1941), which is played at the Congressional hearings on the matter, a year after Huston's death.

1987 *Innerspace* turns out just fine, except that (a) hardly anybody goes to see it, and (b) every other person who does thinks that it's a Steven Spielberg movie. Dante, meanwhile, is determined to break out of the Spielberg orbit and make a movie for grown-ups. To that end, he devotes extensive effort to the development of a project called *Little Man Tate*, about the difficulties faced by a child genius and his mother. An interesting script called "Matinee" comes his way in September, but pre-production chores on *Little Man Tate* take precedence for the remainder of the year. Meanwhile, after several years of trying to figure out how to make a *Gremlins* sequel without Dante's help, Warner Bros. comes to him, late in the year, with an offer he can't refuse (or doesn't, at any rate).

1988 Things fall apart; things change. *Little Man Tate* is canceled, but within a couple of months Dante finds himself on the Universal backlot, moving famous TV houses around in preparation for *The 'Burbs*. Happy to be working at all during the Writers Guild strike, Dante wraps the picture up by the first of August, although much subsequent time is spent concocting a more satisfactory ending, which is shot in November. Meanwhile, throughout the year, *Gremlins 2* scripts are coming over the transom, although it's not until the appearance of a writer named Charlie Haas that anybody is able to make much of one. Haas comes up with a couple of sure-fire narrative gimmicks, and by the end of the year it looks pretty certain that Dante will overcome his reluctance to work with gremlins again. (Legend has it that Victor Fleming felt the same way about "those goddamn Munchkins.")

1989 Just as 1983 had been eaten up by *Gremlins*, so is 1989 the year during which not much else happens besides the production of *Gremlins 2: The New Batch* – "not much else," in this case, being the February release of *The 'Burbs*, which is met with an inexplicably vitriolic response from the nation's film critics, who are apparently deeply offended – no, *shocked* – that the recently-Oscar-nominated Tom Hanks has chosen such a strange film with which to follow up *Big*. Dante can only shake his head and wonder how much worse the response would have been if they'd killed Hanks's character off, as the original draft of the script had called for. Anyway, from May to December it's gremlins, gremlins and more gremlins.

1990 The second *Gremlins* movie proves just as perplexing to Warner Bros. executives as the first one had been, but despite some late-inning haggling over tone and content, the film goes out pretty much as Dante wants it to, although the public response is not particularly overwhelming. In July, he films a trio of 30-second commercials for M&M's, which convinces him to never do *that* again. When his intended next film for Warner Bros. release, called *Matinee*, hits a rough script-development patch, he calls again on Charlie Haas, whose writing services had proved so valuable on *Gremlins 2*, and who comes through again with flying colors. Also on the agenda is a project close to the cartooniest part of Dante's heart: a movie to be made in collaboration with Chuck Jones – a tale of the great Warner Bros. animators to be based on Jones's memoir, *Chuck Amuck*, and to be called *Termite Terrace*. Yes, it was to be all those things – but in the end it was not to be, as you'll see.

1991 Warner Bros. loses interest in *Matinee*; Dante and Finnell lose interest in making movies for Warner Bros. (which will complicate the further development of *Termite Terrace*), and when their deal with the studio runs out, they enter into a two-year "first look" arrangement with Universal Pictures. As a pre-existing Renfield project, *Matinee* must still go looking for outside financing; several arrangements are made, but subsequently fall through. The middle of the year provides a pleasant diversion in Dante's involvement with the offbeat TV series *Eerie, Indiana*, for which he directs the pilot, acts as "creative consultant", directs four additional episodes, and portrays a version of himself in the series finale. The series is canceled after a short network run during the 1991/92 season, but a good time is had by all. On the development front, Charlie Haas takes a little time off from *Matinee* to bring his expertise to bear on a rewrite of *Termite Terrace*, a task he finishes about two weeks before Renfield's deal with Warner Bros. expires. Fate… or Destiny?

1992 When the *third* independent financing source for *Matinee* falls through, Universal (already set to distribute the film) agrees to cough up the production money, and the film starts shooting in Florida in April. That same month, coincidentally, Universal loudly announces that they have purchased a script for Renfield to develop entitled "Kidstuff," about a macho airline pilot who gets "zapped through magical circumstances and shrunken to doll size" and must then do battle with the "violence-oriented action figures" he himself has purchased for his son's birthday. And the *very next day* it's reported that Spielberg's Amblin Entertainment has paid a lot of money for a script entitled

"Small Soldiers," described as "a fantasy adventure about a young boy's escapades with an army of toy soldiers who come to life." Haas continues to toil away on *Termite Terrace*, turning in a revised draft of the script in March, with which the oxymoronic "Creative Group" at Warner Bros. professes to be "thrilled." Meanwhile, Renfield's Universal deal gets them involved in the early stages of preparation for a new version of *The Mummy* (1932).

1993 *Matinee* is released on Super Bowl Weekend, traditional low point of the movie-attendance year, ensuring that the film will make even less money than everyone expected. (*MANT!*, on the other hand, is a smashing success for Lawrence Woolsey – who, alas, vanishes while on a promotional tour for *Galligator* and is never heard from again.) Towards mid-year, Dante accepts an offer to remake an AIP film for cable TV; he picks *Runaway Daughters* (1956) – which he has, amazingly, *never seen* – and gets Haas to re-imagine the original story for his remake. The new version, shot in just 12 days in November, proves once again that he has not forgotten the lessons learned at New World Pictures. And this is the year that, alas, we must bid farewell to *Termite Terrace*, as it sinks slowly into the blue Pacific, doomed by Warner Bros.' lack of enthusiasm for its own cartoon heritage. (Meanwhile, in the world of sports, basketball superstar Michael Jordan leads the Chicago Bulls to their third straight NBA championship, announces his [first] retirement, and starts looking for other ways to spend his time. The relevance of this will become apparent in a few years.) Supplanting *Termite Terrace* at the top of Renfield's development charts is *The Mummy:* preparation proceeds throughout the year, with Rick Baker engaged in planning make-up and animatronics, and John Sayles called in for a re-write in November; meetings are held, casting is discussed, scripts begin to be sent to actors' agents, etc. And speaking of agents, Dante changes his (temporarily, as it turns out) during this year, news of which permits *Daily Variety* to observe that "Dante's trademark is to mix comedy with other genres," while characterizing Garry Marshall (a fellow client at his new agency) as "more of a concept-driven auteur."

1994 Development Hell! The flurry of activity around *The Mummy* peaks at the beginning of the year... then the project crumbles into dust when Universal decides that $25 million is too much to spend on a mummy movie, at least on a Joe Dante mummy movie. (A few years later, a new batch of Universal executives will decide that $25 million isn't nearly enough, so they give somebody else three times that much to do the film.) Meanwhile, although a lot of other projects are put on the burner, nothing comes to a boil. Around mid-year, Dante is announced as director for both *The Phantom* (an Alan Ladd Jr.-Robert Evans project for Paramount) and *Cat & Mouse* (for TriStar); he goes as far as Australia to prepare for shooting the former, before the producers postpone it due to alleged weather and/or casting problems, take your pick. (*The Phantom*, too, is given a second life later on, with no further participation from Dante, despite his name remaining on the 1996 release as one of its four executive producers.)

In lieu of *The Phantom*, Dante realizes a small dream (and grabs yet another opportunity to mix comedy with another genre) by making his first and so far only Western, "Lightning." No matter that it's just half-an-hour long and is buried in an obscure cable TV series – it's got Brian Keith and a burro in it, and some of it is shot in Bronson Canyon, just like *Robot Monster*! Also in 1994, novelist Caleb Carr comes to Renfield with an idea for a science fiction TV series to be called *The Osiris Chronicles*, which interests Dante but is put on the back burner after some initial development.

1995 Development continues on *Cat & Mouse*, a sort of reverse-*Roger Rabbit* concerning the adventures of two animated characters in the real world. Haas dutifully comes up with a revised draft screenplay in July, before the project is shelved. *The Osiris Chronicles* is revived around August, as deals are made with Paramount Network Television and CBS for production of a pilot and possible series; the two-hour pilot, under Dante's direction, is shot in late November and December.

1996 *The Osiris Chronicles* goes nowhere with CBS, and the completed pilot is stuck on the shelf until early 1998. Dante's own TV chronicles continue with the preparation and production of *The Second Civil War* for HBO. And in the Injury to Insult Dept.: in November, Warner Bros. – the studio that couldn't justify making *Termite Terrace* in tribute to their great animators – releases *Space Jam*, an animated basketball game masquerading as a movie, with Bugs Bunny, Daffy Duck and Michael Jordan.

1997 Dante is now offered *Small Soldiers* – fresh off five years' worth of "fast-track" development – by DreamWorks SKG (the "S," of course, being Spielberg). Meanwhile, *The Second Civil War* unveils on HBO to little fanfare but gets a prestigious showcase as an official selection of the Venice Film Festival. Shooting of *Small Soldiers* begins in November, with a script that's on its eighth and ninth writers and continues to be revised almost daily throughout production – keeping actors, technicians and toy soldiers all standing around waiting to be told what to do. Dick Miller's last line of dialogue in the picture nicely sums up the experience: "Toys is Hell."

1998 *Small Soldiers* is completed and released in time to promote the merchandise. Dante flees – er, flies – to Switzerland to receive the Locarno Film Festival's "Leopard of Honor" tribute. Returning home, he resumes his ongoing search for a project that will engage his sensibilities and be worth spending a year of his life on. "All I want to do," he is reported to have said earlier in his career, "is make movies that are as good as movies used to be before they got so bad."

1999 The search for a worthwhile project continues. It's prematurely announced in the trades that he will direct *The Sixth Day* (2000) with Arnold Schwarzenegger, but he can't quite get his head around the basic story foundation – Arnold as Everyman – and decides to pass. Following through with a plan that had been set in motion the previous year, the Locarno Film Festival mounts an exhaustive retrospective of Dante's oeuvre, including TV commercials, outtake reels, and a presentation of *The Movie Orgy*. This event, which also celebrates "the Second Corman generation" and involves many of Dante's cohorts from his New World days (including Corman himself), results in the publication of not one but two books about Dante's work – one in French and the other in Italian.

2000 Back in Hollywood, where it seems that very few executives are impressed by what a bunch of Europeans have to say, Dante's career goes almost completely dark for the first time in a quarter-century. There is one brief report, in the trades, about him serving as an executive producer on the Showtime cable TV series *Jeremiah*, about a future society afflicted by a deadly virus. Eventually the series would enjoy a two-season run (2002–2004), which Dante observed from the sidewalk, he and Mike Finnell having been "aced out of the production after developing and flogging it around town for two years." Let's just call this year a Millennial Hiatus, and leave it at that.

2001 The dark curtain of inactivity begins to lift a bit when Dante is engaged by Dan Angel and Billy Brown to direct two half-hour episodes of their destined-for-obscurity horror/sci-fi anthology show *Night Visions* for Fox. His pleasure at getting back behind the camera is further elevated by the happy experience of working with actress Bridget Fonda, who turns in a tour-de-force performance under Dante's direction in his episode "The Occupant." He is less fonda the fact that this particular gig takes

him, for the first time, over the Canadian border into Vancouver, aka "Hollywood North," which runs counter to his longstanding preference for making movies in good old Hollywood, U.S.A. But there comes a time (and this is it) when a man's gotta work where a man's gotta work, and the lure of a paycheck in any currency is a powerful thing. Fortunately, as it turns out, he speaks tolerably good Canadian for a guy who grew up in New Jersey.

2002 Chuck Jones passes away on February 22, after 89 years of unparalleled ingenuity. A month or so later, in an unrelated but almost painfully ironic development, Dante is offered the directorial reigns on *Looney Tunes: Back in Action* by Warner Bros., at the behest of the film's screenwriter, Larry Doyle. Dante, understandably leery of big budget studio production by this point, vows (out of loyalty to Jones) to do whatever he can to prevent the studio from making another *Space Jam*, little realizing that the project will eat up the next year and a half of his life, and take a few bites out of his soul, as well. Principal photography starts in July and lasts for tortuous month after month of near-constant rewrites, reshoots and studio meddling. At one low point, Dante ejects two bickering studio executives from his set, and at an *even lower* point slinks away for a few hours to catch a flick at the local multiplex – the first (and only) such "walkoff" of his career.

2003 Reeling (or unreeling) a bit in the backwash of the *Looney Tunes* shoot, Dante retains his equilibrium by fantasizing about a more pleasant future project – and by golly if it doesn't materialize, in the form of a screenplay that he encounters on his porch one May evening, entitled "Sunshine Boulevard." It's a fact-based dramatization of Roger Corman's experience shooting *The Trip* (1967), written by Tim Lucas and Charles Largent. Dante reads the whole thing in one sitting and calls the writers to tell them he wants to make it. With Corman's approval, Dante and producer Elizabeth Stanley dive headfirst into the search for financing the film. Meanwhile, an unnamed Academy Award-winning writer is brought in for yet more rewrites on *Looney Tunes*. Despite falling out with Doyle and the producers, Dante and animation director Eric Goldberg gallantly see *Looney Tunes* through to the bitter end, slaving away at post-production for eight grueling months. Adding one more lost battle to the chronicle of the troubled production, Dante's petition for co-director credit for Goldberg is denied by the Directors Guild of America. The film, which becomes the costliest that Dante has ever been and will likely ever be involved in, is released in the U.S. on 2,903 screens in November, earning less than a fifth of its estimated budget. At some point during the year, Dante manages to find time for a commission from the Busch Entertainment amusement park people, a 3D short in the 70mm/5 perforation format entitled *R. L. Stine's Haunted Lighthouse*. The film runs at SeaWorlds parks and Flamingo Land in the U.K., enhanced with such classy "4D" gimmicks as seat buzzers and water cannons aimed at audience members – the latter harking back, no doubt unwittingly, to the wet t-shirt glory days of New World Pictures. Lawrence Woolsey would be proud.

2004 The end of an era: composer Jerry Goldsmith, who had worked with Dante on all of the director's studio projects since 1983, dies of cancer at age 75. His imaginative score for *Looney Tunes: Back in Action* – one artistic bright spot in a project that otherwise involved a nearly endless string of compromises – would be his last. Dante and Stanley continue to work on *Sunshine Boulevard* (which has now been retitled *The Man with Kaleidoscope Eyes*, in a nod to Corman's *X: The Man with the X-Ray Eyes*), commissioning veteran screenwriters Michael Almereyda and James Robison to jazz up certain elements in Lucas's and Largent's original.

2005 Filmmaker Mick Garris creates and produces the Showtime anthology series *Masters of Horror*, enlisting Tobe Hooper, John Carpenter, Larry Cohen, Dario Argento, Takashi Miike, and Dante, among others, as part of the auteur-driven project. Enraged by the escalating Iraq War, Dante designs his episode, *Homecoming*, as a piece of anti-Dubya administration agit-prop. Showing as a stand-alone film, it wins over European audiences in particular, garnering awards at film festivals in Sitges and Torino.

2006 On the heels of the *Homecoming* success, Dante is brought back for a second-season episode of *Masters*. The result, *The Screwfly Solution*, about a virus that turns men into bloodthirsty psychos, is one of his bleakest efforts. The same year marks Dante's short contribution to an omnibus film titled *Trapped Ashes*; he passes on the producer's initial offer to shoot a full segment (a "vampire tits"-themed story that strikes him as "sub-New World"), instead opting to film the wraparound segments, which gives him the pleasure of working again with actor Henry Gibson, who will pass away in 2009. (Ken Russell steps in to handle the vampire tits.) Strictly for the amusement of a few personal friends (or so he thinks), Dante uploads trailers from his personal collection to the Internet for *Attack of the 50 Ft. Woman* (1958), *The Terror* (1963), *From Hell it Came* (1957), *The Unearthly* (1957), and *Daughter of Dr. Jekyll* (1957) with his own running commentary. From this tossed-off acorn, the mighty oak of Trailers from Hell shall grow (see below).

2007 Financing remains elusive for *The Man with Kaleidoscope Eyes*, although the project is shopped around the globe. Dante decides to take a payday when producer Peter Lenkov calls him to direct a Halloween-themed episode of *CSI: NY* entitled "Boo." He also helms a brief segment for a TV movie collaboration called *The Greatest Show Ever* that's never finished (but, to his chagrin, remains stuck on his IMDb page). Trailers from Hell continues to evolve as marketing and new media guru Jonas Hudson, *Kaleidoscope Eyes* scribe and graphic artist Charlie Largent, and producer Elizabeth Stanley team up to launch a website, while also commissioning new trailer commentaries from John Landis, Edgar Wright, John Sayles, Eli Roth, Guillermo del Toro, Jack Hill, Roger Corman, Jon Davison, Larry Cohen, and dozens of others. In the *Plus ça change* Department, one might observe that Dante, the 61-year-old Hollywood veteran, has come full circle to his youthful days as the New World Pictures trailer-cutting whiz. Cue the exploding helicopter!

2008 Betty Moos, a stalwart presence at Renfield Productions for more than two decades, passes away at age 79, and Forrest J Ackerman, who fanned the flames of young Joe's monster-movie passions, moves on to the next realm after 92 years in this one. The trades say that Dante will direct *Bat Out of Hell*, an indie horror project about "a red-eye flight from L. A. to New York during which hijackers confront the monstrous cargo" (per *Variety*), but the money never comes through. He signs on instead for Bold Films' supernatural thriller *The Hole*, his first full-fledged feature since the *Looney Tunes* debacle. Dante convinces the producers to shoot the film in 3D; production starts late in the year and goes over into Christmas.

2009 Roger Corman invites Dante to dinner and, over pizza with *lots* of tomato sauce, proposes that he direct an interactive video-on-demand series for Netflix called *Splatter*, the main conceptual gimmick being that the audience gets to decide which of the show's characters lives or dies. Dante's acceptance marks his first collaboration with Corman since *Piranha* (and at $250,000 also his lowest-budgeted production since then), and the long hours entailed by the production are distinctly reminiscent of his days in Roger's trailer department. Meanwhile, *The Hole* is completed and ready for release, but the saturation of the U.S. market with faux-3D product has left no holes in the booking schedules of domestic theaters. In the end, *The Hole* premieres in Venice, where it wins a 3D award sponsored by eyeglass company Persol ("A lot of good that did me," says Dante looking back into the 4th Dimension.)

2010 *Piranha* joins the ranks of the Unnecessarily Remade; restyled as *Piranha 3D* by "splat pack"-generation filmmaker Alexandre Aja, it flops around, and dies. (*Variety* opines that "unlike the Joe Dante-directed, John Sayles-scripted 1978 version, this latest *Piranha* has no underlying political agenda.") *CSI: NY* producer Lenkov invites Dante to direct another Halloween-themed TV series episode, this one for his *Hawaii Five-o* reboot. Dante and Stanley put together a deal to make *The Man with Kaleidoscope Eyes* after a certain well-known British thesp signs on to play Corman. Unfortunately, when this Actor soon thereafter wins accolades for his "breakthrough performance" in another film, his Hollywood agent deems *Kaleidoscope Eyes* unworthy of his client's newly-ascendant talents (and probably salaries), effectively killing the deal.

2011 Dante is attached to a 3D romantic thriller to be called *Monster Love*, involving "two star-crossed lovers, a werewolf and a vampire." Helped by the fact that he has recently acquired an Italian passport, the film is packaged out of France as a Euro co-production; as of 2013, the director reports its status as "ongoing," which may be a euphemism for "undead." Also during the year, Magnet Media Group approaches Dante about directing a $50 million budget "sci-fi actioner" titled *O2* to be shot in Germany and the U.K., but the Magnet comes unstuck, the financing doesn't materialize, and the producers disappear. Dante doesn't go looking for them.

2012 Yet another uncalled-for *Piranha* remake – this time eloquently titled *Piranha 3DD* (im-plying exactly what you think it implies) – opens, if you can call it that, and sinks without a ripple, adding yet more lustre to the "classic" status of the original. Dante gets strung along on yet another project for a horror film set on an airplane called *Air Disturbance*, until it belatedly dawns on the producers that *three other films* with similar plots are set for almost-simultaneous production, and they decide to redirect their investment. Before year's end, Dante is connected to *Burying the Ex*, a zombie comedy to be shot in Los Angeles or New Orleans, although in the short term it looks like it might not be shot anywhere.

2013 Dante is now a *Hawaii Five-o* regular, directing two episodes in a single year. The Austrian Film Museum, the Vienna */slash* film festival and Slovenian Cinematheque approach Dante about staging a comprehensive retrospective and publishing a book (this book!), the first English language volume solely dedicated to his work. Reports appear about a project called *Casting the Runes*, based on the same source material as Jacques Tourneur's *Night of the Demon* (1957). Simon Pegg is attached but drops out due to scheduling problems, and the producers postpone production for next year. Meanwhile, Franco-Tunisian producer Saïd Ben Saïd, whose impressive track record includes films by Brian De Palma, Roman Polanski, and André Téchiné, is in talks with Dante and Stanley to finance *The Man with Kaleidoscope Eyes*, a.k.a. *The Project That Wouldn't Die*. And – because you can't keep a good zombie down – it appears as of this writing that *Burying the Ex* will go into production in November.

Filmography

Edited by Nil Baskar
With Annotations by Howard Prouty

The Movie Orgy

USA 1966–2009

CONCEIVED, PRODUCED, EDITED AND PERFORMED BY Joe Dante
and Jon Davison
16 MM (ORIGINAL), LATER TRANSFERRED TO DIGITAL VIDEO, B/W &
COLOR, VARYING LENGTHS / 280 MINUTES ("Ultimate Version")

What would ultimately become known as *The Movie Orgy* was conceived by Dante in early 1966, during his second year at the Philadelphia College of Art. The primary inspiration for its creation came from the then-popular revival screenings of the 1943 serial *Batman*, which had begun in July of 1965 at the Playboy Theater in Chicago. Shown at first in the more-or-less traditional one-chapter-daily manner, *Batman* proved unexpectedly popular; on October 9, however, the theater decided to try a different format, unspooling the entire 15-chapter serial in a single screening. "An Evening with Batman and Robin," as it was billed, was an immediate hit.

It also played about that time at the World Theater in Philadelphia, where it was seen by Dante, who had by then become a film programmer at PCA. Inspired directly by *Batman*, and influenced by Susan Sontag's famous 1964 essay "Notes on 'Camp,'" he decided to stage a "Camp Movie Night." Securing a rental print of another vintage chapter play, *The Phantom Creeps* (1939), Dante proceeded to put on a 7-hour show by interspersing reels of the 12-episode serial with whatever bits struck his fancy: pieces of features, old TV shows and commercials, industrial films, cartoons, etc. In this nascent form, *The Movie Orgy* was a smashing success.

For its first year or so, the show was limited to occasional re-stagings on the Philadelphia campus. Its content changed with each running, as Dante gained access to additional films and generally experimented with the format; it soon developed into a two-projector "performance," usually put on by Dante and his friend Jon Davison. The main feature would be threaded up on the first projector, and "when the boring part started," the other projector, with the "alternate" film pieces, would take over.

The Movie Orgy hit the "big time" early in 1970 with a screening at New York's legendary rock concert venue, the Fillmore East, an account of which appeared in the March 21, 1970 issue of *The New Yorker*. This somewhat unanticipated bit of nation-wide publicity for what had, until then, been essentially an "underground" event, "made us paranoid," says Dante, because "we didn't own the rights to any of these films!" Until then, the shows had continued to be constructed around 16mm rental prints, but Dante and Davison now realized that "we'd have to get our own prints" if they were to continue putting on the *Orgies*.

The *New Yorker*'s coverage of the Fillmore

show also brought the *Orgy* to the attention of the Schlitz Brewing Company, which offered to sponsor its presentation on college campuses. Under corporate sponsorship, the "Schlitz Movie Orgy" became a somewhat less bacchanalian event than its title implied: mindful of the possible adverse effects that might result from the combination of bad movies and beer-sodden undergraduates, the company asked Dante to reduce the length of the show to approximately three hours. This also made the show more manageable from a distribution-exhibition standpoint, and eventually the actual work of putting on the performances was sub-contracted to various friends. Although Dante's personal involvement with the *Orgy* diminished over time, it continued to provide him with a source of supplementary income.

The *Orgy* died a more or less natural death around the mid-1970s. According to Dante, it had never stopped evolving, but "after a certain amount of time, the material we were having to use – *The Man from U.N.C.L.E.* (1964–68) and so forth – was itself a bit too self-referential" to maintain the original "camp" ethos of the *Orgy*, and "the whole thing just wasn't much fun anymore." He also attributes its demise in part to the shift towards conservatism that marked many campuses in the mid-1970s: "When the Richard Nixon footage wasn't getting laughs any more, we knew it was time to pack it in."

(H. P.)

~

The All Night Once in a Lifetime Atomic Movie Orgy, as Dante and Davison would eventually call their presentation, was a flashback that kept evolving. It was also a performance. The pair worked with two projectors. Davison's was for the features that provided the basis for the show's grand interlocking narrative. *Earth vs. the Flying Saucers*, *Attack of the 50 Foot Woman*, and *College Confidential* were favorites; Dante recalled that, when they found the insane hillbilly drag-strip JD [Juvenile Delinquency] flick *Speed Crazy*, "we knew we'd struck gold."

Dante's projector was used to interpolate reedited TV shows, hygiene films, and newsreels. Filled with sly inserts, these dense montage sequences provided nutty eruptions in already delirious features. Dante specialized in one-minute digests, cutting from the opening credits of *Tales of the Texas Rangers* to highlights of the next week's episode to the closing credits, reducing something called *This Is America* to a blithely white-supremacist skit followed by "The End." But some were more complex: a commercial in which "good cold milk" is the beverage of choice at Ozzie and Harriet Nelson's twist party (Brando's *Wild One* looking on in disgust) segues into the twist madness of *College Confidential*, complete with mutant Marilyn clone Mamie Van Doren and Elvis imitator Conway Twitty, sliding into the scene where sociology professor Steve Allen scandalizes his student-subjects with… Richard Nixon's Checkers speech.

Projectors positioned outside the booth, Dante and Davison took their cues from the audience in switching back and forth from the edited material and the feature's premarked sections. *The Movie Orgy* had its first big public screening at NYU. Davison had entered the school in 1967 and almost immediately went into exhibition, showing double bills three nights a week at the East Village storefront he called the St. Mark's Cinematheque: "The programming was strictly Sarris," he remembered, but there were light shows and live music too, and before long Davison was selecting movies to be projected between acts at the Fillmore East. *The Movie Orgy* would be shown twice at the 2,700-seat Fillmore. An ad Davison placed in *The Village Voice*, promoted the March 8, 1970, screening (only two days after the Weather Underground inadvertently blew up a Greenwich Village townhouse only blocks away) as "7 incredible hours of thrills, violence, nostalgia & eyestrain. See Chicago police attacked by Giant Insects! See Thousands of performers in the roles that earned them Obscurity! See Singing cowboys, neurotic werewolves, maladjusted Indians, bosomy starlets that never made it, and Conway Twitty!" Admission was $1.50, calculated as 21 cents per hour.

The anonymous *New Yorker* writer who showed up left the only published account of Dante and Davison in action. The reporter noted a seamless cut back and forth between the peplums *Ulysses* and *Hercules*, the Abbott and Costello "Susquehanna Hat Company" routine, a French Dristan commercial, a 1936 Alf Landon campaign film, a public service announcement in which Ann-Margret endorses the War in Vietnam, a newsreel of President Eisenhower and his cabinet demonstrating civil defense preparedness and another entitled *Pivotal Egypt Guardian of the Suez Canal*. To judge from the fixed version of *The Movie Orgy* that Dante would eventually reconstruct, "The Talk of the Town" item might have equally mentioned the *Green Berets* trailer, chunks of a *Superman* TV episode, the WAC guide to menstruation, the clip where affable game-show MC Art Linkletter torments a woman with a box supposedly containing two rats, and *The Movie Orgy*'s single most cited bit: a bit of televised Dada worthy of Ernie Kovacs in which kiddie host Andy Devine, an animal puppet, and an actual cat lead the studio audience in an enthusiastic rendition of "Jesus Loves Me."

Casually blasphemous but relentless in its anti-militarism, *The Movie Orgy* anticipates the Reagan-era Cold War collage *The Atomic Café* as well as the delirious found footage polemics by Craig Baldwin and the nominally more soberminded Adam Curtis, not to mention Dante's own pop-culture shpritzes. Building in intensity, cutting from one apocalypse to another in the fashion of *Duck Soup* (itself referenced in a gunfight montage), *The Movie Orgy* climaxes in a crescendo of tumultuous screaming panic, followed by a long goodbye of Hollywood farewells, a montage of *The Ends*, and, finally, a version of the Roy Rogers-Dale Evans theme song, "Happy Trails." That's all, kids…

(J. Hoberman, "Across the Movi-verse," *Film Comment*, vol. 48, no. 2, March-April 2012)

Hollywood Boulevard

USA 1976

CO-DIRECTOR Allan Arkush **WRITER** Patrick Hobby (i.e. Danny Opatoshu) **CINEMATOGRAPHER** Jamie Anderson **EDITORS** Amy Jones, Allan Arkush, Joe Dante **ART DIRECTOR** Jack DeWolfe **COSTUME DESIGNER** Jane Ruhm **SPECIAL EFFECTS** Roger George **MUSIC** Andrew E. Stein **PRODUCER** Jon Davison (New World Pictures) **CAST** Candice Rialson, Mary Woronov, Rita George, Jeffrey Kramer, Dick Miller, Richard Doran, Tara Strohmeier, Paul Bartel, John Kramer, Commander Cody and His Lost Planet Airmen, Joseph McBride, Barbara Pieters, Godzina, Todd McCarthy, Jonathan Kaplan, Lewis Teague, Joe Dante, Allan Arkush
RELEASE DATE March 1976
35 MM, COLOR, 83 MINUTES

Befitting a film that almost immediately achieved cult status, the story of *Hollywood Boulevard*'s creation has become the stuff of modern Hollywood legend. The film's budget has been reported as anywhere from $50,000 to $90,000 (although $60,000 is the most often-quoted figure), and by most accounts it was indeed a "ten-day wonder," shot in approximately that many days during late September and early October of 1975. Documentation of this is noticeably scant, however – which among other things points up how unusual the production was, even in light of the notoriously loose and semi-improvisational methodology prevalent at New World Pictures in the mid-1970s.

It's clear that from the time that Dante and Arkush got involved with the project, they took its conception in the direction of a kind of "found-footage assemblage," the idea being that the film's primary narrative could be comprised of newly-shot scenes interspersed with footage from New World's other films. One rather glib version of the film's genesis has Dante and Arkush simultaneously cutting trailers for several disparate New World releases – *Street Girls* (1975), *TNT Jackson* (1974) and Fellini's *Amarcord* (1973) – and mixing up the footage, thereby getting the idea that "we could make one of these pictures." Roger Corman, in his memoir *How I Made a Hundred Movies in Hollywood and Never Lost a Dime*, remembers it as a bet proposed by Jon Davison over lunch that "he could produce a picture for $90,000, cheaper than anything New World had done."

The film's tiny budget and short schedule made a division of the directorial labor a necessity. They could only afford one set of sound recording gear, and Dante recalls that "I shot the dialogue sequences, and Allan did the stuff without sound." As the pair assembled the film in the editing room, however, they discovered that they actually had "made a movie," and that the need to plunder the New World vaults was less acute than expected. In the end, the previously-existing footage comprised no more than 10 of the film's 83 minutes. Notably excerpted in *Hollywood Boulevard* are: *The Hot Box* (Joe Viola, 1972), *The Big Doll House* (Jack

Hill, 1971), *The Big Bird Cage* (Hill, 1972), *Big Bad Mama* (Steve Carver, 1974), *Crazy Mama* (Jonathan Demme, 1975) and *Death Race 2000* (Paul Bartel, 1975). There are also various bits of "found footage," and as a homage to Corman, an excerpt from his 1963 classic *The Terror*, used rather poignantly in the scene at the drive-in in which Dick Miller watches himself on-screen with Boris Karloff.

The film attained almost-immediate cult status among cognoscenti of low-budget "exploitation" filmmaking. As early as November 1976, Dante, Arkush and Davison found themselves discussing its making at a "film analysis forum" at the Art Center College of Design in Pasadena. Nearly a quarter-century later, *Hollywood Boulevard* appears most valuable for its offhand, near-documentary depiction of a type of film production, exemplified by New World Pictures in its heyday, that has essentially vanished from the Hollywood landscape.

(H. P.)

~

You don't work for Roger Corman because you want to be rich; you work for Roger Corman because you want to make movies. When you know that going in, it's a lot easier to deal with not getting any money. You're never going to have the opportunity elsewhere that you have at New World to learn about how to do lots of stuff at once. You do the titles, you do the counts, you do the IPs, you do the opticals. It's tremendous education. It *is* film school.

(Joe Dante, in: David Chute, "Dante's Inferno," *Film Comment*, vol. 20, no. 3, May–June 1984)

Piranha
USA 1978

WRITER John Sayles, from a story by Richard Robinson and John Sayles CINEMATOGRAPHER Jamie Anderson EDITORS Mark Goldblatt, Joe Dante ART DIRECTORS Bill Mellin, Kerry Mellin COSTUME DESIGNER Linda Pearl SPECIAL EFFECTS Jon Berg CREATURE DESIGN AND ANIMATION Phil Tippett MAKE-UP EFFECTS Rob Bottin, Vincent Prentice MUSIC Pino Donaggio PRODUCER Jon Davison (Piranha Productions, New World Pictures) CAST Bradford Dillman, Heather Menzies, Kevin McCarthy, Keenan Wynn, Barbara Steele, Dick Miller, Belinda Balaski, Melody Thomas, Barry Brown, Bruce Gordon, Paul Bartel, John Sayles, Joe Dante RELEASE DATE July 1978 35 MM, COLOR, 94 MINUTES

Both Dante and Allan Arkush had wanted to get behind the camera again following *Hollywood Boulevard*, and Corman eventually presented them with two possibilities: *Rock 'n' Roll High School* and *Piranha*. They both preferred the former, but Dante deferred to Arkush's much stronger interest in doing a rock-themed musical film, and accepted *Piranha*.

Despite the full awareness of all concerned that *Piranha* was calculated to capitalize on the phenomenal success of Steven Spielberg's *Jaws* (1975), Dante recalled in a 1979 interview that the script (by Richard Robinson) had actually been written prior to the release of *Jaws*. In the same interview, Jon Davison called that script "considerably different and considerably worse" than what was finally shot, while Dante stated bluntly that "we refused to do Robinson's script."

At the urging of his valued story editor, Frances Doel, Corman turned to John Sayles, whose renown as one of the most independent of America's independent filmmakers (and one of Hollywood's most reliable script doctors) then lay entirely in the future. Doel had read his work, however, and recognized his talent, and on *Piranha* he came through with flying colors. According to Dante, "John solved the main script problem, which was how to get people back into the water once the piranhas had been discovered." Sayles's name alone appeared on the film's final script, and although Dante maintained that "the only things [from the Robinson script] that still exist are the piranhas and the little girl," a Writers Guild arbitration resulted in a shared story credit for Robinson.

The shooting of *Piranha* was a period of stress and uncertainty for Dante: "I was convinced I was making the worst movie in history and that it was going to be a huge flop. I thought it was so bad I didn't even go to the wrap party. I was still editing, because I thought it needed every second of attention I could give it before the deadline." In one sense, though, Dante felt himself fortunate: "We were lucky that *Avalanche* was being made [by Corey Allen] at the same time and Roger was off supervising that. So he left us alone, and we got to do pretty much whatever we wanted. We didn't have to show it to him until we thought it was in half-decent shape."

The end result was a box-office hit. After its first three weeks in release (during which it grossed over $2 million), Corman predicted correctly that it would become New World's highest-grossing film to date. Reviews were generally positive, with many critics appreciating the film's tongue-in-cheek humor. Perhaps the most important notice came from the man whose own box-office smash it was designed to capitalize upon: Steven Spielberg, who famously complimented *Piranha* as "the best of the *Jaws* rip-offs," and marked Dante as a filmmaker to watch. (H.P.)

Rock 'n' Roll High School
USA 1979

DIRECTORS Allan Arkush, Joe Dante (uncredited) **WRITERS** Richard Whitley, Russ Dvonch, Joseph McBride, from a story by Allan Arkush and Joe Dante **CINEMATOGRAPHER** Dean Cundey **EDITORS** Larry Bock, Gail Werbin, Joe Dante (uncredited) **ART DIRECTOR** Marie Kordus **COSTUME DESIGNER** Jack Buehler **SPECIAL EFFECTS** Frank DeMarco, Roger George **GIANT MOUSE CREATOR** Rob Bottin **MUSIC** Ramones, Chuck Berry, Alice Cooper, Devo, MC5, Todd Rundgren, The Velvet Underground, Brian Eno a.o. **PRODUCER** Michael Finnell (New World Pictures) **CAST** P.J. Soles, Vincent Van Patten, Clint Howard, Dey Young, Mary Woronov, Paul Bartel, Dick Miller, Don Steele, Alix Elias, Loren Lester, Joey Ramone, Johnny Ramone, Dee Dee Ramone, Marky Ramone, Rodney Bingenheimer, Darby Crash, Allan Arkush, Joe Dante **RELEASE DATE** April 1979
35 MM, COLOR, 93 MINUTES

While *Rock 'n' Roll High School* unquestionably belongs in the Allan Arkush *oeuvre*, Dante made several contributions to the film – the least of which, ironically, is reflected in the on-screen story credit he shares with Arkush. That credit

traces back to the original treatment for the film, entitled "Girls Gym," which is said to have been dictated into a tape recorder by the pair over a two-day period in 1977, then typed into screenplay format by another New World staff member. The only extant printed version of "Girls Gym" in Dante's files is a 78-page screenplay dated July 14, 1977, which bears virtually no resemblance to the completed film.

Dante had had "no connection to the project" after collaborating with Arkush on the aforementioned treatment and script, but that all changed on December 19, 1978, the 17th day of *Rock 'n' Roll High School*'s grueling 20-day shooting schedule. Thanks to Arkush's dedication and energy (and more than a few 16-hour workdays), the production was only slightly behind schedule, but the demanding pace had taken its toll. As journalist Michael Goodwin wrote in *Penthouse*: "Suddenly, at dusk, Arkush is literally overcome with exhaustion; he heads for home, and Dante [who was on location helping out with second unit work] finds himself directing the first unit." After completing the scene in progress (in the school cafeteria), Dante headed home to bed. The next morning,

Arkush valiantly appeared on the set at 6:30, only to be taken away in an ambulance shortly thereafter – and Dante was awakened by a phone call from Mike Finnell asking him to take over direction of the film.

Unable to decipher the scribbles that comprised Arkush's shooting plan, Dante did what five years at New World had taught him to do best: improvise under pressure. ("What would Hitchcock have done?" he is reported to have muttered for the benefit of the note-taking Goodwin.) By the end of the week, he had finished shooting the film, on schedule. With barely a breather for the Christmas holiday, cutting began (with Dante helping out until Arkush had recovered and returned to work) and by the end of January the picture was completed.

For the record, Dante's directorial contributions were: a portion of the aforementioned school cafeteria scene; the entire musical number in the girls' gym (ironic, given the original script title); the scene where Soles's character, Riff Randell, wins tickets to the Ramones concert from a radio call-in show; the long-take mirror shot (which Dante laughingly called "Sirkian") in the girls' bathroom; and some shots contained in the montage of the kids wrecking the school ("I remember a roomful of kids in suds"). Dante estimates that "no more than five minutes" of footage directed by him is contained in the released version of *Rock 'n' Roll High School*. (H.P.)

The Howling

USA 1981

WRITERS John Sayles and Terence H. Winkless, based on
the novel by Gary Brandner **CINEMATOGRAPHER** John Hora
EDITORS Mark Goldblatt, Joe Dante **ART DIRECTOR** Robert A.
Burns **COSTUME DESIGNER** Jack Buehler **SPECIAL EFFECTS** Roger
George **MAKE-UP EFFECTS** Rob Bottin **MUSIC** Pino Donaggio
PRODUCERS Michael Finnell, Jack Conrad (Avco Embassy
Pictures Corp., International Film Investors) **CAST** Dee
Wallace, Patrick Macnee, Dennis Dugan, Christopher
Stone, Belinda Balaski, Kevin McCarthy, John Carradine,
Slim Pickens, Elisabeth Brooks, Robert Picardo, Margie
Impert, Kenneth Tobey, Dick Miller, Roger Corman,
Jonathan Kaplan, John Sayles, The Round Oak String Band
PREMIERE January 1981 (Avoriaz Fantastic Film Festival)
35 MM, COLOR, 91 MINUTES

The film rights to *The Howling*, a lurid paper-back novel by Gary Brandner published in 1977, were first acquired by Jack Hyatt Conrad and Steven Lane, who with producer Daniel Blatt packaged the project for Avco Embassy Pictures. Blatt, who had recently set up shop as an independent producer, had co-executive produced *I Never Promised You a Rose Garden* for New World release in 1977, and had met both Finnell and Dante on that production. Blatt hired Finnell, fresh off the production of *Rock 'n' Roll High School*, to handle the producer's chores on *The Howling*. Pre-production stalled, however, due to Jack Conrad's insistence on directing his own script and Avco Embassy's reluctance to entrust that task to an untried director. Ultimately, Conrad and Lane agreed to step aside and allow Blatt to continue with the project in exchange for receiving producer/executive producer credits on the finished film.

Dante was approached by Finnell about *The Howling* in the fall of 1979, at a point when *Jaws 3, People 0*, which he had spent several months preparing at Universal, was close to cancellation. The studio's abandonment of that project left Dante free to concentrate on *The Howling*; the Conrad screenplay was scrapped and Terence Winkless was hired to attempt a new adaptation of the novel. Dante came to believe that the book's narrative was unadaptable to film, and after the resulting Winkless screenplay was still unsatisfactory, he turned to his *Piranha* collaborator, John Sayles. Sayles later wrote that "the main problem with the story they had… was that there wasn't any consistency in what the werewolves could and couldn't do, so in one afternoon Joe and I wrote down the rules for werewolves." According to Dante, he and Sayles "wanted to make a kind of a modern, more urban, and somewhat more sophisticated werewolf picture," and he credits the writer with suggesting the idea of satirizing Californian obsessions with psychoanalysis and interpersonal relationships, embodied in the notion of "The Colony," the werewolves' Esalen-like sylvan retreat. "Once we had that idea, everything else came together."

Dante, though highly knowledgeable about prior werewolf movies, wanted to do something different, particularly with regard to the actual man-to-werewolf transformations. The desire to break new ground with the werewolf transformation effects led him to make-up wizard Rick Baker. In the middle of preparation on the film, however, Baker had to bow out and Rob Bottin, his protégé, stepped in and assumed responsibility for the work. The film's budget (although generous, at $1.8 million, in comparison to New World standards) occasioned many compromises, but the finished effects – involving an ingenious combination of make-up effects, facial casts, masks with hydraulics inside, werewolf-head puppets, even some stop-motion animation – were startling and subsequently much-imitated.

While breaking new ground, Dante in typical fashion also managed to include in *The Howling* various homages to the genre whose traditions he had been absorbing since childhood. At one point, Dugan and Balaski are seen watching Universal's *The Wolf Man* (1941) on television, and most of the film's major characters were named after directors of past werewolf films, with references to a few others (John Brahm, Stuart Walker) slipped into the dialogue. Perhaps of greatest personal significance for Dante, however, was his casting of veteran actor (and star of innumerable low-budget horror films) John Carradine in a supporting role as "Erle Kenton."

Not only did *The Howling* prove successful at the box-office, but it also made Dante somewhat of a "star" director within the community of horror/science fiction film devotees, who could not have missed the extensive coverage of the film, its special effects, and its young director – who had, after all, risen from among their own ranks – in such genre-centered magazines as *Fangoria*, *Cinefantastique*, and of course the venerable *Famous Monsters of Filmland* itself (a couple of issues of which can be glimpsed in the hands of its editor, Forrest J Ackerman, during his brief cameo appearance as a customer in Walter Paisley's bookstore). (H.P.)

Police Squad! (TV)

USA 1982

EXECUTIVE STORY EDITOR David Misch **CINEMATOGRAPHER** Sherman Kunkel **EDITOR** Tom Benko **ART DIRECTOR** Seymour Klate **MUSIC** Ira Newborn **PRODUCER** Robert K. Weiss (Paramount Television) **REGULAR CAST** Leslie Nielsen, Alan North, Rex Hamilton, Ed Williams, William Duell, Peter Lupus

Joe Dante directed two episodes of the series which ran on ABC for one season and six episodes.

"RING OF FEAR" ("A Dangerous Assignment"; Episode 2) **WRITERS** Tino Insana and Robert Wuhl **ADDITIONAL CAST** Rudy Solari, Patrick St. Esprit, Tessa Richarde, Floyd Levine, Irwin Keyes, Grand Bush, Georg Stanford Brown **AIR DATE** March 11, 1982 **35 MM, COLOR, 24 MINUTES**

"TESTIMONY OF EVIL" ("Dead Men Don't Laugh"; Episode 6) **WRITERS** Tino Insana and Robert Wuhl **ADDITIONAL CAST** Claudette Nevins, Dick Miller, Danny Dayton, Jerry Layne, Wayne Winton, Dick Clark, William Conrad **AIR DATE** July 8, 1982 **35 MM, COLOR, 24 MINUTES**

Dante had known "ZAZ" (Jerry Zucker, Jim Abrahams and David Zucker) since the mid-1970s, and was brought in to direct two of the six episodes of the trio's short-lived cop-show spoof. An attempt to apply the crammed-full-of-gags-parody approach to comedy that had so invigorated their 1980 hit *Airplane!* (produced by Jon Davison) to a TV series, *Police Squad!* was a dismal ratings failure on U.S. television, and

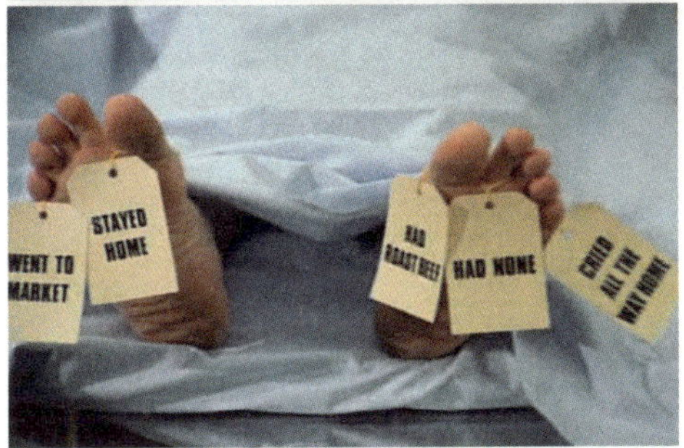

was abruptly canceled after four weeks of its scheduled six-week run on the ABC network. The series almost immediately achieved cult status, however, and subsequently re-emerged into the mainstream with a series of three "Naked Gun" movies, beginning with *The Naked Gun: From the Files of Police Squad!* (1988).

Dante's general unflappability, a legacy of his New World apprenticeship, served him well in his first foray into the medium of series television, as *Police Squad!* proved to be a relatively loose (not to say chaotic) production. "[ZAZ] treated me the way they treat each other," he recalled, "which is that you'd start to shoot the scene, and you'd shoot the angle this way, and then you'd relight and start to shoot the scene this way. And they came in and said to me, 'Oh, geez, we just thought of a great joke.' And I said, 'Well, yeah but I already…' 'But you got to get it. You got to do it.' … It was really a lot of fun to work on that show. It was great." (H.P.)

Twilight Zone: The Movie
USA 1983

DIRECTORS John Landis (Prologue and "Time Out"), Steven Spielberg ("Kick the Can"), Joe Dante ("It's a Good Life"), George Miller ("Nightmare at 20,000 Feet") **PRODUCTION DESIGNER** James D. Bissell **MUSIC** Jerry Goldsmith **PRODUCERS** Steven Spielberg, John Landis (Warner Bros.) **RELEASE DATE** June 24, 1983
35 MM, COLOR, 101 MINUTES

"IT'S A GOOD LIFE" (Segment 3)
WRITER Richard Matheson, based on the novel by Jerome Bixby **CINEMATOGRAPHER** John Hora **EDITOR** Tina Hirsch **COSTUME DESIGNER** Deborah Lynn Scott **SPECIAL EFFECTS** Mike Wood **MAKEUP EFFECTS** Rob Bottin **ANIMATION SUPERVISOR** Sally Cruikshank **CAST** Burgess Meredith (voice), Kathleen Quinlan, Jeremy Licht, Kevin McCarthy, Patricia Barry, William Schallert, Dick Miller, Cherie Currie
26 MINUTES

Dante got involved with *Twilight Zone: The Movie* more or less by being in the right place at the right time. Although he was not enthusiastic about the producers' idea of remaking episodes of the original *Twilight Zone* television series, he ultimately agreed to take on "It's a Good Life" because he felt that by working from the original source material, a 1953 short story by Jerome Bixby, he could find a way "to tell the story from a different viewpoint" than Rod Serling had chosen for his 1961 TV adaptation.

Working over a period of several months with screenwriter Richard Matheson Dante re-

shaped the original material to fit his own vision. From a straight horror-story adaptation of the Bixby original, it gradually came to contain much of the dark humor that often marks Dante's films, as well as the television/cartoon style that ultimately became the film's hallmark. Dante once referred to the final result as "somewhat like an off-Broadway cartoon designed by Chuck Jones." This also marked the beginning of Dante's friendship and occasional collaboration with Jones himself, whose advice he sought during the development of the episode.

The inescapable central fact of any account of the production of *Twilight Zone: The Movie* will always be "the accident": the tragic helicopter crash on July 23, 1982, during the filming of the John Landis-directed segment, that claimed the life of actor Vic Morrow and the two children (Renee Chen and Myca Dinh Le) that his character was ironically carrying across a river to safety in the scene being filmed. However, while this event cast a pall over the entire production, it had no direct effect on the filming of Dante's episode – and, in fact, may have been perversely beneficial. In the wake of the

accident, Warner Bros. put the entire project on hold; even after the decision was made to proceed with production, Landis, Spielberg and the studio were all anxious to distance themselves from the film, while Dante was given a remarkably free hand during production.

In addition to his episode, Dante also directed two other short segments of *Twilight Zone: The Movie*, only one of which was used in the final film. The unused piece was an original coda for his own segment, featuring the Kathleen Quinlan character hitchhiking on a deserted road, where she is picked up by the Dan Aykroyd character, featured in the film's Landis-directed prologue. Dante's other small contribution to the film took place at the very end of production, in February 1983, when he was called in to direct a newly-concocted ending for George Miller's "Segment 4." This short sequence, with a strait-jacketed John Lithgow being loaded into an ambulance, became the ending of the film as released.   (H.P.)

~

I wish I could have put all the outtakes into the film, because I had all these people eating junk food, for, like, a week. Kevin McCarthy would eat anything we put in front of him. He would eat candied apples, he would eat potato chips, he would eat all the time. Then he'd go out to lunch, and he'd come back and between takes he would eat whatever was left on his plate. It was astonishing. Maybe he felt that a rush of sugar to his brain would help his performance. You know, this was my first studio picture, and I thought people would be running onto the set saying, "What are you doing? All these potato chips! Make them stop eating!" But nobody ever did that.

(Joe Dante, in: David Chute, "Dante's Inferno," Film Comment, vol. 20, no. 3, May–June 1984)

Gremlins
USA 1984

WRITER Chris Columbus **CINEMATOGRAPHER** John Hora **EDITOR** Tina Hirsch **PRODUCTION DESIGNER** James H. Spencer **COSTUME DESIGNERS** Norman Burza, Linda Matthews **GREMLINS CREATED BY** Chris Walas **SPECIAL EFFECTS** Robert MacDonald, Sr. **MUSIC** Jerry Goldsmith **PRODUCER** Michael Finnell (Amblin Entertainment, Warner Bros.) **CAST** Zach Galligan, Phoebe Cates, Hoyt Axton, Polly Holliday, Frances Lee McCain, Judge Reinhold, Dick Miller, Glynn Turman, Keye Luke, Scott Brady, Corey Feldman, Harry Carey Jr., Don Elson, Belinda Balaski, Nick Katt, Kenneth Tobey, Chuck Jones
RELEASE DATE June 8, 1984
35 MM, COLOR, 106 MINUTES

"I think I was in my crummy little office," Dante told an interviewer in 1984, "which was across from a bowling alley in a cheesy part of Hollywood, waiting around for a picture called *The Philadelphia Experiment* to get made… and things were looking pretty grim… All of a sudden, this script arrives – from Steven Spielberg. It was *Gremlins*. There was a note attached asking if I would read the script and would I like to meet with Mr. Spielberg… I figured they must have sent it to the wrong address."

Dante liked the script and took the meeting – at which, he recalled, his first action was to apologize to Spielberg "for ripping off *Jaws*" – and discovered that his selection to receive the *Gremlins* script had been no mistake: Spielberg had seen and admired both *Piranha* and *The Howling*, and had recognized a sensibility in Dante's work that he thought would mesh well with the spirit of *Gremlins*. And while Dante had heard the widely-circulated rumors about Spielberg's meddling with Tobe Hooper's direction of the *Poltergeist* (1982), his enthusiasm for the script, and Spielberg's assurance that the situation would not recur, overcame his trepidations.

Script problems, differing conceptions about the style and scale of the film, and the considerable technical challenge of designing the gremlins themselves, for which Chris Walas was engaged in April 1982, all contributed to a protracted pre-production period. Dante, meanwhile, was far from idle: now in the Spielberg orbit, he was offered – and accepted – the opportunity to direct one of the segments of the Spielberg-John Landis production *Twilight Zone: The Movie*, which occupied much of his time from mid- to late 1982.

Principal photography on *Gremlins* occupied 69 shooting days, and the post-production shooting another 50. Even with the film "in the can," protracted discussions with Warner Bros. executives over its tone and content continued during the editing phase. The scene which came to be emblematic of the divergence between Dante's vision of the film and the studio's was the "Santa Claus scene," in which Phoebe Cates tells Zach Galligan the grisly tale of discovering her father's corpse in the chimney of the family home. Dante had always loved the scene and insisted on keeping it in the film; the studio had just as adamantly opposed it. Spielberg, despite his own distaste for the disputed scene, supported Dante's well-articulated position and put the issue to rest in a memo to Barry Reardon, Warner Bros. Distribution president.

Released in June of 1984, *Gremlins* was not only an immediate financial success – Warner Bros. crowed that the film had earned $100 million at the box-office in just six weeks, "faster than any other motion picture in company history" – but also became a genuine phenomenon. *Gremlins* will no doubt remain, for better or worse, the film that Joe Dante's name is most permanently identified with. He once expressed the view that *Gremlins* "became a hit all out of proportion to its quality as a movie, and you're lucky if you have one of those in your life."

(H. P.)

~

As a producer *and* director, Steven Spielberg seems limited to two subjects: power and magic. The power that interests him is, of course, the power that he commands, and the magic is that of his medium. Put these together and add the input of director Joe Dante, another film buff, and you get a movie about movies, triple-distilled. And the curious achievement of *Gremlins* is that it makes such self-absorption commercially viable, at the same time that it refuses to conform to any single, sustained social meaning. Much as the depiction of Vietnam in Coppola's *Apocalypse Now* was designed to placate hawks and doves alike, *Gremlins* is cleverly contrived to please skeptics as well as believers, optimists as well as pessimists about the American way of life. Thanks to a disconnected episodic structure that suggests several separate movies crammed together – a strategy that re-creates the fragmented, discontinuous flow of TV watching – viewers of *Gremlins* are invited to chart out their own justifications for enjoying Dante and Spielberg's treasure trove.

One justification is offered by the movie's plot, which gives us a cautionary Christmas fable set in a Frank Capra universe. [...] So much for the moral, upstanding movie some viewers want, which *Gremlins* dutifully supplies. What about the film's immoral, irresponsible aspects? Are viewers interested in these also? The filmmakers seem to think so. *Gremlins* offers them in such abundance that it conjures up a second movie, diametrically opposed to the first, which delights in assaulting everything the other movie stands for: Christmas, Norman Rockwell's America, consumer society, family entertainment, and so on. And while the moral side of *Gremlins* can be taken in two possible ways (as sincere or cynical), the amoral side seems to break up like the gremlins themselves into an infinity of possible meanings. The evil beasties can be plausibly read at various times as (a) adolescents, (b) blacks, (c) Native Americans, (d) good ole boys, (e) people who like Walt Disney (or Steven Spielberg) movies, (f) mischievous kids, (g) hoboes, (h) monsters – anyone can add to the list.

Because Dante concentrates so much on individual shots and ideas and so little on over-riding concepts, *Gremlins* seems ideally suited for home video. As an inspired (if unruly) collection of bits, it virtually cries out for the pause button – not to mention forward and backward searches. Film freaks can freeze-frame in order to pinpoint the multiple movie references. Splatter hounds can leapfrog from one flamboyant, grisly death to the next. Special-effects aficionados can linger on the loving gremlin crowd scenes, in a tavern, movie theater, and elsewhere.

Sometimes the most subversive and complex thing to do in a Hollywood movie is to give audiences exactly what you think they want, never hesitating to pursue the resulting contradictions to the limit. Perhaps no viewer can swallow the concoction whole without incurring a little bit of heartburn; but each is guaranteed to get more than he or she bargained on.

(Jonathan Rosenbaum, "Gremlins,"
Video Times, December 1985)

~

In the original version of the story, which was incredibly gruesome, the gremlins were more… well, they ate the kid's dog, OK? I mean, they used to bite people, and that was pretty much it. Although there was this one great scene where the kids go into a McDonald's, and all the people have been eaten – but not the burgers. As you might imagine, it would have been not a little gory. So when Mike Finnell and I came on the picture, we suggested using the gremlins the way they were in old World War II stories, where they turned technology against people. That suddenly opened up a whole new avenue of being clever about it, rather than just letting people get their legs bitten.

(Joe Dante, in: David Chute,
"Dante's Inferno," Film Comment, vol. 20,
no. 3, May–June 1984)

Explorers

USA 1985

WRITER Eric Luke **CINEMATOGRAPHER** John Hora
EDITOR Tina Hirsch **PRODUCTION DESIGNER** Robert F. Boyle
COSTUME DESIGNER Rosanna Norton **VISUAL EFFECTS** Bruce
Nicholson **MAKE-UP EFFECTS AND ALIEN CHARACTERS** Rob Bottin
MUSIC Jerry Goldsmith **PRODUCERS** Edward S. Feldman,
David Bombyk (Paramount Pictures) **CAST** Ethan Hawke,
River Phoenix, Jason Presson, Amanda Peterson, Dick
Miller, Robert Picardo, Leslie Rickert, James Cromwell,
Dana Ivey, Bobby Fite, Bradley Gregg, Georg Olden,
Eric Luke
RELEASE DATE July 12, 1985
35 MM, COLOR, 109 MINUTES

The script for *Explorers*, one of Dante's most personal films – and most troubled productions – was submitted to him personally by Paramount production chief Jeffrey Katzenberg, not long before the release of *Gremlins*. While Dante liked the script by Eric Luke, the back-to-back productions of his *Twilight Zone: The Movie* segment and *Gremlins*, in particular the grueling post-production schedule on the latter, had left him exhausted. Katzenberg persisted, however: Dante remembered that he "kept calling me like every 15 minutes about the script [and] finally, it occurred to me that either I was going

to do it, or somebody else was going to do it. So, I figured, 'Well, gee, maybe I ought to do it,' so I did."

From the beginning, what Dante initially thought might be a welcome change – "a nice little movie, with kids" – seemed to have the deck stacked against it. Luke's script had been in development at Paramount since early 1983, and at some point the studio had fixed on the idea that *Explorers* would be their major release for the summer of 1985. To achieve this end, they saddled Dante with a demanding schedule: his contract specified a delivery date of July 15, 1985, meaning that the entire production would have to be completed within the space of one year.

Various delays put the company behind schedule, and on Saturday, December 1, matters were further complicated when one of the film's young co-stars, Ethan Hawke, fractured a bone while riding a dirt bike. Hawke's foot was in a cast for several weeks, necessitating a series of schedule changes and script revisions in order to work around his limited mobility. Principal photography dragged on until February 25, 1985, at which point the production was 13 days behind schedule; post-production

shooting, which took place at Industrial Light & Magic in San Rafael, commenced immediately and wrapped in 15 days.

By then, too, there had been an important change of cast in Paramount's executive suites: at the end of January, Jeffrey Katzenberg, who had been so instrumental in putting *Explorers* into Dante's hands, departed the studio to follow his former boss, Michael Eisner, to the Walt Disney Studio. This left *Explorers* in an extremely vulnerable position. As Dante later wrote, the film "turned into a classic example of an 'orphan' production. When the original powers-that-be departed to another studio, the incoming regime viewed this conspicuously on-going, needlessly over-budgeted project as nothing more than an embarrassing white elephant left over from the previous administration. Acrimony reigned and it became discouragingly apparent as early as February that the picture was doomed."

On July 12, *Explorers*, befitting its status as Paramount's major release for the summer, opened on 1,750 screens across the U.S. One of the broadest releases of the year, it soon became one of the shortest: performing poorly at the box-office from the outset, it was pulled from release after only two weeks, having taken in a mere $7.4 million (less than one-third of its production cost). The failure of *Explorers* hit Dante hard, and in several interviews he has revealed a variety of attitudes towards the film.

Perhaps the rawest expression of his profoundly mixed feelings can be found in the draft of his note to a friend, written not long after the film's release, in which he called it "my favorite picture so far, despite the maddening fact that, creatively, it's the worst experience I ever had... *Explorers*, whatever else it may be, will always be a work in progress, full of unrealized, even unintended possibilities." (H.P.)

Twilight Zone (TV)
USA 1985

Joe Dante directed the first of three segments of episode 10, season 1 of the series (1985–89), which ran on CBS for three seasons and 65 episodes.

"THE SHADOW MAN"
WRITER Rockne S. O'Bannon **CINEMATOGRAPHER** Bradford May **EDITOR** Tom Pryor **ART DIRECTOR** John Mansbridge **VISUAL EFFECTS** Bruno George **MUSIC** Merl Saunders, The Grateful Dead **PRODUCER** Harvey Frand (CBS Entertainment Productions, London Films, Persistence of Vision Films) **CAST** Jonathan Ward, Jason Presson, Michael Rich, Heather Haase, Jeff Calhoun, Kathleen Coyne, Tricia Bartholome, Julia Hendler, Melissa Moultrie **AIR DATE** November 29, 1985 **35 MM, COLOR, 18 MINUTES**

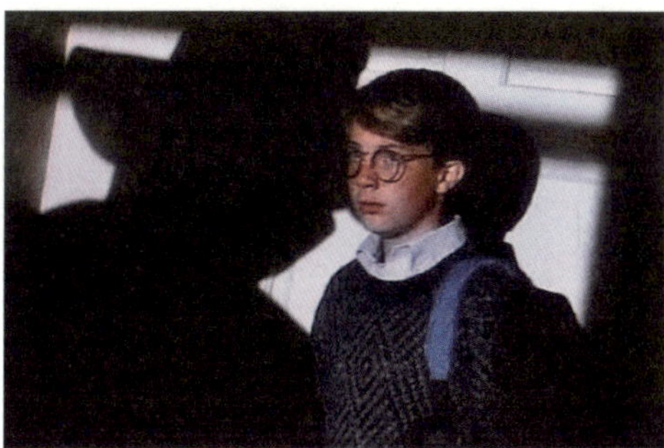

"The thing that I remember most vividly about doing the *Twilight Zone* episode," Dante says, "was that the production values – especially in contrast to *Amazing Stories*, which I'd already done my first show for – were almost shockingly low, like Poverty Row. But for all that, I think the show itself was a lot more effective,

because they put a lot of effort into getting the scripts right. The script for 'The Shadow Man' was by the series' story editor, Rockne O'Bannon, and it was a nice, tight little piece which I shot pretty much as written. It was done in just a few days out at the old Republic lot, in a very tight, studio-bound kind of way, which actually enhanced that sort of oppressive, nightmarish mood that the story required. If 'The Shadow Man' had been an episode of *Amazing Stories*, they probably would have built an entire street set so that the Shadow Man could be fifty feet tall and lift the roof off the kid's house to carry him off to Hell or something." (H.P.)

Amazing Stories (TV)
USA 1986

PRODUCER David E. Vogel (Amblin Entertainment, Universal) Joe Dante directed two episodes of the series (1985–87) which ran on NBC for two seasons and 45 episodes.

"BOO" (Season 1, episode 17)
WRITER Lowell Ganz, Babaloo Mandel **CINEMATOGRAPHER** Robert Stevens **EDITOR** Steven Kemper **PRODUCTION DESIGNER** Rick Carter **VISUAL EFFECTS** Joseph Roveto **MUSIC** Jerry Goldsmith **CAST** Eddie Bracken, Evelyn Keyes, Bruce Davison, Andrea Marcovicci, Robert Picardo, Wendy Schaal, Taliesin Jaffe, Heidi Zeigler **AIR DATE** February 16, 1986 **35 MM, COLOR, 24 MINUTES**

"THE GREIBBLE" (Season 2, episode 6)
WRITER Mick Garris, based on the story by Steven Spielberg **CREATIVE CONSULTANT** Richard Matheson **CINEMATOGRAPHER** Robert Stevens **EDITOR** Steven Kemper **PRODUCTION DESIGNER** Rick Carter **THE GREIBBLE DESIGNED AND CREATED BY** Rob Bottin **MUSIC** John Addison **CAST** Hayley Mills, Dick Miller, Justin Mooney, Don McLeod, Frank Welker, Jim Jansen **AIR DATE** November 3, 1986 **35 MM, COLOR, 23 MINUTES**

Neither of the two episodes that Dante would direct for Steven Spielberg's *Amazing Stories*, was much more than a trifle – but in the wake of the *Explorers* debacle, Dante felt the need to retreat from the pressures of feature filmmaking, and thankfully his association with Spielberg and the brief mid-1980s revival of anthology television series (e.g. *The Twilight Zone*) presented several opportunities of this type.

Amazing Stories, conceived at a time when Spielberg was still riding high from the success of *E.T. the Extra-Terrestrial* (1982), was a deliberate attempt to expand the reach of Amblin Entertainment from movies to television. The fact that NBC committed to a full two seasons of the program solely on the strength of Spielberg's name – in other words, without requiring the production and approval of a pilot episode – was seen as a measure of his stature in the entertainment industry at the time, just as the series' ultimate failure was a clear sign of the limitations of that stature.

Critics of the program liked to point out that the *Amazing Stories* weren't all that "amazing," but Dante thinks the basic problem was that most of the entries were rather weak as *stories*. "I never saw a single episode of the series where I didn't know exactly where it was going within the first five minutes," Dante said, "and that, I have to admit, includes the ones I did. The series was vastly over-produced – as an example, Steven insisted that all the shows be shot, and finished, on film… Unfortunately, the sumptuousness of the production values just served to emphasize the skeletal nature of the stories."

Dante feels that although there was great creative freedom on *Amazing Stories*, and no lack of talent either in front of or behind the cameras (other contributing directors, besides Spielberg, included Clint Eastwood, Martin Scorsese and Paul Bartel), that somehow "nobody really did their best work on that series." The program never caught on with either critics or the public in its two years on the air: as the critic for *The New York Times* put it, *Amazing Stories* was "not so much monumentally dreadful as consistently disappointing." (H.P.)

Innerspace
USA 1987

WRITER Jeffrey Boam and Chip Proser, based on the story by Chip Proser **CINEMATOGRAPHER** Andrew Laszlo **EDITOR** Kent Beyda **PRODUCTION DESIGNER** James H. Spencer **COSTUME DESIGNER** Rosanna Norton **SPECIAL EFFECTS** Rob Bottin, William George, Harley Jessup, Dennis Muren, Kenneth Smith **MUSIC** Jerry Goldsmith **PRODUCER** Michael Finnell (Amblin Entertainment, Guber-Peters Company, Warner Bros.) **CAST** Dennis Quaid, Martin Short, Meg Ryan, Kevin McCarthy, Fiona Lewis, Vernon Wells, Robert Picardo, Wendy Schaal, Harold Sylvester, William Schallert, Henry Gibson, John Hora, Kevin Hooks, Kathleen Freeman, Archie Hahn, Dick Miller
RELEASE DATE July 1, 1987
35 MM, COLOR, 120 MINUTES

Innerspace was not a project to which Dante was naturally drawn: he disliked spy films generally, and he regarded the original version of the script by Chip Proser as little more than an uninspired variation on *Fantastic Voyage* (1966). Although some preliminary contract negotiations took place between his agent and Universal regarding the project, Dante ultimately passed on *Innerspace* in favor of *Explorers*. Producer Peter Guber (who, Dante was astonished to learn, had no knowledge of *Fantastic Voyage*) kept the project alive, however, hiring Jeffrey Boam to rewrite the script as a comedy.

By early 1986, when *Innerspace* was again proposed to Dante, he was in a different state

of mind than he had been in 1983, having experienced in the interim both the phenomenal success of *Gremlins* and the dismal failure of *Explorers*. Following his brief retreat into relatively low-pressure work, he had decided that his return to feature film directing should be "a real Hollywood movie, a picture that wasn't coming out of my warped psyche." The revamped *Innerspace* promised to fill that need, and Dante was sold on the project when Boam told him that he had re-imagined the story as having the premise of a Dean Martin and Jerry Lewis movie: what if Dean were shrunk and put inside Jerry? "I want to make *that* picture," Dante remembers saying. "That sounds great!"

In a 1989 interview, Dante said that *Innerspace* had "probably the best script I've ever worked with." There was certainly nothing in the development of the screenplay that remotely resembled his experiences on *Gremlins* or *Explorers*, and the overall result was a much more straightforward production. There was also adequate post-production time scheduled to meet the July 1, 1987 release date, including the allowance for a typical studio preview process. Small adjustments were made as a result of audience reactions, but by the time of the nationwide sneak preview on June 20, Warner Bros. had reason to anticipate a smash hit. *Variety*'s review stated that *"Innerspace* has b.o. smash written all over it," and the film received generally excellent notices from critics across the country.

Unfortunately, the film (at least in the U.S.) did not fulfill these predictions. Opening over a three-day holiday weekend, it grossed only $4.7 million. Warner Bros. pressed a backup ad campaign into service, but without notable improvement. Ultimately, however, *Innerspace* was far from the disaster that *Explorers* had been, and its overseas success compensated somewhat for its reception in America. It also achieved a measure of distinction when its visual effects team (William George, Harley Jessup, Dennis Muren, and Kenneth Smith) received the Oscar for Visual Effects at the 60th Academy Awards ceremony – making *Innerspace* Dante's only film to have been thus honored.

Innerspace also marked the only time that Dante has agreed to take the so-called "possessory credit" – i.e., "A Joe Dante Film." He strongly dislikes the credit, which he thinks is seldom justified: "It's not fair to the writer, for one thing. If the writer and director are the same person, well, maybe – but no matter how exalted the credits make the director sound, if the camera crew and the sound guys and the script supervisor and all those other indispensable people decide to take the week off, who will it be 'a film by' then?" In the case of *Innerspace*, it was only at the insistence of Spielberg that

Dante agreed to the credit, although on the condition that its use be confined to the film's advertising.

It is also worth noting that Dante's brief appearance in *Innerspace* – approximately two seconds of screen time during the laboratory takeover scene, in which he is sprayed in the face by one of the invaders – qualifies as one of the most humorously self-deprecating directorial cameos in the history of cinema.   (H.P.)

~

Filmmakers Joe Dante, Nicholas Meyer, and Robert Zemeckis, each in his own way, buttress the theory of directorial authorship as the dominant influence on visual effects. Even before he employed Industrial Light & Magic (cf. *The Howling*), Dante's unerring, uncanny instinct for effects expanded the grammar of genres. He continues in various modes of discourse, to fascinate and surprise. Dante's ILM films, *Explorers* (1985) and *Innerspace* (1987), rank among the house's most impressive achievements, and his non-ILM work [...] shows similar sensitivity to effects' expressive potential.

Explorers is, even today, a model of how certain effects should be art-directed, accomplished, and integrated – such as the effect of an invisible force ricocheting around a boy's basement, the carnival-ride movement of boys within a flying bubble. *Innerspace*, a study in scale, begins with a visual pun on subliminal seduction: a murky environment turns out to be microphotography of scotch on the rocks. The director continually relates characters within the story space to the effects surrounding them,

even when they themselves are skeptical: a submersible shrinks with a Tasmanian Devil spin via a laser scalpel of proprietary design, coupled to "what would be a common home carpet sweeper." Dante prepares the audience's response to the crucial effects by undercutting any pretense to scientific realism foregrounding their whimsical cartoonish quality. Much like Spielberg (who exec-produced several of the films), Dante has an acute ear for the note an effect strikes in a film, and he tunes his characters just as adroitly. His effects have a peculiar tonal effect on his films' inner and outer space. He frees his audience to have fun.

(Gregory Solman, "The Illusion of a Future," *Film Comment,* vol. 28, no. 2, March–April 1992)

Amazon Women on the Moon
USA 1987

DIRECTORS Joe Dante (5 segments), Carl Gottlieb (3 segments), Peter Horton (1 segment), John Landis (5 segments), Robert K. Weiss (6 segments) **WRITERS** Michael Barrie, Jim Mulholland **CINEMATOGRAPHER** Daniel Pearl **EDITORS** Bert Lovitt, Marshall Harvey, Malcolm Campbell **PRODUCTION DESIGNER** Ivo Cristante **COSTUME DESIGNER** Taryn DeChellis **MUSIC** Ira Newborn **PRODUCER** Robert K. Weiss (Westward Productions, Universal Pictures)
RELEASE DATE September 18, 1987
35 MM, COLOR AND B/W, 85 MINUTES

The collective film *Amazon Women on the Moon* features 20 segments in the theatrical version and 22 segments in the TV version. Joe Dante directed the following: **"HAIRLOOMING"** with Joe Pantoliano and Stanley Brock (5th segment; 1 minute) **"BULLSHIT OR NOT"** with Henry Silva and Sarah Lilly (9th segment; 3 minutes) **"CRITICS CORNER"** with Archie Hahn, Belinda Balaski, Justin Benham, Erica Gayle, Al Lohman and Roger Barkley (10th segment; 4 minutes) **"ROAST YOUR LOVED ONE"** with Belinda Balaski, Robert Picardo, Justin Benham, Erica Gayle, Rip Taylor,

Slappy White, Jackie Vernon, Henny Youngman, Charlie Callas, Steve Allen, Archie Hahn (12th segment; 9 minutes) **"RECKLESS YOUTH"** with Carrie Fisher, Paul Bartel, Herb Vigran, Tracy Hutchinson, Mike Mazurki and Frank Beddor (20th segment; 5 minutes) **"FRENCH VENTRILOQUIST'S DUMMY"** with Dick Miller, Robina Suwohl and Phil Bruns (TV-version only; 4 minutes)

Amazon Women on the Moon is generally regarded as a misfired attempt by John Landis to recapture the spirit of *The Kentucky Fried Movie*, with which he had scored a major success in 1977. The appeal to Dante was obvious enough: along with his recently-completed television episodes, it was another in the string of low-key efforts in which he had taken refuge after the draining experience of *Explorers*. "It was very much an ad hoc project," Dante recalls. "By the time I was asked to participate, unfortunately, a couple of the segments I'd have liked to do were already taken (particularly the 'Invisible Man' parody)."

Though it was of little consequence to Dante, *Amazon Women* proved to be an unqualified dud at the box-office, the consensus being that material which might have seemed fresh at the time of *The Kentucky Fried Movie* was, ten years later, labored and pointless. Dante feels that the film was tampered with too much during the year-and-a-half that it sat on the shelf after completion. "There was a lot of funny stuff in *Amazon Women* that just didn't make the final cut," he says – including one of his own episodes, "French Ventriloquist's Dummy," which featured Dick Miller as a ventriloquist who discovers that his dummy has been swapped for another, and that he's gone onstage with a French dummy. The loss of this episode gives *Amazon Women on the Moon* the dubious distinction of being the only Dante feature without an appearance by Dick Miller. (The segment was restored, however, for the TV version of the film.)

Dante could take some consolation from the fact that several of his episodes – particularly "Reckless Youth," his parody of a 1930s venereal-disease melodrama – were among those singled out for whatever scant critical praise the film received. Shot in black-and-white in just two days, on hilariously flimsy sets and in perfect technical mimicry of Depression-era exploitation films, "Reckless Youth" is second only to *Matinee*'s "*MANT!*" in Dante's sub-oeuvre of perfectly-realized genre spoofs. In a nod to his own *Hollywood Boulevard*, the segment ends with the Miracle Pictures logo and legend: "If It's a Good Picture, It's a Miracle."

(H.P.)

The 'Burbs

USA 1989

WRITER Dana Olsen **CINEMATOGRAPHER** Robert Stevens
EDITOR Marshall Harvey **PRODUCTION DESIGNER** James H.
Spencer **COSTUME DESIGNER** Rosanna Norton **VISUAL EFFECTS**
VCE Inc., Peter Kuran **MUSIC** Jerry Goldsmith **PRODUCERS**
Michael Finnell, Larry Brezner (Imagine Entertainment)
CAST Tom Hanks, Bruce Dern, Carrie Fisher, Rick Ducommun, Wendy Schaal, Corey Feldman, Courtney Gains,
Henry Gibson, Gale Gordon, Dick Miller, Robert Picardo,
Brother Theodore, Dana Olsen
RELEASE DATE February 17, 1989
35 MM, COLOR, 102 MINUTES

Like all of Hollywood in early 1988, Dante found himself nervously anticipating the impact of a threatened strike by the Writers Guild of America. In the first week of March, the writers rejected the producers' final contract offer and voted to strike. "It looked like nobody was going to be working for a year," Dante recalled. "And I figured, if I don't work this year… my filmography is going to have a two-year gap in it, and people are gonna think I was in a detox center or something." A solution arrived, however, in the form of a script entitled "Bay Window," sent to him from Imagine Entertainment, the independent production company headed by Ron Howard and Brian Grazer. *Bay Window* had been close to production under another director (Rod Daniel), but had fallen through at the last minute – fortuitously, at least for Dante. Mike Finnell remembered that "we wanted to make the film pretty quickly, because we had another commitment [*Gremlins 2*, then in active script development] behind this."

Concluding that the only way to get the film made within the available time-frame was on a studio backlot, Dante and Finnell settled on Universal's "Colonial Street" as the most likely possibility. They asked production designer James Spencer if he could revamp the Universal street to match the script in six weeks. Spencer said yes, and the production came together with remarkable rapidity. The Writers Guild strike was by then in full swing, which posed a dilemma for screenwriter Dana Olsen – who, although a daily presence as the film's co-producer, was contractually forbidden from any writing. Dante compensated by encouraging his cast to explore their characters, and improvise where necessary. This was appropriate to what he viewed as a "behavioral movie" and the result was "free-form, almost experimental… probably the loosest movie I ever did."

An added bonus was being able to shoot on one of Hollywood's legendary backlots. Some of the structures on the "Colonial Street" were familiar to Dante (and millions of American moviegoers and TV viewers) through their reuse in hundreds of productions; others, equally familiar, were relocated from other parts of the lot, as Spencer reconfigured the street into the cul-de-sac where the story takes place. Included on the "hybrid street," as Dante called it, were:

the house in which James Stewart lived in *Harvey* (1950); Deanna Durbin's house from her Universal musicals of the 1930s and 1940s; the Gothic mansion occupied by *The Munsters* in the campy 1960s TV series; and the archetypical American TV house, the Cleavers' residence from *Leave It to Beaver* (1957–63). "Back lots are kind of magical to me," Dante told an interviewer. "I grew up with all the Universal horror pictures, and when I got onto this back lot and actually saw the places where they shot that stuff … it was kind of moving."

For reasons that are still a bit of a mystery to Dante, *The 'Burbs* became "the worst-reviewed picture I ever had. I think there were two good reviews, but for the most part the critical opinion ran the gamut from 'mediocre' to 'abysmal.'… Maybe it had something to do with the fact that it came out just after Tom Hanks received his first Oscar nomination [for *Big*], and something 'more' was expected of him than this dark and kind of weird little comedy." (H. P.)

~

In the case of *The 'Burbs*, the moral choices available to the viewer are even broader [than in *Gremlins*, *Explorers*, or *Innerspace*]. The movie can be read as a satire about suburban conformists and snoops – xenophobic busybodies who can't tolerate the presence of any sort of eccentricity in their midst. Or the movie is a cautionary tale about the dangers of insulation and ignorance – minding one's own business and being unaware of the horrible things that are happening right next door. Or, finally, one can take the noncommittal stance assumed by the teenage characters in the movie, who are as undisturbed about the mysterious neighbors as they are amused by the xenophobic snoops trying to uncover them; the kids are simply around to enjoy the show.

By building all three seemingly contradictory attitudes into one movie, Dante and screenwriter Dana Olsen don't abdicate their moral responsibility. It might be more accurate to say that they honor the pluralistic and democratic possibilities of their story, and do so in a way that the viewer doesn't have to adopt any one of these three attitudes exclusively. *The 'Burbs*, which has no pretensions at all about "making a statement" or addressing a social issue, implicitly respects an audience's ability to consider events rather than merely react to them, and to do so from more than a single perspective. […]

The 'Burbs is small and modest entertainment rather than a broadside, so one doesn't want to make too much of its clever strategies, which convert its three adult heroes into children, their wives into mothers, and the neighborhood kids into relatively mature grown-ups. Some of the pleasures to be found in the margins of this romp are the inside references that tend to be a Dante specialty, ranging from a box of *Gremlins* breakfast cereal to the name of the author of a dusty volume called *The Theory and Practice of Demonology* (one Dr. Julian Karswell, a character played by Niall MacGinnis in Jacques Tourneur's classic *Curse of the Demon*).

(Jonathan Rosenbaum, *"The 'Burbs,"*
Chicago Reader, February 24, 1989)

Gremlins 2: The New Batch

USA 1990

WRITER Charlie Haas, based on characters by Chris Columbus **CINEMATOGRAPHER** John Hora **EDITOR** Kent Beyda
PRODUCTION DESIGNER James Spencer **COSTUME DESIGNER** Rosanna Norton **GREMLIN AND MOGWAI EFFECTS** Rick Baker
SPECIAL EFFECTS Ken Pepiot **VISUAL EFFECTS** Dennis Michelson
BUGS BUNNY & DAFFY DUCK ANIMATION Chuck Jones **MUSIC** Jerry Goldsmith **PRODUCER** Michael Finnell (Amblin Entertainment, Michael Finnell Production, Warner Bros.)
CAST Zach Galligan, Phoebe Cates, John Glover, Robert Prosky, Robert Picardo, Christopher Lee, Haviland Morris, Dick Miller, Jackie Joseph, Gedde Watanabe, Keye Luke, Kathleen Freeman, Henry Gibson, Don Stanton, Dan Stanton, Shawn Nelson, Archie Hahn, Jerry Goldsmith, Rick Ducommun, Belinda Balaski, Paul Bartel, Kenneth Tobey, Charlie Haas, Leonard Maltin, Hulk Hogan
VOICE CAST Howie Mandell, Tony Randall, Frank Welker
RELEASE DATE June 15, 1990
35 MM, COLOR, 106 MINUTES

From the moment it became apparent that they had a monster hit on their hands with *Gremlins*, Warner Bros. attempted to get Dante to sign on to doing a sequel. His resistance, at first, was absolute: "I will never live down the fact that I said I'd never do it," he said in a 1995 interview, "but I swear I meant it; I didn't want to make *Gremlins 2*." Dante's files, however, show that he and Mike Finnell attended a meeting on a *Gremlins* sequel on April 10, 1985, at which Steven Spielberg, Warner Bros. executive Lucy Fisher, and writers Ed Solomon and Chris Matheson were also present. The notes of that meeting reveal a significant comment by Dante:

"Joe suggested 'breaking the frame' – that is; take risks and have fun with the medium. For instance, we could present the film with an overall awareness that it is a film. For instance, we could have another MOVIE THEATER SCENE; however, for this movie we could have the gremlins in OUR movie theater – meaning we would pretend there are gremlins screwing with the projector, for instance, as we watch. We could have the film run on leader tape for a while – or get cut – or who knows…"

This could hardly be a clearer blueprint for the underlying ethos of *Gremlins 2: The New Batch* as finally realized five years later, but apparently it made little impression on that day. Solomon and Matheson were instructed to proceed with the development of the storyline and turned out a 26-page "rough outline" the following month; a few weeks later Terry Jones (of the Monty Python troupe) came up with yet another short outline, set in New York City. Dante remembered Jones's approach as "very funny [and] *somewhat* irreverent, and I don't think that endeared it to Warner Bros., who have come to look upon [the gremlins] as sacrosanct."

Dante had always liked the "Gremlins in New York" idea that had first surfaced in Jones's treatment, but it wasn't until he brought Charlie Haas onto the project in mid-1988 that he found a writer who was able to make something of the idea. In Haas's first draft, the majority of the action takes place inside the "Clamp Plaza," a giant office-retail-media complex run by a real-estate tycoon modeled in equal parts after Donald Trump and Ted Turner. This was Haas's innovation, and Dante credits it as the key that finally made the project viable. From a practical point of view, keeping the action confined to one location meant the budget could be held to a realistic level.

Having largely suppressed his natural inclination towards self-referential movie-buff humor in *Innerspace* and *The 'Burbs* – feeling that it would be inappropriate for those fairly straightforward films – Dante saw no reason to refrain from including such gags in *Gremlins 2*. He also indulged his long-standing desire for a full-fledged creative collaboration with famed animator Chuck Jones, with whom he had been friendly for a number of years (and whom he had cast in cameo roles in both *Gremlins* and *Innerspace*), by asking him to create animated sequences featuring Bugs Bunny and Daffy Duck for the film's opening and closing credits.

The shooting of *Gremlins 2* lasted nearly eight months, and was followed by a period of wrangling with Warner Bros. executives over the film's final shape. As with *Gremlins*, the studio was concerned about the violence ("make it less gruesome and goopy," reads one studio note from February 1990), and was keen on building up the merchandizable character of Gizmo. "They even wanted to eliminate Chuck Jones's animated credits sequence," Dante remembers, "because one executive didn't like the way Bugs Bunny looked!" On balance, though, "the picture was so wacky there really wasn't much they could do to it." Dante was able to hold his ground against major changes, and later professed to be "very happy with the way *Gremlins 2* came out; in fact, it was one of my happiest experiences in terms of a picture turning out the way I had wanted it to."

What did not prove so satisfying, however, was the film's reception at the box-office. Despite good reviews and preview results, the film did not meet Warner Bros.' expectations in its initial release, for which Dante blames the studio's marketing decisions (specifically, opening the film on the same weekend as Touchstone's heavily-promoted *Dick Tracy* [1990]), but he also disdains the marketing practices of modern Hollywood in general. "They think they know what's going to be a hit because they have research," he told an interviewer in 1995. "They can always drag out this research to tell why it's okay that they have no ads for your movie, or why this *terrible* ad was really a good ad. The answer to everything is always 'the numbers, the numbers,'… and these people believe in this crap…"

When *Gremlins 2* was released on videocassette, Dante convinced Warner Bros. that the gremlins-taking-over-the-movie theater sequence – which featured a quite convincing effect of film breaking in the projector gate – would not play well on the small screen. They agreed to let him create an entirely new sequence to insert in its place, which applies the same idea but is structured as though the video tape is being disrupted by the gremlins; different film clips were used in the new segment (primarily from the John Wayne film *Chisum* [1970]) than in the feature. (H. P.)

Gremlins is grounded in a fundamental division in American popular culture, between the sweetness and sociability of the Disney features, and the unbridled id of Warner Brothers' Looney Tunes shorts. If the forces of Disney win in the first film – the gremlins are lulled into complacency by a screening of *Snow White and the Seven Dwarfs* – the barbarian hordes of Warner Brothers dominate the sequel. Beginning with an animated prologue featuring Bugs Bunny and Daffy Duck, directed by the Warners animator Chuck Jones, *Gremlins 2* abandons Disney's rural settings for an environment far more congenial to the Looney Tunes ethic, New York City.

After more than two decades some of the gags in *Gremlins 2: The New Batch* are still disturbingly topical. Most of the action takes place in a Midtown office tower redolently named "The Clamp Premiere Regency Trade Center," named after its developer, a certain Daniel Clamp (John Glover), who combines his healthy ego and real estate rapaciousness with some Ted Turner-like tendencies. (His cable network offers *Casablanca* "now in color and with a happier ending.") Other jokes may require footnotes (Hulk Hogan, anyone?), while others seem eerily ahead of their time. Christopher Lee makes an impeccably timed entrance as a research scientist working on genetically altered Frankenfood.

Dante's cheerful, everything-into-the-blender approach recalls one of the great nonsense comedies, H. C. Potter's 1941 adaptation of Olsen and Johnson's manically improvised stage show *Hellzapoppin.'* But *Gremlins 2* is also a horror movie, though in a distinctively Dantean way. Where the recent wave of zombie splatter comedies has amply demonstrated one basic principle of audience psychology – when things become too scary, they become funny, as anxiety finds an outlet in laughter – Dante has long worked from the opposite, more provocative position.

(Dave Kehr, "Exotic Creatures, Naughty and Nice," *The New York Times*, June 15, 2012)

M&M/Mars Television Commercials (TV)
USA 1990

"THE LANDING" / "THE HUNT" / "THE TAKEOFF"
COPY WRITER Jon Krevolin **CINEMATOGRAPHER** John Hora
ART DIRECTOR Catherine Gates **VISUAL EFFECTS** Mike McAlister
PRODUCERS Karen Rohrbacher (Lucasfilm Commercial Productions), Nancy St. John (Industrial Light & Magic), Marc Falcone (Backer Spielvogel & Bates, Inc.), Andrea Waldman (MARS) **CAST** T. J. Evans, Nicolas Rutherford, Jeremy Jackson, Jenny Drugan, Penny Peyser **AIR DATE** exact dates unknown (Dante remembers that the commercials were "part of a special promotion, so I think they only ran for a couple of weeks or so.")
35MM, COLOR, 3 × 30 SECONDS

"The story of doing these commercials is basically the story of why I don't do commercials," says Dante. "I wanted to do them for two reasons: first, because I wanted to work with the computer-based character technology, which was then quite new; and secondly, because I wanted to go through the process of doing a commercial, just to see what it was like... All in all, an extremely unrewarding experience, and one that I'm not eager to repeat..."

The three commercials formed a mini-narrative, in which aliens come to Earth in search of candy so they can celebrate Halloween on their planet. The first two were essentially teasers, leading up to the third, which was intended to display symbols which would then appear in the next day's *USA Today*, as the key elements of a promotional contest. (H. P.)

Eerie, Indiana (TV)

USA 1991–92

CREATED BY Karl Schaefer, José Rivera **CREATIVE CONSULTANT** Joe Dante **COSTUME DESIGNER** Melissa Binder **PRODUCERS** José Rivera, Walter Barnett, Gary Markowitz, Jon Poll, Michael Cassutt (Unreality Inc., Cosgrove/Meurer Productions, Hearst Entertainment Productions) **REGULAR CAST** Omri Katz, Justin Shenkarow, Mary-Margaret Humes, Francis Guinan, Julie Condra

35 MM, COLOR, 24 MINUTES PER EPISODE

Joe Dante directed five episodes of the series which ran on NBC for one season and 19 episodes.

"FOREVERWARE" (Episode 1)
WRITERS Karl Schaefer, José Rivera **CINEMATOGRAPHER** John Hora **EDITOR** Jon Poll **PRODUCTION DESIGNER** Charles Hughes **MUSIC** Gary Chang **ADDITIONAL CAST** Louan Gideon, Belinda Balaski, Nathan Schultz, Nicholas Schultz, Dan Stanton, Don Stanton **AIR DATE** September 15, 1991

"THE RETAINER" (Episode 2)
WRITERS Karl Schaefer, José Rivera **CINEMATOGRAPHER** Jonathan West **EDITOR** Jon Poll **PRODUCTION DESIGNER** Charles Hughes **MUSIC** J. Peter Robinson **ADDITIONAL CAST** Vincent Schiavelli, Patrick LaBrecque, Lou Cutell, Lauri Hendler, Aron Kincaid **AIR DATE** September 22, 1991

"THE LOSERS" (Episode 4)
WRITER Gary Markowitz, based on the story by Gary Markowitz and Michael R. Perry **CINEMATOGRAPHER** Jonathan West **EDITOR** Jon Poll **PRODUCTION DESIGNER** Charles Hughes **MUSIC** J. Peter Robinson **ADDITIONAL CAST** Henry Gibson, Dick Miller, Russell Gannon, Billy Million **AIR DATE** October 6, 1991

"HEART ON A CHAIN" (Episode 7)
WRITER José Rivera **CINEMATOGRAPHER** Jonathan West **EDITOR** Tom Meshelski **PRODUCTION DESIGNER** Michael Corenblith **MUSIC** J. Peter Robinson **ADDITIONAL CAST** Cory Danziger, Danielle Harris, Jim Jansen, Sarah Lilly, Henry Brown, Steven Peri **AIR DATE** November 3, 1991

"THE HOLE IN THE HEAD GANG" (Episode 13)
WRITER Karl Schaefer **CINEMATOGRAPHER** Jonathan West **EDITOR** Terry Blythe **PRODUCTION DESIGNER** Donald Light-Harris **MUSIC** J. Peter Robinson **ADDITIONAL CAST** Jason Marsden, Claude Akins, John Astin, Archie Hahn, Belinda Balaski, Erin Braun, Michelle Braun **AIR DATE** March 1, 1992

Joe Dante: "It's always been kind of a dream of mine to be involved in a television series in some fashion – for one thing, it gives you something to do while you're waiting around for your next feature to get off the ground. The guys who created *Eerie, Indiana*, Karl Schaefer and José Rivera, came to me with the pilot script around the spring of 1991, when we were still trying to get *Matinee* together. I loved it, and signed on as the director without hesitation – but I also told them I liked the whole premise of the series, and wanted to stay involved in some fashion. They said, well, you can be 'creative consultant,' and I said, sure. And although it might sound like a meaningless title, it turned out to be a much better job than I expected: I *was* consulted, *and* I got to be creative!… It was really a terrific, very positive experience – and I loved that we got to shoot it on the old Republic Studios backlot [now the CBS Studio Center] in Studio City. The show, unfortunately, was somewhat ahead of its time, and as so often happens when a network is faced with something that's kind of odd or unusual – and *Eerie* was certainly that – they really didn't know what to do with it. So in their wisdom, they put it into probably the most competitive time-slot in American network TV, opposite *60 Minutes* on Sunday evenings. That pretty much sealed its doom. But it's something I'm very pleased to have been a part of."

The series is also notable for what is perhaps Dante's best acting performance – as himself – in the final episode, entitled "Reality Takes a Holiday," in which the young hero learns that his life has become a TV show entitled *Eerie, Indiana*: his hometown is a movie set, his family and friends are just actors, and the script calls for him to be "written out" of the series by being killed! Dante loved the idea, and had originally been set to direct the episode himself, but pre-production chores on *Matinee* made it impossible, and Ken Kwapis took over as director.

Repeat airings of the original series on the Disney Channel and the Fox Network have given *Eerie, Indiana* something of a cult following in the U.S., but in early 1998 it was replaced by a new series, produced in Canada, entitled *Eerie, Indiana: The Other Dimension*, which is generally regarded as inferior in quality to the original (and with which Dante has no creative involvement).   (H. P.)

Matinee

USA 1993

WRITER Charlie Haas, based on the story by Jerico (Stone) and Charlie Haas **CINEMATOGRAPHER** John Hora **EDITOR** Marshall Harvey **PRODUCTION DESIGNER** Steven Legler **COSTUME DESIGNER** Isis Mussenden **VISUAL EFFECTS** Dennis Michelson **MANT/ANT DESIGNER** James McPherson **MUSIC** Jerry Goldsmith **PRODUCER** Michael Finnell (Renfield Productions, Universal City Studios, Inc.) **CAST** John Goodman, Cathy Moriarty, Simon Fenton, Omri Katz, Kellie Martin, Lisa Jakub, Robert Picardo, Lucinda Jenney, Jesse Lee, Jesse White, Dick Miller, John Sayles, Belinda Balaski, Charlie Haas, Archie Hahn, Naomi Watts, Robert Cornthwaite, William Schallert, Kevin McCarthy
RELEASE DATE January 29, 1993
35 MM, COLOR AND B/W, 98 MINUTES

Matinee was unquestionably Dante's most personally resonant feature since *Explorers* (and perhaps his most low-tech since *Hollywood Boulevard*). "The kid is sort of the way I was at that age," he once said, "going to the kind of movies I went to see, reading the kind of magazines I used to read." When the story had first come his way in 1987, in a draft script by Jerico Stone, the action began in the present day, as three men who had been boyhood friends gathered to watch the demolition of an old movie palace. The main narrative was presented in flashback, as they recalled their long-ago adventure in the theatre and their reverie veered into fantasy. "The script ended with the theater being demolished to make way for a video store," Dante recalls.

The whole notion of an "adventure at the Saturday matinee" clearly held a strong appeal for Dante, and a second writer, Ed Naha, was engaged to develop the story further. The flashback structure was eliminated, and in the last draft prepared by Naha in October 1988, the story took place in late 1962, at the time of the Cuban Missile Crisis (although nothing is made of the event except for the inclusion of a "duck-and-cover" scene at the school). But although the setting was made a bit more geographically relevant for Dante – it was now set in a fictional New Jersey town, "Lineville" – the uneasy mixture of fantasy and reality remained.

Without a satisfactory script, *Matinee* languished, while Dante's energies were fully engaged by *Gremlins 2*. Fortuitously, that production brought Charlie Haas into Dante's circle of collaborators, and in July of 1990, with *Gremlins 2* finally released, Dante asked Haas to try his hand at re-writing *Matinee*. Haas's first outline, completed in just a couple of weeks, made a number of vital changes: the fantasy element was jettisoned entirely; the Cuban Missile Crisis was given prominence as the historical backdrop throughout the film; and, most importantly, a new character was introduced, a schlock horror-film producer who comes to town to promote his latest film. With these elements in place, the project was fully revived and ready to move forward.

One element of *Matinee* had been present, in one form or another, from the very beginning: the film-within-a-film entitled *MANT!* ("Half Man! Half Ant! – All Terror!" screams the ad line) – in fact, at least one of the *MANT!* scenes in the film appears almost verbatim in the 1987 script. Dante clearly relished the notion of making a "nuclear-mutation" movie – even if only a few pieces of one – in the mold of those that had so enthralled him as a child. As the story developed, and the "atomic-fear" theme assumed greater prominence, *MANT!* became a more integral part of the overall film – to the point where it ultimately became necessary to shoot a full 15 minutes of *MANT!* for inclusion in *Matinee*.

Perhaps no other filmmaker could have risen so successfully to the challenge of replicating the look and tone of a 1950s-era monster epic, but Dante, with typical modesty, has been known to decline the credit in favor of another auteur: "Lawrence Woolsey made *MANT!*, not me." To extend the illusion of *MANT!* as a film existing outside the boundaries of *Matinee* itself, a set of authentic-looking *MANT!* publicity stills was produced and most of the supporting cast of *MANT!* itself (including Dante stalwarts Kevin McCarthy and William Schallert) was not listed in *Matinee*'s credits. The illusion was completed, Dante says, when "somebody actually approached me with an offer to finish *MANT!* and put it out as a full-length feature!"

Dante found the experience of making *Matinee* very satisfying, especially after the demanding production of *Gremlins 2*, and given his company's role in producing the film, was able to assemble the final cut with relatively little studio interference. And although *Matinee* did poorly at the box-office, Dante claims that doesn't matter. "I was just happy to be able to make *Matinee* at all," he says. "I was very pleased with both the reviews and the audience response to the movie. Besides, no one ever really thought it would make any money – the head of Universal Pictures even admitted to me that he had no idea how to sell the picture."

(H. P.)

~

As luck would have it, I saw Joe Dante's ferocious and lighthearted new comedy, *Matinee* – about John F. Kennedy "standing up to" Nikita Khrushchev while the world held its breath – barely an hour after reading in the paper that the world was holding its breath to see if Bill Clinton, in his first days of office, would "stand up to" Saddam Hussein. Despite the intriguing coincidence I doubt that many in the audience would jump to the conclusion that Dante made a movie with anything at all to say about the way we live and think today. [...]

A horror-movie schlockmeister is the central character in *Matinee* – a jovial showman named Lawrence Woolsey (John Goodman) who's clearly modeled on William Castle, master of the horror-exploitation gimmick (and underrated director of some earlier noirish B-films like *When Strangers Marry* and *The Whistler*). Woolsey's relation to the Cuban missile crisis is clarified when he takes on the role of surrogate father to 15-year-old Gene Loomis (Simon Fenton), who has recently moved to Key West with his family. Gene's father, who's in the Navy, has been "sent out" to parts unknown on the day the story opens, shortly before a spe-

cial bulletin interrupts Art Linkletter's TV show *People Are Funny* to bring on President Kennedy demanding the withdrawal of offensive missile sites recently spotted in Cuba.

In fact, Gene's father never puts in a single appearance in *Matinee* – unless one counts some brief glimpses of him in a home movie his wife (Lucinda Jenney) tearfully watches – so one might say that, mythically and emotionally, Kennedy in his sole TV appearance is the father's replacement. But Woolsey – "America's number-one frightmaster," as he calls himself – is present in the opening scene, in a trailer for his latest horror production, which Gene watches; shortly thereafter we learn that Woolsey will be appearing in person at the theater, on Saturday, to present a special matinee preview of his film. In fact, as soon as Woolsey appears in the flesh, not long after Kennedy's speech, he becomes the movie's most important patriarch, supplanting Kennedy, Adlai Stevenson (who appears briefly at UN hearings on TV), and Gene's missing father – a more ideal version of all of them.

Soon after Woolsey arrives for his show – which involves an elaborate setup with buzzers under the seats and apparitions in the aisles, neatly summarizing some of Castle's most celebrated gimmicks – the panicky theater manager (Robert Picardo) objects that the country is "on red alert." "Exactly," says Woolsey. "What better time to open a horror movie?" And as we discover, Woolsey's arsenal of scare tactics is every bit as effective as Kennedy's. Just as the fear of nuclear holocaust creates a hoarding panic among shoppers at the supermarket, Woolsey's own show reduces his audience to hysterical popcorn fights even before the movie starts. Similarly, the two scaremasters prove equally successful at inspiring hasty retreats; shortly after Woolsey averts disaster by conjuring up a fake nuclear holocaust to drive the audience out of the theater, it is reported in the news that the implied threat of nuclear holocaust has attained comparable results with the Soviets: Khrushchev has promised that the missiles in Cuba will be dismantled. [...]

Inhabiting a corner of junk heaven in all his pictures, Dante clearly regards each project as a fresh opportunity to show off his appreciation of pop culture. His pleasure in using familiar bit players such as Jesse White (here the owner of a theater chain) and Dick Miller and John Sayles (members of Citizens for Decent Entertainment) is palpable. As a TV illiterate, I can't comment on the way TV shows past and present have affected casting decisions and the dialogue, though when it comes to movies Dante has obviously taken full advantage of his resources. It doesn't seem accidental, for instance, that Cathy Moriarty – Woolsey's somewhat resigned girlfriend, leading lady, and all-around assistant – reminds us through her accent of her debut role in *Raging Bull*.

We also glimpse a profusion of 1962 "one-sheet" movie posters in the lobby of the film's theater, the Key West Strand – a pantheon including *The Man Who Shot Liberty Valance*, *Hatari!*, *What Ever Happened to Baby Jane?*, *Lonely Are the Brave*, and *Confessions of an Opium Eater*. It seems Dante is ticking off his favorites, even if this means working in many more posters than one could imagine such a theater displaying at once. He's also created many "excerpts" from movies showing in the theater – including a *MANT!* trailer, *MANT!* itself (both in black and white), and something called *The Shookup Shopping Cart*, a color feature that suggests both Frank Tashlin and live-action Disney. At the same time that Dante has a field day brutally satirizing our desire to scare ourselves and others, he also re-creates early-60s clichés with a relish and a feeling for detail that come very close to love.

(Jonathan Rosenbaum, "War Fever:
On *Matinee*," *Chicago Reader*,
February 5, 1993)

Runaway Daughters (TV)
USA 1994

WRITER Charlie Haas, based on the story by Lou Rusoff and Charlie Haas **CINEMATOGRAPHER** Richard Bowen **EDITOR** Mark Helfrich **PRODUCTION DESIGNERS** Brian Spencer Kasch, Kathleen M. McKernin **COSTUME DESIGNER** Susan Bertram **SPECIAL EFFECTS** F. Lee Stone **MUSIC** Hummie Mann **PRODUCERS** Debra Hill, Louis S. Arkoff, Willie Kutner (Arkoff/Hill/Kutner production, Drive-In Classics Cinema, Showtime Networks Inc.) **CAST** Julie Bowen, Holly Fields, Jenny Lewis, Paul Rudd, Chris Young, Dick Miller, Dee Wallace Stone, Christopher Stone, Cathy Moriarty, Robert Picardo, Wendy Schaal, Joe Flaherty, Belinda Balaski, Roger Corman, Julie Corman, Samuel Z. Arkoff **AIR DATE** August 12, 1994 **35 MM, COLOR, 82 MINUTES**

Fourth of the ten feature films presented on Showtime under the umbrella title "Rebel Highway," inspired by *Runaway Daughters* (Edward L. Cahn, 1956)

"*Runaway Daughters* was my AIP movie – really my valentine to AIP," Dante says. "I'd grown up watching all those Samuel Z. Arkoff-James Nicholson productions – many of which were directed by Roger Corman, of course – and had a great fondness for them, and had always thought that it would just be great to be able to do a movie like that."

The "Rebel Highway" project was made to order to help Dante realize that ambition. It was conceived as a series of ten made-for-cable features, each of which would take as its starting point one of the classic "teen angst" films produced by American International Pictures in the 1950s. The idea was to replicate the low-budget, short-schedule conditions under which the originals had been produced, but otherwise to bring a 1990s sensibility to the new versions.

Dante confirms that he was never expected to produce a "remake" of the original *Runaway Daughters*, which wouldn't have interested him anyway. Oddly enough, though, given his reputation as a walking movie encyclopedia, Dante admits that *Runaway Daughters* was the only film among the available titles that he hadn't seen, and that when he screened it he was "somewhat underwhelmed." "All the producers really gave us," he remembers, "was a packet of advertising material related to the original film; we were completely free to develop the story however we wanted."

For this task, Dante immediately thought of Charlie Haas, who "is just terrific at re-imagining older material like this." Just a few weeks after Dante signed on to the project in May 1993, Haas had produced an outline, which he prefaced with the comment that "the hook in this story is mainly the same observation about the '50s that colors the Douglas Sirk pictures… that a lot of unruly human heat was boiling away under a conformist-materialist surface, and that the heat kept erupting in the form of juvenile delinquency, racial and class friction, beatnik stuff, Elvis, etc…" Despite the serious underpinnings, the writer felt that "we can get some character comedy out of the rituals of the time (both kid-world and adult-world) [and] we can be a little tongue-in-cheek at times with that Sirk style of dialogue (aphoristic, fatalistic, bluntly self-declaring, etc.). However… it would be a mistake to get real broad and campy."

Dante always saw the project as a perfect opportunity "to comment on those movies while I also got to make one." He felt that *Runaway Daughters* was one of the most successful of the series, that they had managed to update the basic material while still retaining "a kind of innocence" that was faithful to the spirit of the AIP originals. "It was the only film in the group with no nudity," he points out, also noting that at 76 minutes, exclusive of credits, it was "as short as the original film (which ran 92 minutes) *should* have been." A number of critics agreed with his assessment, often singling out Dante's feature for special praise. As one wrote: "It's enough to make you want to rebuild the drive-ins."

(H.P.)

~

Seeking to avoid camp, the "Rebel Highway" movies aspire to a kind of historical revisionism, with fascinating if uneven results. On a conventional level, the best of the four I've seen is Dante's *Runaway Daughters*, the only one that plausibly captures the period in which it's set – 1957, shortly after Sputnik went into orbit and the year after the original *Runaway Daughters* was made. Scripted by Dante's usual

writer, Charles Haas, the movie careens from an opening newsreel montage of 50s events to a double-date make-out session at a drive-in showing *I Was a Teenage Werewolf*. [...] Reportedly sticking closer to his source than most of the other series directors, Dante gives his material charm, wit, and verve by working gracefully with his likable cast (including such familiar faces as Joe Flaherty, Robert Picardo, Fabian, John Astin, and even Cathy Moriarty in an uncredited cameo). He seems wholly at ease with both the period and the AIP mode, both of which he affectionately parodies. A typical spin on the material comes when AIP (and Dante) regular Dick Miller, playing a private detective investigating the girls' disappearance, lectures four of their parents: "Do you people ever sit down and talk to your kids? I mean really talk to them about sex and sexual diseases, about peculiar practices? About the strange night world of twisted kicks [an electronic instrument starts to warble on the sound track, evoking 50s SF movies], of weird rituals and equipment? Of whips and chains and rubber balls and dildos and handcuffs?" A little later, gazing at the poster for the original *Runaway Daughters* at a drive-in, Miller sighs, "Ah, they don't make 'em like they used to" – Dante's sentiments exactly.

(Jonathan Rosenbaum, "The Way We Weren't," *Chicago Reader,* November 18, 1994)

Picture Windows (TV)

USA 1995

Joe Dante directed the first segment of the second trilogy of the *Picture Windows* mini-series broadcast on Showtime.

"LIGHTNING"

WRITER Jim Byrnes, based on the short story "Tappan's Burro" by Zane Grey **CINEMATOGRAPHER** Jamie Anderson **EDITOR** David Hickes **PRODUCTION DESIGNER** Nanette Vanderbilt **COSTUME DESIGNER** Beverly Hong **MUSIC** Hummie Mann **PRODUCERS / SERIES CREATORS** Scott J. T. Frank, Dan Halperin, David Wesley Wachs (Yorktown Productions, Skyvision Entertainment, Showtime Networks) **CAST** Brian Keith, Kathleen Quinlan, Ron Perlman, Henry Jones **AIR DATE** October 29, 1995 **35 MM, COLOR, 31 MINUTES**

The other two segments were directed by Bob Rafelson ("Armed Response") and John Boorman ("Two Nudes Bathing"). The segments in the first trilogy were directed by Peter Bogdanovich ("Song of Songs"), Jonathan Kaplan ("Language of the Heart") and Norman Jewison ("Soir Bleu").

"I'd always wanted to do a western," Dante says of how "Lightning" came about, "but the chances these days are pretty rare. The Zane Grey story that "Lightning" is based on was actually something we were developing with Jim Byrnes, but we really didn't know where to go with it. Luckily, these people came along with the concept for what was then called 'The Painted Word.'" The 1992 proposal states the premise as follows: "Each program starts off with an internationally recognized work of art, which then magically springs to life, as characters from the masterpiece enact a story of the time period by a similarly renowned author." "It was kind of a strange idea," Dante says, "but it was the perfect opportunity for us to get our Zane Grey story filmed."

Originally, the idea was to link the story thematically (per the proposal) with the painting "The Prospector," by N. C. Wyeth, but according to Dante, "there was just no way to match the background of the painting without building it, which would have been sort of silly. So we ended up working backward from a freeze-frame of our opening shot, making it look like a Frederic Remington etching, and then throwing in some real Remingtons that sort of matched it, and worked with the premise of the series."

"It was fun to do. We shot it in just five days, on the same type of 'western' locations around L.A. – Bronson Canyon and so forth – that they always used to use for all those dozens of TV westerns in the 1950s. And Brian Keith! – just a great actor, and I was really happy to do a show with him."

(H. P.)

The Second Civil War (TV)

USA 1997

WRITER Martyn Burke **CINEMATOGRAPHER** Mac Ahlberg **EDITOR** Marshall Harvey **PRODUCTION DESIGNER** Joseph P. Lucky **COSTUME DESIGNER** Dan Moore **SPECIAL EFFECTS** Gregory Landerer, Lee Allan McConnell **VISUAL EFFECTS** Gene Warren, Jr. **MUSIC** Hummie Mann **PRODUCER** Guy Riedel (HBO Pictures, Baltimore Pictures) **CAST** Beau Bridges, Joanna Cassidy, Phil Hartman, James Earl Jones, James Coburn, Dan Hedaya, Elizabeth Peña, Denis Leary, Ron Perlman, Kevin Dunn, Brian Keith, Kevin McCarthy, Dick Miller, William Schallert, Roger Corman, Robert Picardo **AIR DATE** March 15, 1997 **35 MM, COLOR, 96 MINUTES**

Canadian-born novelist and occasional filmmaker Martyn Burke was the primary creative

force behind *The Second Civil War*, a satirical treatment of American attitudes toward immigration, which was developed for HBO by Barry Levinson's Baltimore Pictures. Starting with the thesis that the traditional "melting pot" principle, on which American's immigration policy has been founded for over a century, is no longer compatible with the political and economic realities of the present day, Burke contrived a black comedy in which politicians, the news media, and home-grown American xenophobia all come under fire.

Dante was offered the job in June of 1996. "Although the script at that point was too long, and sort of unwieldy, I really liked the ideas and the characters, and it seemed like a great opportunity to do something with some substance to it, instead of another movie with kids and lots of special effects. And what proved to be really remarkable was that all during the process of making the film – while working on the script, during shooting, and on into post-production – every time I opened up a newspaper, there would be something going on that was just like something in the film." As is more or less typical with American made-for-TV fea-

228

tures, the remaining pre-production time after Dante was hired was fairly compressed, and the necessary script work had to be handled concurrently with location scouting and casting – the latter being no small matter in a production that has nearly 90 speaking roles.

"The cast was just terrific," Dante says, "maybe the best overall that I've ever worked with, and since the re-writing continued while we were shooting, a lot of what we ended up with was a result of the actors' input." The actual shooting, done on a tight 38-day schedule, "was a lot of fun. HBO basically left us alone all during the shoot." That situation changed, however, after Dante delivered his first cut to HBO in mid-December, and the film was put through the standard 4-week "HBO preview period." Dante notes that "HBO has this sort of assembly-line preview procedure, during which they show the film to 36 people at a time, in a room in their headquarters building. It was presented to the preview audience as a comedy, and because it had a rather serious opening – and in any case is darker and more satiric than it is laugh-out-loud funny – it just didn't go over with these little groups of people."

HBO immediately began to press for changes, and what had until then been a good experience for Dante became, he says, "my second most negative experience making a film." The biggest battle was over the film's opening. Dante felt strongly that it was necessary "to get the audience grounded in the emotional reality of the situation, out of which the black comedy can then emerge," and to that purpose had opened his cut with an H-bomb explosion. "But the HBO people said 'No HBO movie can begin with an H-bomb going off!', and ultimately they held the power to make the film what they thought it should be." Although there is much he still likes about *The Second Civil War*, in summation Dante says that "in terms of how good I knew the film could have been, before all the post-production meddling, the end result was very disappointing – more so than any other movie I'd done since *Explorers*."   (H. P.)

~

Properly speaking, this skillful made-for-cable satire directed by Joe Dante qualifies as the middle feature in his so-called war trilogy, preceded by *Matinee* and followed by *Small Soldiers*. Viewers who consider it the best of the threesome may have a point, though its lack of a theatrical run in this U.S. makes it somewhat better known overseas. Beau Bridges plays the governor of Idaho who decides to close his state borders to a plane full of Pakistani orphans fleeing a nuclear disaster, and the action is crosscut with national government deliberations and various kinds of frantic media spin. Barry Levinson set this project in motion, so the parallels with *Wag the Dog* aren't accidental, but one of the essential ingredients brought to it by Dante, the least Swiftian of satirists, is that nobody's a villain, even when behaving like an idiot and/or a hypocrite. The governor, for instance, plays shamelessly to his xenophobic constituency while remaining smitten with his Mexican mistress, a reporter played by Elizabeth Peña, and the movie is determined to view him simply as a lovable asshole.

(Jonathan Rosenbaum, *"The Second Civil War," Chicago Reader,* April 28, 2006)

The Osiris Chronicles (TV)

USA 1998

WRITER Caleb Carr **CINEMATOGRAPHER** Jamie Anderson
EDITORS Marshall Harvey **PRODUCTION DESIGNER** Sandy
Veneziano **COSTUME DESIGNER** Deborah Everton **SPECIAL**
EFFECTS Ric Zarro **VISUAL EFFECTS** Deena Burkett **MUSIC** Karl
Lundeberg **PRODUCERS** Dan Dugan, Bill Millar, Rene Garcia,
Thomas R. Polizzi (Renfield Productions, Paramount Pic-
tures Corporation) **CAST** John Corbett, Rod Taylor, Carolyn
McCormick, John Pyper-Ferguson, Elisabeth Harnois,
J. Madison Wright, Darryl Theirse, Marjorie Monaghan,
Joel Swetow, Phillip Moon, Lilyan Chauvin, Rhino
Michaels, Dick Miller **AIR DATE** January 27, 1998
35 MM, COLOR, 92 MINUTES

The Osiris Chronicles was the brainchild of
writer Caleb Carr, best known for his bestselling novels *The Alienist* (1994) and its follow-
up *The Angel of Darkness* (1997). He told *Starlog*
magazine that the idea originated with "his life-
long fascination with *Star Trek*"; also a histo-
rian, Carr says that, in watching *Star Trek* in all
its many incarnations, he had often "wondered
what would happen when the Federation [the
intergalactic government] fell apart."

Dante, for his part, had spent relatively little
of his life thinking about *Star Trek* at all: "I've
never been a huge fan of space shows," he said,
"They're very hardware-oriented and technical

for me." But he and Mike Finnell had worked
with Carr a few years earlier on an unproduced
project at Universal (*The Green Hornet*) and had
established a good working relationship, and
when Carr brought his *Osiris* proposal to Renfield Productions, they agreed to develop it for
TV. Dante had always been attracted to the
idea of series television, and also happened to
love Carr's concept and pilot script, which he
saw as "only incidentally science fiction… The
whole look of the show is that civilization has
collapsed and everybody's back to wearing the
wardrobe from *The Undead*."

Renfield convinced Paramount's Network
Television Division to back the show, and CBS
made a deal for Carr to develop scripts for six
additional episodes in case they decided, on the
basis of the pilot, to turn the show into a series.
Development of these scripts proceeded concurrently with the production of the pilot
episode under Dante's direction. As it turned
out, however, none of additional scripts were
needed. According to Dante, "CBS had made
the deal for *Osiris* at a time when they were trying to change their image as the 'old-fogey' network, to appeal to a 'younger demographic,' as
they say. By the time we got done making the
pilot, however, they'd changed their mind,
and *The Osiris Chronicles* was a type of show
they had decided they were no longer interested in."

Completed in April 1996, the pilot sat on the
shelf for well over a year after being rejected by
CBS. Attempts to sell it elsewhere were unsuccessful, and finally Paramount, in an effort to
recoup some of their investment, decided to re-
fashion the pilot into a two-hour TV movie.

"This was done without our participation," says Dante. "The problem was that it wasn't originally designed as a self-contained two-hour movie with a definite beginning, middle and end… They changed the narration and re-cut it in an attempt to make it work as a story, but it just didn't. And then they gave it that really stupid title – "The Warlord" is the *bad guy*, for God's sake!" As *The Warlord: Battle for the Galaxy*, it was given its premiere broadcast on Paramount's own United Paramount Network on January 27, 1998. (H. P.)

Small Soldiers

USA 1998

WRITERS Gavin Scott, Adam Rifkin, Ted Elliott, Terry Rossio **CINEMATOGRAPHER** Jamie Anderson **EDITORS** Marshall Harvey, Michael Thau **PRODUCTION DESIGNER** William Sandell **COSTUME DESIGNER** Carole Brown-James **ACTION FIGURES DESIGN** Stan Winston **VISUAL EFFECTS** Stefen Fangmeier **ANIMATION** David Andrews **MUSIC** Jerry Goldsmith **PRODUCERS** Michael Finnell, Colin Wilson (DreamWorks Pictures, Universal Pictures) **CAST** Kirsten Dunst, Gregory Smith, Jay Mohr, Phil Hartman, Denis Leary, Kevin Dunn, Robert Picardo, Ann Magnuson, Dick Miller, Wendy Schaal, David Cross, Jacob Smith **VOICE CAST** Frank Langella, Tommy Lee Jones, Ernest Borgnine, Jim Brown, Clint Walker, Bruce Dern, George Kennedy, Sarah Michelle Gellar, Christina Ricci **RELEASE DATE** July 10, 1998 **35 MM, COLOR, 110 MINUTES**

Gavin Scott's original screenplay "Small Soldiers," a fantasy-adventure about a young boy whose army of toy soldiers come to life, was purchased by Steven Spielberg's Amblin Entertainment in April 1992, for a reported $400,000. While Dante's strong identification with the *Gremlins* films made him a natural choice for a project of this sort, he wasn't overly enchanted with the idea of directing yet another little-

creatures-on-the-rampage movie. Given one of the early script revisions to read by Amblin, he found it uninspiring, and passed on the project.

By mid-1997, however, when Dante was approached again, there were several things that made the enterprise more attractive. Perhaps most significant was that Dante himself, in the wake of *Matinee*'s disappointing box-office performance and several projects that had failed to come to fruition, had by then gone nearly five years without directing a feature. *Small Soldiers*, in the meantime, had also "migrated" from Amblin to Spielberg's newest production venture, DreamWorks SKG, and Dante knew well that directing a film for Hollywood's hottest studio could go a long way toward reinvigorating his career. The advances in the use of CGI in film production had by 1997 also made *Small Soldiers* a much more feasible undertaking than it had seemed even a few years before.

Dante, always attracted by cutting-edge technology, acknowledges that it was the opportunity to work so extensively with CGI that finally convinced him to sign on. "They showed me the character models, the storyboards, all sort of things having to do with the visual design of the film, and I agreed to do it," Dante remembers; "…then they showed me the script." To his dismay, Dante found that despite four years of work (by four writers), the script for *Small Soldiers* "still didn't work." With his commitment to direct, however, pre-production got under way in earnest, while two new writers set about in another attempt to fix the script in the four months before shooting was scheduled to begin.

However vital the presence (or absence) of a coherent screenplay may have been to Dante and his team, in a larger sense it was almost incidental to the creation of *Small Soldiers*. At the time Dante came aboard the project, the film was already set upon its inexorable course toward the marketplace, for one simple reason: toy manufacturer Hasbro Inc. had signed a deal with DreamWorks to produce and market a wide range of products (action figures, computer games, etc.). The toys were in production, and already set for release in the summer of 1998: the movie would simply have to be ready at the same time.

Principal photography began on November 3, 1997 with, as Dante remembers, "about 60 approved script pages" (less than half the length of the full script), and the situation did not improve. The troubled production dragged on for four months, with principal photography finally wrapping on March 10, 1998. Script revision had only ceased a few weeks before: the "script as used on final day of shooting" (in Dante's files) bears the names of nine writers and lists *forty* separate dates on which pages were added during shooting. The "production schedules" file is bulging with revisions to the shooting sched-ule, issued throughout the production – sometimes more than one in a single day! – as new scenes were written and old material was dropped. "Of course, *Casablanca* and *Son of Frankenstein* were made this way, too," Dante quipped, "but they turned out better."

The completion of principal photography did not bring an end to the film's troubles. One major problem arose when another of the film's major licensees, Burger King, learned that *Small Soldiers* would likely receive a PG-13 rating from the MPAA. With a multi-million-dollar promotional campaign in the works, centered around the inclusion of *Small Soldiers* toys in each of their Kids Meals – targeted for children aged 2 to 8 years – Burger King brought considerable pressure on the producers to reduce the amount of the violence depicted in the movie. This was a factor – as were the film's continuing narrative problems – in scheduling the additional nine days of reshooting, which took place in late April and early May.

Until the Burger King pressure reached its apex, Dante felt that he'd done the best he could with the project under very difficult circumstances. It was clear that the cuts, though, would not earn the film the desired PG rating, and when it appeared that he would be forced to make still deeper incisions, Dante seriously contemplated quitting the production and removing his name from the film. Ultimately, Burger King accepted the PG-13 rating, and instituted last-minute adjustments to its marketing campaign (although they still became the target of criticism in light of the general public perception that the film was "too violent" for younger children).

In considering the arc of Dante's career, it is irresistible to point out that *Small Soldiers*, at a reported cost of $61 million, was almost one thousand times as expensive as *Hollywood Boulevard* – yet it does not seem to have been any better organized. (H. P.)

~

Dante's satire doesn't simply target war and warmongering but the everyday cultural violence that encompasses them, by which I mean the violence in pop culture as well as the violence of pop culture. With the possible exception of *Innerspace*, just about all of Dante's best work is concerned with this cultural violence – cuddly Spielbergian pets in *Gremlins*; animated cartoons in "It's a Good Life," his segment of *Twilight Zone: The Movie*; TV in the finale of *Explorers* and practically all of *The Second Civil War* (his prescient and neglected 1997 made-for-cable satire); xenophobia in *The 'Burbs* (despite the confusing ending); war fever in *Matinee*; corporate merchandising in *Gremlins 2: The New Batch* – and part of the exciting achievement of *Small Soldiers* is to combine all of these concerns into one streamlined statement.

Part of the kick of Dante's cheerful scorn is that it takes on not only the more obvious targets like *The Dirty Dozen* (by employing members of the original cast to speak the voices of the Commandos), but also the less obvious ones, like *Apocalypse Now* – already perceived by many as an antiwar film and hence something of a sacred cow, even in the nineties – while adroitly exposing the innate childishness of the overblown epic and heroic stances in all of them. The self-importance of a supposedly "balanced" portrait like *Patton* (Richard Nixon's favorite movie) is made to seem just as ludicrous as an imperialist adventure like *Rambo*, and the consumerist aspect of war films in general is kept in the foreground. This pointedly includes the hypocrisy of such flag-waving "history lessons" as the exploded and severed body parts in *Saving Private Ryan*, which are contrived simultaneously to sell tickets and to provide moral correctives to other war movies – though the movies being corrected often upped the violence quotient in their own eras with identical rationalizations and mixed motives.

(Jonathan Rosenbaum, "At War with Cultural Violence: The Critical Reception of *Small Soldiers*," in: *Movie Wars: How Hollywood and the Media Conspire to Limit What Films We Can See*, Chicago: A Cappella, 2000)

~

Unlike, say, Oliver Stone's *Natural Born Killers*, *Small Soldiers* is not the kind of high-minded satire that heedlessly exploits the very conditions it mocks. Instead, Dante exploits those conditions with heed. He generates real and unabashed pleasure from the junk. Take, for instance, the film's most bravura sequence, in which the toy soldiers implant the war-mongering computer chips into a group of "Gwendy" dolls. Transformed into a demonic girl gang of grotesqueries (complete with bulging eyes, bald pates, and screws and stitching protruding from all over), they seductively prance around the bedroom spouting stream-of-conscious trendyisms ("She's gone postal," "That haircut is so five minutes ago," "Don't hate me because I'm beautiful") and launching a vicious attack against their teenage girl owner. That these maniacal Courtney-Love-cum-Barbie-Beautiful toys are capable of doing major damage is one point the director is trying to put across; but that these are also gorgeously weird, deliciously menacing creations (the kind only possible in an overstuffed, hyperpop universe) is most certainly another. Dante makes the pranksterism cut both ways here, and it proves to be his smartest move. He recognizes the threat being posed to our fun, but he refuses to empower that threat by treating it seriously. Or, to put it in explicitly militaristic terms: He wins the war by defeating his enemies at their own game.

Will children get any of this? Probably not, but I don't want to sell the kid's movie appeal of *Small Soldiers* short. Dante understands that children can respond to the rudeness, excitement, and anarchy of the satire, even if they aren't getting all the jokes. And he's also made certain that they respond to the excitement of the film by focusing, in sublimely child-like fashion, almost entirely on visceral and kinetic pleasure. Indeed, like a child lost to the world in his own after-school fantasies, Dante has created a completely pure "play" universe, a film that refuses to abide by any adult (or Hollywood) rules of logic or propriety. A toy soldier chases and then desperately tries to scale a live-action moving bicycle as it speeds down the street; the soldiers bind and gag the heroine's younger brother and then lock him up in the closet; in the final battle sequence, they deliriously launch flaming tennis balls through a family's living room windows, only to have the balls shot right back at them by a mom with a fierce backhand. Dante skirts along ecstatically and infectiously; he seems determined that every frame of his movie explode in a burst of rowdy excitement. And whereas other directors might have shaped the same material into a treacly *E.T.*-like ode to childhood imagination, Dante's rambunctiousness allows *Small Soldiers* to become something far more practical (and funny): an owner's manual for children on how to use imagination as a weapon.

(Christopher Kelly, "Toys in the Attic," *Film Quarterly* vol. 53, no.4, Summer 2000)

Night Visions (TV)

Canada / USA 2001

CINEMATOGRAPHER Andreas Poulsson **MUSIC** Frank Macchia, George S. Clinton **PRODUCTION DESIGNER** Lance King **PRODUCERS** Dan Angel, Billy Brown (Angel/Brown Productions, Warner Bros. Television)

Joe Dante directed two segments of the series (2001-02) which ran on FOX for one season (13 episodes with two segments each).

"QUIET PLEASE"
WRITER Jim Leonard, based on the story by Joseph Beyer and Jim Leonard **EDITORS** Bill Luciano, Michael Ruscio **ART DIRECTOR** Mark Soparlo **COSTUME DESIGNER** Cynthia Summers **SPECIAL EFFECTS** Randy Shymkiw **CAST** Cary Elwes, Brian Dennehy, Gus Lynch, Henry Rollins **AIR DATE** July 19, 2001
35 MM, COLOR, 21 MINUTES Second segment of the third episode; first segment directed by Bill Pullman

"THE OCCUPANT"
WRITERS Billy Brown, Dan Angel **EDITORS** Ken Bornstein, Michael Ruscio **ART DIRECTOR** Mark Soparlo **COSTUME DESIGNER** Cynthia Summers **SPECIAL EFFECTS** Randy Shymkiw **CAST** Bridget Fonda, Dion Luther, Anthony Harrison, Chris Kelly, Jessica Sloan, Henry Rollins **AIR DATE** August 9, 2001
35 MM, COLOR, 21 MINUTES Second segment of the sixth episode; first segment directed by Po-Chih Leong

See Chronology (p. 191) for more information.

R. L. Stine's Haunted Lighthouse

USA 2003

WRITER Sam Hamm, based on the story by R. L. Stine
CINEMATOGRAPHER Sean MacLeod Phillips **EDITOR** Marshall
Harvey **VISUAL EFFECTS** Sean MacLeod Phillips, Alan G.
Markowitz **MUSIC** Chris Stone **PRODUCERS** Neal Allen,
Yvonne Bernard, Jini Dayaneni, Michael Finnell (Busch
Entertainment Corporation, Lookout Entertainment)
CAST Sara Paxton, Lea Thompson, Christopher Lloyd,
Michael McKean, Matt Weinberg, Bobby Edner,
"Weird Al" Yankovic **RELEASE DATE** March 7, 2003
70 MM (DUAL-STRIP 3D), COLOR, 22 MINUTES

A short "4D" film (3D screening with multi-sensory effects such as water and air jets, and buzzing seats) which debuted in SeaWorld theme parks in San Diego and San Antonio.

Shooting with 70mm cameras, as Dante recalls in a 2010 interview, is a "nice process when it's done, but it's very tedious to shoot." The cameras were "strapped together like a big Buick" and the whole rig took "six guys to push it on the track and there's so much noise you've got to loop everything."

See Chronology (p. 192) for more information.

Looney Tunes: Back in Action

USA / Germany 2003

ANIMATION DIRECTOR Eric Goldberg **WRITER** Larry Doyle
CINEMATOGRAPHER Dean Cundey **EDITORS** Marshall Harvey,
Rick W. Finney **PRODUCTION DESIGNER** Bill Brzeski **ANIMATION
ART DIRECTOR** John Kleber **COSTUME DESIGNER** Mary E. Vogt
VISUAL EFFECTS Chris Watts **MUSIC** Jerry Goldsmith **PRODUCERS**
Paula Weinstein, Bernie Goldmann, Joel Simon (Warner
Bros., Baltimore/Spring Creek Pictures, Goldmann Pictures)
CAST Brendan Fraser, Jenna Elfman, Timothy Dalton, Joan
Cusack, Bill Goldberg, Heather Locklear, Steve Martin, Ron
Perlman, Robert Picardo, Mary Woronov, Don Stanton,
Dan Stanton, Dick Miller, Kevin McCarthy, Roger Corman
VOICE CAST Joe Alaskey, Jeff Bennett, Billy West, Eric
Goldberg, Brendan Fraser
RELEASE DATE November 9, 2003
35 MM, COLOR, 91 MINUTES

I don't know who controlled the final cut on *Looney Tunes: Back in Action* – which seems even more personal than *Small Soldiers* – and the screen credits don't tell us much. Dante avoids taking any writing credit on his movies. According to a *New York Times* story by David Edelstein, the only credited writer on this movie, Larry Doyle, "pulled out of [the film] after vehement disagreements over animation, character voicing and jokes," and twenty-eight other writers, none of them credited, "were involved in varying capacities." So it's hard to say who deserves credit for authoring *Looney Tunes*, especially when one considers that the cartoon characters that dominate the action come mainly from the work of Tex Avery, Robert Clampett, Friz Freleng, Chuck Jones, and Frank Tashlin – all dead and uncredited. And one has to be careful not to limit the cast list to the on-screen actors, because one actor, Joe Alaskey, furnished the voices of the two leads, Bugs Bunny and Daffy Duck, and those of three secondary characters, Beaky Buzzard, Mama Bear, and Sylvester. In any case, Dante's stamp is evident on almost every frame, in part because he's not simply a creator but a creative filter, assiduously minimizing all elements that aren't Dante-esque.

What does his stamp consist of? For one thing, a faithful reliance on a stable of secondary actors, the most prominent of whom include Dick Miller (as a security guard), Roger Corman (as a Warners director), and Kevin McCarthy (returning briefly as the hero of the original *Invasion of the Body Snatchers*) – all of them associated with Dante's experience as a movie fan in the '50s and '60s and an employee of Corman's in the '70s. For another thing, there's a reliance on horror and SF movies of the '50s and early '60s – from *The Man From Planet X* and *This Island Earth* to *Forbidden Planet* and *Psycho* – as well as Warners cartoons dating back to the '30s, all supplemented by other pop-movie references. Finally, there's an affection for both monsters and cartoon characters and a cheerful contempt for powerful institutions and what they commonly represent – a position that becomes full of contradictions once it's directed at such powerful institutions as

Warner Brothers and Acme, the generic manufacturer of products ordered by Wile E. Coyote in Road Runner cartoons. These two multinational entities are mocked more than others in *Looney Tunes*; a Wal-Mart that appears in the Nevada desert gets only a cameo: "Is it a mirage or just more product placement?" asks Bugs.

The putative human heroes in any Dante work tend to be bland and dumb, while the putative human villains tend to be regarded with amusement rather than rancor. The main human heroes in *Looney Tunes* are Brendan Fraser, playing an aspiring stunt man for Brendan Fraser, and Jenna Elfman, playing a Warners executive. The main villain is Steve Martin, playing Mr. Chairman, the mad, scheming head of Acme. It's no surprise that the Warner brothers – much closer to bluenose villains than good guys – are played by Dante semi-regulars (identical twins Don and Dan Stanton) and are much less lively than Mr. Chairman. It might seem curious that the Warners company employs Bugs Bunny and Daffy Duck (along with Fraser and Elfman), while the Acme company employs Wile E. Coyote (along with the Tasmanian Devil, Ron Perlman, and Dante regular Mary Woronov); but these two institutions, unlike their employees, are offered as parallel monolithic and monopolistic enterprises rather than as competitors. The ultimate aim of Acme, we discover, is to turn everyone on earth, except Mr. Chairman, into monkeys that can provide cheap labor to churn out products, then back into humans who can buy these products. The ultimate aim of the Warner brothers is to turn everyone except them into monkeys that churn out *Looney Tunes: Back in Action*, then back to humans who can buy tickets and ancillary products. That Fraser, whose character works for Warners, also supplies the voices of the Tasmanian Devil and She-Devil, who both work for Acme, only underlines this moral equivalence.

It's characteristic of Dante to be brazenly yet offhandedly honest rather than cynical about these discrepancies. What makes him unusual as a satirist is that he's an equal-opportunity ridiculer, showing just as much affection for Beau Bridges, the putative villain of his 1997 TV movie *The Second Civil War*, as for any of the more sensible characters. Though he clearly cares more for the cartoon characters here than for any of the live-action ones, he gamely allows Steve Martin to try to compete with them by mugging his head off – though of course the poker-faced reaction shots of Bugs and Wile E. Coyote always elicit more laughs. Indeed, viewers are likely to come away from *Looney Tunes* concluding that the cartoon characters are far more real, substantial, and sympathetic than any of the humans – not my conclusion after watching Robert Zemeckis's much slicker *Who Framed Roger Rabbit*. This superiority is less peculiar than it sounds: after all, many more human hours – adding up to decades rather than weeks – have been invested in the creation, elaboration, and perpetuation of the cartoon figures. As collective creations, they make me think of the Chartres Cathedral – which paradoxically makes Dante's appreciation of them singular and not at all collective. […]

As a comedy, *Looney Tunes* is closest to *Gremlins 2*, though I doubt Dante was given such a free hand with it. And it's hard to tell whether it has as much meaning for kids who don't catch the film references and don't know or care who Dante is; its life in the marketplace probably depends more on its status as an anonymous factory product than its charm as a nostalgic personal manifesto. (This was also true of *Small Soldiers*, though that movie generally scored better with kids than with the uptight adults whose taste for war it ridiculed – which is probably why it did better on video than in theaters.)

In a related way, the difference I see today between two Bob Hope comedies littered with in-jokes – Frank Tashlin's *Son of Paleface* in 1952 and Hal Walker's *Road to Bali* of the same year – is probably less apparent to people simply looking for laughs than it is to auteurists like me. I loved both movies as a kid, but today the Tashlin looks snappy and sweet, while the Walker looks tired and sour. That's partly a consequence of how Tashlin and Walker made their films, and partly the result of my reading their films differently today. But I won't have to wait another fifty years to see that *Looney Tunes* is lovable and *Who Framed Roger Rabbit* is only likable. Robert Zemeckis isn't a Hal Walker, but Joe Dante's right up there with Tashlin, Avery, and Jones.

(Jonathan Rosenbaum,
"Joe Dante Calls the Toon," *Chicago Reader*,
November 21, 2003)

Masters Of Horror (TV)

Canada / USA / Japan 2005 / 2006

CREATED BY Mick Garris **PRODUCERS** Tom Rowe, Lisa Richardson (IDT Entertainment [2005], Nice Guy Productions, Industry Entertainment, Reunion Pictures, Starz [2006–2007])

Joe Dante directed two episodes of the series (2005–07). It ran on Showtime for two seasons with 13 episodes each.

HOMECOMING (Season 1, episode 6)
WRITER Sam Hamm, based on the short story "Death & Suffrage" by Dale Bailey **CINEMATOGRAPHER** Attila Szalay **EDITOR** Marshall Harvey **PRODUCTION DESIGNER** David Fischer **COSTUME DESIGNER** Lyn Kelly **MAKE-UP EFFECTS** Gregory Nicotero, Howard Berger **VISUAL EFFECTS** Lee Wilson **MUSIC** Hummie Mann **CAST** Jon Tenney, Thea Gill, Wanda Cannon, Terry David Mulligan, Robert Picardo, Beverley Breuer, Karen Austin, Daniel Wesley, Jason Emanuel
AIR DATE December 2, 2005 **DIGITAL, COLOR, 58 MINUTES**

THE SCREWFLY SOLUTION (Season 2, episode 7)
WRITER Sam Hamm, based on the short story by James Tiptree, Jr. (i.e. Alice Sheldon) **CINEMATOGRAPHER** Attila Szalay **EDITOR** Marshall Harvey **PRODUCTION DESIGNER** David Fischer **COSTUME DESIGNER** Lyn Kelly **MAKE-UP EFFECTS** Gregory Nicotero, Howard Berger **VISUAL EFFECTS** Lee Wilson **MUSIC** Hummie Mann **CAST** Jason Priestley, Kerry Norton, Linda Darlow, Brenna O'Brien, Steve Lawlor, Elliott Gould, Don House
AIR DATE December 8, 2006 **DIGITAL, COLOR, 59 MINUTES**

At once galvanic and cathartic, Dante's film uncorks the rage that despondent progressives promptly suppressed after last year's election and that has only recently been allowed to color mainstream coverage of presidential untruths and debacles. For all its broad, bludgeoning satire, *Homecoming* is deadly accurate in skewering the callousness and hypocrisy of the Bush White House and the spin industry in its orbit.

Zombie flicks, with their built-in return-of-the-repressed theme, have always served as allegories of their sociopolitical moments. Dante, the Roger Corman protégé who went on to direct *Innerspace* and both *Gremlins* movies, has been known to embed wayward subversions in Hollywood genre pieces (he also previously attempted an all-out political satire in the 1997 HBO movie *The Second Civil War*). But *Homecoming*, very much a movie on a mission, casts aside metaphor – it derives its power from its disconcerting literalness. The zombies do not represent – but *are* – the unseen costs of this futile war. Implicit in the film's unapologetic bluntness is a sickened urgency, an insistence that this is no time for subtlety.

"If you're going to code the message, which is the way horror movies have always done it, that's fine, but it's not going to reach an audience like a movie that's overt, and this is not exactly subtle," says Dante. "Somebody has to start making this kind of movie, this kind of statement. But everybody's afraid – it's uncommercial, people are going to be upset. Good, let them be upset. Why *aren't* people upset? Every minute, somebody's dying in this war, and for nothing. To establish a religious theocracy in Iraq? It doesn't seem to me quite worth it." […] Dante hopes *Homecoming* functions as a wake-up call – not so much for politicians but for filmmakers. "If this spurs other people into making more and better versions, it will have done its job. I want to see more discussion," he says. "Nobody is doing anything about what's going on now – compared to the '70s, when they were making movies about the issues of the day. This elephant in the room, this Iraq war story, is not being dramatized."

"You don't have to be a rocket scientist to see what a fucking mess we're in," he continues. "It's been happening steadily for the past four years, and nobody said peep. *The New York Times* and all these people that abetted the lies and crap that went into making and selling this war – now that they see the guy is a little weak, they're kicking him with their toe to make sure he doesn't bite back. It's cowardly. This pitiful zombie movie, this fucking B movie, is the only thing anybody's done about this issue that's killed 2,000 Americans and untold numbers of Iraqis? It's fucking sick."

While gratified by the warm reception to *Homecoming* in Turin [Torino Film Festival], Dante says he's eager for the right-wing punditocracy back home to see it: "I hope this movie bothers a lot of people that disagree with it – and that it makes them really pissed off, as pissed off as the rest of us are."

(Dennis Lim, "Dante's Inferno,"
Village Voice, November 22, 2005)

~

Because of its trendy politics, Joe Dante's overpraised *Homecoming* was the only *Masters of Horror* from last season to get the attention of the alternative press. Realizing this, producers have asked their slate of horror auteurs to emphasize politics above all else for the second season of the series, except Dante has gone way beyond the call of duty, stuffing his new experiment in terror, *The Screwfly Solution*, with enough hot-button provocation to not only expand your mind but to also blow it to pieces. Shunning metaphor, Dante imagines a frightening apocalypse when the human reproductive cycle is invaded by an insect virus. The effects are chilling (men, aroused by sex, take out their violent aggressions against women), and as this bioterrorist threat spreads, the world explodes in a testosterone madness that informs housing policies and flights plans. The film's murders are vicious spectacles of sexual aggression and the flight of one woman to Canada away from her scientist husband (played by Jason Priestley) becomes a nightmare journey for survival that ponders a strange alien interference. In one scene, a star falls from the sky only to change its direction, teasing a would-be wisher; this is Dante's haunting way of suggesting our political noise has caused a rip in the cosmos. Dante understands the earth as an organism at a precarious point in its evolution, envisioning a planet fighting to resist the pressures the human populace has placed on it, and though the director's notion of religious zealotry as an automatic symptom of the story's bioterror is specious to the point of insult, all bases are hit with a startling sense of attention and logic (there's even a moment during which the effects of the virus on gay men is addressed).

Dante is deeply attuned to the way the story's crisis messes with humanity, forcing us to make startling concessions. In short: Dante has given us a great cautionary tale.

(Ed Gonzales, "Masters of Horror: Season Two," Slant, January 8, 2007)

Trapped Ashes

USA/Japan 2006

DIRECTORS Joe Dante ("Wraparound"), Ken Russell ("The Girl With Golden Breasts"), Sean S. Cunningham ("Jibaku"), Monte Hellman ("Stanley's Girlfriend"), John Gaeta ("My Twin, The Worm") **WRITER** Dennis Bartok **CINEMATOGRAPHER** Zoran Popovic **EDITOR** Marcus Manton **PRODUCTION DESIGNER** Robb Wilson King **COSTUME DESIGNER** Toni Rutter **VISUAL EFFECTS** Robert Skotak **MUSIC** Kenji Kawai **PRODUCERS** Yoshi-fumi Hosoya, Yuko Yoshikawa, Dennis Bartok (Independent Film Financing, Cinema Investment, Tokyo Broadcasting System, Asmik Ace, Elephant Studio/Five Windows) **CAST** Amelia Cooke, Jayce Bartok, Lara Harris, Luke MacFarlane, Scott Lowell, Michèle-Barbara Pelletier, Tahmoh Penikett, John Saxon, Henry Gibson, Dick Miller **PREMIERE** September 12, 2006 (Toronto Film Festival) **35 MM, COLOR, 105 MINUTES**

Gross-out comedy about male discomfort with female sexuality dominates this horror anthology scripted by Dennis Bartok. Joe Dante directed the frame – about a movie-studio tour, guided by Henry Gibson, in which customers can escape from a haunted house only by telling a gruesome story – and Monte Hellman directed the best segment, premised on the early Hollywood career of Stanley Kubrick. Their craft gives this feature most of its interest, though bad-movie buffs may enjoy the stylistic overkill of Ken Russell's tale about a starlet getting transplanted breasts that prove deadly to others, and the other standard-issue crudities and improbabilities found in John Gaeta's and Sean C. Cunningham's stories.

(Jonathan Rosenbaum, "Trapped Ashes," Chicago Reader, August 24, 2007)

The Greatest Show Ever (TV)

USA 2007

DIRECTORS Joe Dante, Huston Huddleston, Scott Leva, Stacy Title **WRITER** Huston Huddleston **CINEMATOGRAPHERS** Paolo Cascio, Charles Schner **EDITOR** Jeff Werner **PRODUCER** Nancy Adams (Popoosa Productions)

Joe Dante directed a 2-minute sketch featuring Mickey Rooney and Paul Ganus for this unfinished TV movie. See Chronology (p. 193) for more information.

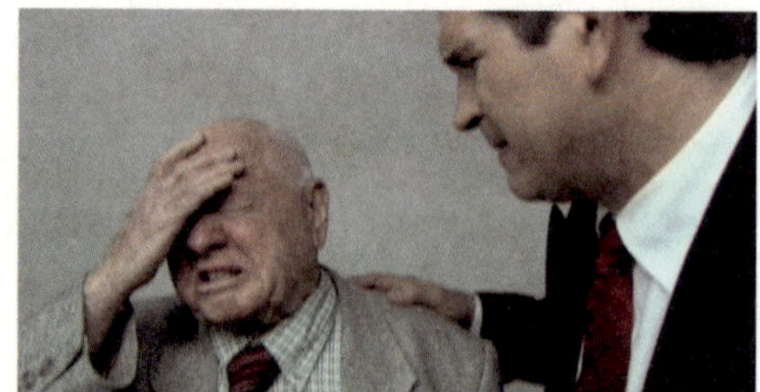

CSI: NY (TV)

USA 2007

Joe Dante directed one episode of the series (2004–13) which ran on CBS for nine seasons with 197 episodes.

"BOO" (Season 4, episode 6)
WRITERS Peter M. Lenkov, Daniele Nathanson
CINEMATOGRAPHER Marshall Adams **EDITOR** Bill Zabala
PRODUCTION DESIGNER Vaughan Edwards **COSTUME DESIGNER**
Elizabeth Palmer **SPECIAL EFFECTS** David Kelsey **MUSIC** Bill
Brown **CREATED BY / EXECUTIVE PRODUCERS** Anthony E. Zuiker,
Ann Donahue, Carol Mendelsohn (CBS Paramount Network Television) **CAST** Gary Sinise, Melina Kanakaredes,
Carmine Giovinazzo, Anna Belknap, Hill Harper, Eddie
Cahill, Robert Picardo, Bruce Dern
AIR DATE October 31, 2007 **DIGITAL, COLOR, 43 MINUTES**

See Chronology (p. 193) for more information.

The Hole

USA 2009

WRITER Mark L. Smith **CINEMATOGRAPHER** Theo van de Sande
EDITOR Marshall Harvey **PRODUCTION DESIGNER** Brentan
Harron **COSTUME DESIGNER** Kate Main **SPECIAL EFFECTS** Darren
Marcoux **MUSIC** Javier Navarrete **PRODUCERS** Michel Litvak,
David Lancaster (Bold Films, Benderspink) **CAST** Chris
Massoglia, Haley Bennett, Nathan Gamble, Bruce Dern,
Teri Polo, Quinn Lord, John DeSantis, Doug Chapman,
Mark Pawson, Peter Shinkoda, Jonathan Bruce, Merritt
Patterson, Ali Cobrin, Chelsea Ricketts, Chord Overstreet,
Dick Miller
PREMIERE September 11, 2009 (Venice Film Festival)
DIGITAL, COLOR, 92 MINUTES

Depth isn't a slapped-on gimmick in *The Hole*, but a metaphor central to its plot. A single mom (Teri Polo) moves into a bland suburban home with her two sons, a teenager (Chris Massoglia) with an awakening interest in girls, and a little boy (Nathan Gamble) with some persistent father issues. When they find a tightly padlocked trap door in the basement of their new house, they enlist the help of

the cute girl next door (Haley Bennett) to pry it open – unleashing a whole range of repressed anxieties, which are different for everyone who looks into the hole's bottomless depths.

The Hole doesn't have the frantic wit of Dante's *Gremlins 2* or the political import of his *Small Soldiers*, but it has something just as satisfying: a thorough understanding of the psychological underpinnings of the genre, placed in the service of warmly drawn characters and a sincerely told story. Its spirit is that of a child-centered fantasy film from the Fifties – like *The Invisible Boy* or *The 5,000 Fingers of Dr. T* – that speaks to primal fears while maintaining a sense of fun and adventure. A genuinely humanist horror movie, *The Hole* is a useful enchantment that deserves to be seen.

(Dave Kehr, "*The Hole:* Into the Black," *Film Comment*, vol. 46, no. 4, July–August 2010)

~

From the black comic *The 'Burbs* (1989), Bruce Dern returns as another crazy neighbour, surrounded by popping lightbulbs in a disused glove factory. Dante's movie-buff world is so well established it's a pleasure to check off the landmarks, including a wordless cameo from recurrent star walk-on Dick Miller, a television clip from *Gorgo* (1961), and the teen heroine's significant night-reading (Dante's "Inferno"). But there has always been more than simple fun in even Dante's most trivia-studded movies, and he never makes a reference which doesn't have an emotional resonance. Here horror boils down to a terrible childhood, one that even suburban heaven – moving next door to a nice girl who looks adorable in a bikini – can't erase.

Chris Massoglia, fresh from the cartoonish teen monster angst of *Cirque du Freak,* is wholly credible as the lead – Dane is understandably wary and difficult, yet not so much of a self-involved mope that it's impossible to care about him. Known for his toothy monsters, represented here by a grinning jester puppet sure to get on the nerves of real-life sufferers from the condition labelled by the script as "Bozo-phobia", Dante is perhaps underappreciated for his rapport with young performers (he drew fine early performances from, among others, Ethan Hawke, River Phoenix, Corey Feldman and Kirsten Dunst), and *The Hole* benefits from the nice interplay between antagonistic brothers Dane and Lucas and girl next door Julie, as they segue from normal kid feuds and flirtations to a methodical probing of the need-it-even-be-said highly metaphorical hole in the cellar.

Dante has worked in 3D before (2003's theme-park attraction *R. L. Stine's Haunted Lighthouse*) and may be uniquely qualified by temperament to use the process for all its gimmick appeal (a ball-tossing bit that evokes a key moment from *House of Wax* and a rickety roller-coaster that echoes *Gorilla at Large*) and make narrative capital of its disorienting strangeness. Even the odd attenuation of space that comes with tridvid lensing is appropriate when delving into the supernatural space of the hole: especially as the teenage Dane is surrounded by overscale furniture and misshapen props (his father's big belt is especially disturbing) which reduce him to the size of a toddler. The film offers well-timed creep-out shocks (an eye that stares from a TV just when everyone – including the audience – is distracted by other business) but stays away from gore and even much in the way of monster effects, quietly confident that a well-told, character-based ghost story can play in the third dimension with as much impact as, say, the slashing of *My Bloody Valentine 3D* or the splatter of *The Final Destination.*

(Kim Newman, *"The Hole," Sight and Sound,*
vol. 20, no. 10, October 2010)

~

I think 3D can be a great storytelling tool, just as color, widescreen and stereo sound became. But there are drawbacks, particularly in poor presentation, which has killed off every previous iteration of 3D. And the preponderance of 2D movies sloppily "converted" after the fact flies in the face of the very idea of 3D. You plan, shoot, design and think in 3D while you're making the movie, not as an afterthought. I used to think 3D had a big future; lately I'm not so sure.

(Joe Dante, in: Toni D'Angela,
"Interview with Joe Dante," *La Furia umana,*
no. 11, winter 2012)

Splatter

USA 2009

WRITER Richard Christian Matheson **CINEMATOGRAPHER** John DeFazio **EDITOR** Karen Smalley **PRODUCTION DESIGNER** Niko Vilaivongs **SPECIAL EFFECTS** Vincent Guastini **MUSIC** Aaron Symonds **PRODUCERS** Roger Corman, Julie Corman (New Horizon Picture Corp.) **CAST** Corey Feldman, Tony Todd, Mark Alan, Tara Leigh, Stuart Pankin, Erin Way
RELEASE DATE October 29, 2009
DIGITAL, COLOR, 10 EPISODES OF VARIABLE LENGTH (7–11 MINUTES)

For this interactive web series commissioned by Netflix, Joe Dante directed all (potential) episodes, only three of which were actually streamed on Netflix, because the audience could vote on which characters they wanted to see killed off in the subsequent installment. Sometime in the future, Dante plans to issue a "party DVD" which includes all episodes and potential endings.

"It's a rock star's funeral and all the mourners are hangers-on and people who basically used him. He's now come back from the dead and he's going to get revenge on all of them. It's based on the idea: 'which characters do the audience want to see die?', which I guess is a negative way to approach it if you're an actor, but it's sort of a triumph if you get picked, because it proves that you managed to be more odious than the person next to you! […] I think the webisode idea in itself is going to survive, but the idea of interactive storytelling has its limits. If the audience gets to choose what happens, it becomes very difficult to have a point to the

story. You can imagine that if *Midnight Cowboy* had been interactive, the audience would have voted for them to strike out earlier on and move to Beverly Hills!"

(Joe Dante, in: Alex Fitch, "*Splatter:* Interview with Joe Dante," *Electric Sheep*, Sept. 24, 2010)

Hawaii Five-O (TV)

USA 2011/2013

DEVELOPED BY / EXECUTIVE PRODUCERS Alex Kurtzman, Roberto Orci, Peter M. Lenkov (Kurtzman Orci Paper Products, 101st Street Productions, CBS) **REGULAR CAST** Alex O'Loughlin, Scott Caan, Daniel Dae Kim, Grace Park, Masi Oka

Joe Dante directed two episodes of the series (2010–) which runs on CBS and is based on the original CBS series *Hawaii Five-O* (1968–1980) created by Leonard Freeman.

"KA IWI KAPU" (Season 2, episode 7)
WRITERS Michele Fazekas, Tara Butters **CINEMATOGRAPHER** James L. Carter **EDITOR** Maja Vrvilo **PRODUCTION DESIGNER** Keith Neely **SPECIAL EFFECTS** John C. Hartigan **MUSIC** Bryan Tyler, Keith Power **ADDITIONAL CAST** Lauren German, Robert Englund, Autumn Reeser, Ryan Devlin, Erin Way
AIR DATE October 31, 2011 **DIGITAL, COLOR, 42 MINUTES**

"OLELO PA'A" (Season 3, episode 20)
WRITERS Peter M. Lenkov, Ken Solarz **CINEMATOGRAPHER** James L. Carter **EDITOR** Roderick Davis **PRODUCTION DESIGNER** Keith Neely **SPECIAL EFFECTS** John Hartigan, Archie Ahuna **MUSIC** Bryan Tyler, Keith Power **ADDITIONAL CAST** Michelle Borth, Jimmy Buffett, Alan Ritchson, Rick Yune, Terry O'Quinn, Robert Picardo
AIR DATE April 15, 2013 **DIGITAL, COLOR, 42 MINUTES**

See Chronology (p. 194) for more information.

Joe Dante's credited and uncredited collaborations and appearances

CREDITED AS EDITOR
GRAND THEFT AUTO Ron Howard, 1977

CREDITED AS PRODUCER
THE PHANTOM Simon Wincer, 1996. Executive producer (one of four)
JEREMIAH (TV) J. Michael Straczynski (series creator), 2002–2004. Executive producer of the series' first 21 episodes, and executive consultant for the subsequent 13 episodes
TRAILERS FROM HELL (VOLUME 1 & 2) 2008; 2011. Producer and commentator on two volumes of the Trailers From Hell DVD release
TRAIL OF BLOOD Joseph Guerrieri & Justin Guerrieri, 2011. Executive producer

CREDITED AS ACTOR
In addition to the single credited role in the final episode ("Reality Takes a Holiday") of *Eerie, Indiana*, where he essentially plays himself ("Director"), and numerous uncredited appearances in his other films (*Hollywood Boulevard, Piranha, Rock 'n' Roll High School, Innerspace* and *Gremlins 2: The New Batch*), Dante has also appeared in a number of films by other directors.
NIPPON CHINBOTSU (TIDAL WAVE) Shirō Moritani, 1973. Dante dubbed a number of voices for the 1975 U.S. release version of the film by New World Pictures (under the title *Tidal Wave*); the original was significantly cut and newly-shot footage was added.
CANNONBALL Paul Bartel, 1976. Dante and Allan Arkush play "Kid" and "Panama," a couple of small-town mechanics who sell a racing car to David Carradine.
BREAKING UP Mick Garris, ca. 1980. A little seen, half-hour comedy, shot for $10,000, in which Dante portrays a stereo salesman
STEPHEN KING'S SLEEPWALKERS Mick Garris, 1992. Dante appears in a single shot as the "Lab Assistant" to John Landis's "Lab Technician."

IL SILENZIO DEI PROSCIUTTI (THE SILENCE OF THE HAMS) Ezio Greggio, 1993. Dante ("Dying Man") is mortally wounded in an absurd shootout between bank robbers and police. Before dying, he gives vital information to John Carpenter.
BEVERLY HILLS COP III John Landis, 1994. Dante ("Jailer") leads Eddie Murphy from a jail cell in two brief scenes, with two lines of dialogue.
THE BUTTERFLY ROOM Jonathan Zarantonello, 2012. In two shots, Dante ("Taxi Driver") loads suitcases in the cab and tries to impress the young heroine's mother despite their difference in height.
BLAST VEGAS (TV) Jack Perez, 2013. In the film's cold open, Dante ("Salesman #2") is again paired with Landis ("Salesman #1") for his most verbose and self-deprecatory bit part in recent times. Unleashing an ancient curse, they both perish before the opening credits.

Over the years, Joe Dante has also participated, appeared on-screen, or received a "special thanks" credit in a great number of short and feature-length documentaries, mainly on the subject of genre cinema, as well as his own work and that of his fellow filmmakers.

IN CREDIT ONLY
In two of New World Pictures' international co-productions, *Fly Me/Il racket del sesso* (Cirio H. Santiago, 1973) and *The Arena/La rivolta delle gladiatrici* (Steve Carver, 1974), Joe Dante is credited as "Dialogue Director" and "Editor," respectively. In reality, Dante was *not* involved with either of these two films; the credits were likely inserted by Jon Davison in an effort to replace original Italian credits with English-sounding names.

In John Landis's *Oscar* (1991), Dante's name appears in the end credits. However, as his character's name ("Face on the Cutting Room Floor") suggests, his cameo scenes did not actually make it into the final cut.

Joe Dante in *Beverly Hills Cop III* (1994)

UNCREDITED CONTRIBUTIONS

DIRTY DUCK Charles Swenson, 1974. Additional editing for the New World-produced animated cartoon

COCKFIGHTER (BORN TO KILL) Monte Hellman, 1974. Additional editing for the 1975 re-release of the film by New World Pictures (under the title *Born to Kill*)

QUI COMINCIA L'AVVENTURA (BLONDE IN BLACK LEATHER) Carlo Di Palma, 1975. Additional editing for the 1977 U.S. release of the film by New World Pictures (under the title *Blonde in Black Leather*)

ALLEGRO NON TROPPO Bruno Bozzetto, 1976. Additional editing for the 1977 U.S. release of the film by Specialty Films

I NEVER PROMISED YOU A ROSE GARDEN Anthony Page, 1977. Additional editing for the New World-produced film

FAST CHARLIE... THE MOONBEAM RIDER Steve Carver, 1979. Additional editing for the film produced by Roger Corman for Universal Pictures

WHITE DOG Samuel Fuller, 1982. Additional editing for the film produced by Jon Davison for Paramount

L'ISOLA DEGLI UOMINI PESCE (SCREAMERS) Sergio Martino, 1979. Additional editing for the 1981 U.S. release of the film by New World Pictures (under the title *Screamers*)

Dante's uncredited work also includes a directing job for the *Twilight Zone*-themed "Tower of Terror" attraction at the MGM-Disney Studios park in Orlando, Florida, which took place sometime in September 1993. The attraction consisted of two elements: footage of Rod Serling introducing a *Twilight Zone* episode (with dubbed-in dialogue) which was displayed in the "hotel lobby"; and newly-shot "ghost footage" which was projected in the drop tower elevator itself. Dante believes that the latter element was probably "seen by more people than most of my real movies!"

Selected Bibliography

Selected writings by Joe Dante

JOE DANTE JR. WITH INPUT FROM FORREST J ACKERMAN,
"Dante's Inferno," *Famous Monsters of Filmland*,
no. 18, July 1962

JOE DANTE, "Joe Dante's Guilty Pleasures: Can even a
confirmed trivia freak admit to liking A. C. Lyles Westerns?,"
Film Comment, vol. 19, no. 3, May–June 1983

JOE DANTE, "Joe Dante Shops for Horror," *American Film:
Magazine of the Film and TV Arts*, vol. 9, no. 10,
October 1984

ROGER CORMAN AND JOE DANTE, "Memories of Vincent Price,"
Sight and Sound, vol. 3, no. 12, December 1993

Books and dossiers on Joe Dante

**BILL KROHN, ROGER GARCIA, JONATHAN ROSENBAUM, AND
CHARLES TESSON,** *Joe Dante et les Gremlins de Hollywood*,
Paris: Cahiers du cinéma; Locarno: Festival International
du Film de Locarno, 1999

BILL KROHN, JONATHAN ROSENBAUM, AND FRANCO LA POLLA,
*Hollywood Boulevard: Joe Dante e l'altro cinema
indipendente*, Milano: Olivares, 1999

FRANK LAFOND, *Joe Dante: L'art du je(u)*, Pertuis:
Rouge Profond, 2011

LA FURIA UMANA, no. 11, Winter 2012. Edited by Toni
D'Angela; a multilingual dossier on Joe Dante with an inter-
view and essays by Jonathan Rosenbaum, Toni D'Angela,
David Cairns, Bill Krohn, Adrien Clerc, L. de La Hire, Julien
Oreste, Gabrielle Lucantonio, Carlos Losilla, Cloe Masotta,
John Kern, Marco Grosoli, David Phelps, Peter Nelhaus,
Gina Telaroli, Maxime Renaudin, Sergi Sánchez, Gino Frezza,
Mónica M. Marinero, Olivier Schefer and Sigismondo
Domenico Sciortino. Available at www.lafuriaumana.it

Selected interviews, articles, and book chapters

JORDAN R. FOX AND ADAM EISENBERG, *"The Howling,"
Cinefantastique*, vol. 10, no. 3, Winter 1980

OLIVIER ASSAYAS, "Hurlements," [*The Howling*] *Cahiers du
cinéma*, no. 320, February 1981

FORREST J ACKERMAN, "Werewolves of the World Unite in
The Howling," *Famous Monsters of Filmland*, no. 174,
June 1981

BILL WARREN, "A Starburst interview with Joe Dante (Part 1),"
Starburst, vol. 3, no. 12, August 1981

BILL WARREN, "A Starburst interview with Joe Dante (Part 2),"
Starburst, vol. 4, no. 1, September 1981

BRUCE KAWIN, "Reviews: *The Funhouse* and *The Howling*,"
Film Quarterly, vol. 35, no. 1, Autumn 1981

CHARLES TESSON, "Profils de monstres (2e partie),"
[*The Howling*] *Cahiers du cinéma*, no. 332, February 1982

BILL KROHN, "La nouvelle génération américaine,"
[*Hollywood Boulevard, Rock 'n' Roll High School,
The Twilight Zone*; Interview] *Cahiers du cinéma*, no. 343,
January 1983

DON SHAY AND PAUL SAMMON, "Shadows and Substance,"
[*Twilight Zone: The Movie*] *Cinefex*, no. 14, October 1983

OLIVIER ASSAYAS, "Voulez-vous jouer à *Twilight Zone* avec
moi?," *Cahiers du cinéma*, no. 356, February 1984

DAVID CHUTE, "Dante's Inferno," [Cover Article and
Interview] *Film Comment*, vol. 20, no. 3, May–June 1984

RICHARD CORLISS AND DENISE WORRELL, "Creature Comforts
and Discomforts," [*Gremlins*] *Time*, June 4, 1984

PAUL M. SAMMON, "Never Feed Them After Midnight,"
[*Gremlins*] *Cinefex*, no. 19, November 1984

KIM NEWMAN, "*Gremlins* Review", *Monthly Film Bulletin*,
vol. 51, no. 611, December 1984

CHARLES TESSON, "Le Gizmo, sec ou à l'eau?," [*Gremlins*]
Cahiers du cinéma, no. 367, January 1985

ADAM EISENBERG, "The Stuff That Dreams Are Made Of,"
[*Explorers*] *Cinefex*, no. 23, August 1985

BILL KROHN, "Le retour des morts-vivants," [*Explorers*]
Cahiers du cinéma, no. 376, October 1985

JONATHAN ROSENBAUM, "*Gremlins*," *Video Times*,
December 1985

JOHN NANGLE, "Joe Dante Blames Paramount for *Explorers* flop," *Cinefantastique*, vol. 15, no. 5, January 1986

RICHARD CORLISS, "A Funny, Fantastic Voyage," [*Innerspace*] *Time*, July 13, 1987

JANINE POURROY, "Inside Martin Short," [*Innerspace*] *Cinefex*, no. 32, November 1987

CHARLES TESSON, "L'enfer de Dante," [*Innerspace*] *Cahiers du cinéma*, no. 403, January 1988

VINCENT CANBY, "Suspicious Goings-On Next Door," [*The 'Burbs*] *The New York Times*, February 17, 1989

JONATHAN ROSENBAUM, "Split-Level Comedy," [*The 'Burbs*] *Chicago Reader*, February 24, 1989

RICHARD CORLISS, "Bad Neighbors," [*The 'Burbs*] *Time*, February 27, 1989

HERVÉ LE ROUX, "*Cheeseburger Film Sandwich*," [*Amazon Women on the Moon*] *Cahiers du cinéma*, no. 418, April 1989

KIM NEWMAN, "*The 'Burbs* Review," *Monthly Film Bulletin*, vol. 56, no. 667, August 1989

RIP RENSE, "Joe 'Gremlin' Dante," *Starburst*, Special no. 6, 1990

DAVID TOLSKY, "*Gremlins 2: The New Batch*," *American Cinematographer* vol. 71, no. 6, June 1990

JONATHAN ROSENBAUM, "We Monsters," [*Gremlins 2*] *Chicago Reader*, June 28, 1990

BILL KELLEY, "*Gremlins 2*," *Cinefantastique*, vol. 21, no. 1, July 1990

IANNIS KATSAHNIAS, "Génération Rank Xerox," [*Gremlins 2*] *Cahiers du cinéma*, no. 434, July–August 1990

TERRENCE RAFFERTY, "Gremlinology," *The New Yorker*, July 2, 1990

TERRENCE RAFFERTY, "*Gremlins 2: The New Batch*," *The New Yorker*, July 16, 1990

IANNIS KATSAHNIAS, "Gizmo" and "La truculence du mal," [*Gremlins 2*] *Cahiers du cinéma*, no. 435, September 1990

BILL KROHN, "Entretien avec Joe Dante," [Interview] *Cahiers du cinéma*, no. 435, September 1990

KIRK ELLIS, "Chuck Jones, entre Bugs Bunny et Joe Dante," [*Gremlins 2*] *Cahiers du cinéma*, no. 435, September 1990

THIERRY HORGUELIN, "Le grand carnaval: *Gremlins 2: The New Batch* de Joe Dante," *24 images*, no. 50–51, Autumn 1990

CHARLES LEAYMAN, "Dante's fun but always suggests an undertow of genuine horror," *Cinefantastique*, vol. 21, no. 3, December 1990

ANTHONY AMBROGIO, "Joe Dante," in Nicholas Thomas (ed.), *International Dictionary of Films and Filmmakers, Volume 2, Directors*, London: St. James Press, 1991

RON MAGID, "Rick Baker revisited," [*Gremlins 2*] *Cinefex*, no. 46, May 1991

MARK DAWIDZIAK, "*Eerie Indiana*," *Cinefantastique*, vol. 22, no. 3, December 1991

GREGORY SOLMAN, "The Illusion of a Future," [*Explorers* and *Innerspace*] *Film Comment*, vol. 28, no. 2, March 1992

BILL KROHN, "Les films TV de Joe Dante," [*Eerie, Indiana*] *Cahiers du cinéma*, no. 463, January 1993

JONATHAN ROSENBAUM, "War Fever," [*Matinee*] *Chicago Reader*, February 5, 1993

RICHARD SCHICKEL, "It Came From Inner Space," [*Matinee*] *Time*, February 8, 1993

STEVE BIODROWSKI, "Joe Dante's B-Movie Memories: *Matinee*," *Cinefantastique*, vol. 23, no. 6, April 1993

TIM LUCAS, "Joe Dante," [Cover Article] *Sight and Sound*, vol. 3, no. 6, June 1993

MARK KERMODE, "Terror Master," *Sight and Sound*, vol. 3, no. 6, June 1993

STEVE BIODROWSKI, "Dante's *Matinee*: *Mant*," *Cinefantastique*, vol. 24, no. 1, June 1993

PAT JANKIEWICZ, "*Matinee* time for Joe Dante," *Starburst*, vol. 15, no. 10, June 1993

PAT JANKIEWICZ, "*Eerie, Gremlins, Innerspace* Joe Dante," *Starburst*, vol. 15, no. 11, July 1993

GREGORY SOLMAN, "The Bs of Summer," [*Matinee*] *Film Comment*, vol. 29, no. 4, July 1993

J. HOBERMAN, "Secret services," [*Matinee*], *Artforum International*, vol. 32, no. 3, November 1993

RICHARD CORLISS, "I was a Teenage Teenager," [*Rebel Highway*] *Time*, August 15, 1994

DAVID EHRENSTEIN, "Joe Dante and *The Howling*," in Jerry Roberts and Steven Gaydos (eds.), *Movie Talk from the Front Lines: Filmmakers Discuss Their Works with the Los Angeles Film Critics Association*, Jefferson, N. C.: McFarland, 1995

MICHAEL SINGER, "Joe Dante," in Michael Singer (ed.), *A Cut Above: 50 Film Directors Talk about Their Craft*, Los Angeles: Lone Eagle Publishing, 1998

MICHAEL HENRY [WILSON], "Joe Dante: Entretien – 'J'ai essayé de conserver ma faculté d'émerveillement,'" [Interview] *Positif*, no. 449/450, July–August 1998

YANNICK DAHAN, "Joe Dante: De horreur anecdotique au drame universel," [Cover Article] *Positif*, no. 449/450, July–August 1998

JANET MASLIN, "The Few, the Proud, the Computer-Generated," [*Small Soldiers*] *The New York Times*, July 10, 1998

DENNIS LIM, "Toys of Summer," [*Small Soldiers*] *The Village Voice*, July 21, 1998

JONATHAN ROSENBAUM, "Cutting Heroes Down to Size," [*Small Soldiers*] *Chicago Reader*, July 24, 1998

JONATHAN ROMNEY, "*Small Soldiers*," *Sight and Sound*, vol. 8, no. 10, October 1998

JODY DUNCAN, "A Small Soldiers Story," *Cinefex*, no. 75, October 1998

BILL KELLEY, "*Small Soldiers*," *Cinefantastique*, vol. 30, no. 9/10, November 1998

JONATHAN ROSENBAUM, "At War with Cultural Violence: The Critical Reception of *Small Soldiers*," in *Movie Wars: How Hollywood and the Media Conspire to Limit What Films We Can See*, Chicago, Illinois, A Cappella Books, 2000

ROSS CARE, "Joe Dante," in Tom Pendergast and Sara Pendergast (eds.), *International Dictionary of Films and Filmmakers, Volume 2, Directors*, (4th edition) London: St. James Press, 2000

CHRISTOPHER KELLY, "Toys in the Attic: The Unsung Pleasures (and Terrors) of *Babe: Pig in the City* and *Small Soldiers*," *Film Quarterly*, vol. 53, no. 4, Summer 2000

JOSHUA KLEIN, "Interview: Joe Dante," *The Onion A. V. Club*, November 29, 2000 [www.avclub.com/articles/joe-dante,13689]

MARTYN BAMBER, "Joe Dante," *Senses of Cinema*, Issue 26, 2003 [http://sensesofcinema.com/2003/great-directors/dante]

DAVID EDELSTEIN, "That's Not All, Folks!," [*Looney Tunes: Back in Action*] *The New York Times*, November 2, 2003

STEPHEN HOLDEN, "Bugs Bunny and Friends Dash Through Movie Lore," [*Looney Tunes: Back in Action*] *The New York Times*, November 14, 2003

DAVID EDELSTEIN, "Wabbit Season: Bugs and Daffy reclaim past glory in *Looney Tunes: Back in Action*," *Slate*, November 14, 2003 [www.slate.com/articles/arts/movies/2003/11/wabbit_season.html]

JONATHAN ROSENBAUM, "Joe Dante Calls the Toon," [*Looney Tunes: Back in Action*] *Chicago Reader*, November 21, 2003

ANDREW OSMOND, "*Looney Tunes: Back in Action*," *Sight and Sound*, vol. 14, no. 3, March 2004

JAMES BELL, "*The Howling*," *Sight and Sound*, vol. 14, no. 10, October 2004

MICHAEL HEINTZELMAN, "The Dante/Goldsmith Project: Nine Films, Nine Scores, One Sensibility," *Film Score Monthly*, vol. 10, no. 6, November 2005

DENNIS LIM, "Dante's Inferno: A Horror Movie Brings Out the Zombie Vote to Protest Bush's War," [*Homecoming*] *The Village Voice*, November 30, 2005

MARK PERANSON, "Dante's Inferno: The Necessary Satire of *Homecoming*," [Interview] *Cinema Scope*, no. 25, Winter 2006

NEIL YOUNG, "Rotterdam 2006: Part Four," [*Homecoming*] *Jigsaw Lounge*, February 11, 2006 [www.jigsawlounge.co.uk/film/reviews/rotterdam-2006-part-four-including-joe-dante-s-homecoming]

LINCOLN GERAGHTY, "Love's Fantastic Voyage: Crossing Between Science Fiction and Romantic Comedy in *Innerspace*," *Extrapolation*, vol. 47, no. 1, Spring 2006

THIERRY MÉRANGER, "Dans Looney Tunes de Joe Dante, Bugs Bunny traverse les toiles," *Cahiers du cinéma*, no. 611, April 2006

MICHAEL SRAGOW, "*Homecoming*," *The New Yorker*, April 17, 2006

GAVIN SMITH, "*Police Squad!*," *Film Comment*, vol. 42, no. 6, November–December 2006

TIM LUCAS, "Joe Dante: Anarchy in L.A.," *Video WatchBlog*, Novemver 28, 2006 [http://videowatchdog.blogspot.com/2006/11/joe-dante-anarchy-in-la.html]

ETHAN DE SEIFE, "Gremlins in the Mix," *16:9*, no. 25, February 2008 [www.16-9.dk/2008-02/side11_inenglish.htm]

LAWRENCE FRENCH, "Supernal Dreams: Joe Dante talks Poe with Roger Corman & Daniel Haller," *Cinefantastique Online*, April 2, 2008 [http://cinefantastiqueonline.com/2008/04/supernal-dreams-joe-dante-talks-about-the-poe-films-with-roger-corman-and-daniel-haller]

STEVE BIODROWSKI, "*Trapped Ashes* – Horror Film Review," *Cinefantastique Online*, July 15, 2008 [http://cinefantastiqueonline.com/2008/07/film-review-trapped-ashes-2006]

TOM CHARITY, "Deep Space," [*The Hole*] *Sight and Sound*, vol. 19, no. 3, March 2009

BILL KROHN, "En profondeur," [*The Hole*] *Cahiers du cinéma*, no. 647, July–August 2009

BILL KROHN, "Entretien avec Joe Dante: Éviter de refaire les erreurs du passé," [Interview] *Cahiers du cinéma*, no. 647, July–August 2009

DAVID CAIRNS, "'I want to give you a piece of my mind': Interview with Joe Dante (Part 1)," *MUBI Notebook*, July 7, 2009 [http://mubi.com/notebook/posts/i-want-to-give-you-a-piece-of-my-mind-interview-with-joe-dante-part-1]

DAVID CAIRNS, "'Fun, Yes, But By No Means Civilized': Interview with Joe Dante (Part 2)," *MUBI Notebook*, July 8, 2009 [http://mubi.com/notebook/posts/fun-yes- but-by-no-means-civilized-interview-with-joe-dante-part-2]

J. R. JONES, "'Shades of Bacchus!': Joe Dante Talks W. C. Fields," *Chicago Reader*, September 16, 2009

DANIEL KASMAN, "TIFF 09: *The Hole*," *MUBI*, September 18, 2009 [http://mubi.com/notebook/posts/tiff-09-the-hole-joe-dante-usa]

SUSAN KING, "*Splatter* is vintage Roger Corman, fresh on the Web," *Los Angeles Times*, October 29, 2009

DAVE KEHR, "*The Hole*: Into the Black," *Film Comment*, vol. 46, no. 4, July–August 2010

TODD VANDERWERFF, "Interview: Joe Dante," *The Onion A. V. Club*, August 16, 2010 [www.avclub.com/articles/joe-dante,44164]

MARTYN CONTERIO, "Joe Dante," [Interview] *Little White Lies*, September 22, 2010 [www.littlewhitelies.co.uk/features/articles/joe-dante-12282]

ALEX FITCH, "*Splatter*: Interview with Joe Dante (part 1)," *Electric Sheep*, September 24, 2010 [www.electricsheepmagazine.co.uk/features/2010/09/24/splatter-interview-with-joe-dante]

JONATHAN ROMNEY, "*Enter the Void*, Gaspar Noé, *The Hole*, Joe Dante," *The Independent*, September 26, 2010

TOM CHARITY, "The Niceties," [Cover Article] *Sight and Sound*, vol. 20, no. 10, October 2010

KIM NEWMAN, "*The Hole*," *Sight and Sound*, vol. 20, no. 10, October 2010

JAMES MOTTRAM, "Serious Mischief," [Interview] *Sight and Sound*, vol. 20, no. 10, October 2010

ALEX FITCH, "*The Hole* in 3D: Interview with Joe Dante (part 2)," *Electric Sheep*, October 27, 2010 [www.electricsheepmagazine.co.uk/features/2010/10/27/the-hole-in-3d-interview-with-joe-dante-part-2]

JESSE P. FINNEGAN, "60-Second Cinema," ["Trailers From Hell"] *Film Comment*, vol. 47, no. 5, September–October 2011

DAVE KEHR, "Saved From Extinction: Classics and Curiosities," [*The Movie Orgy*] *The New York Times*, October 14, 2011

MICHAEL SRAGOW, "*Gremlins 2: The New Batch*," *The New Yorker*, vol. 87, no. 36, November 2011

THIERRY MÉRANGER, "FrankenJoe," [Interview] *Cahiers du cinéma*, no. 674, January 2012

J. HOBERMAN, "Across the Movi-verse," *Film Comment*, vol. 48, no. 2, March 2012

DAVE KEHR, "Exotic Creatures, Naughty and Nice," [*Gremlins 2: The New Batch*] *The New York Times*, June 17, 2012

BEN SACHS AND GABE KLINGER, "The Orgiast: An Interview With Joe Dante (Part 1)," *Chicago Reader*, August 8, 2012 [www.chicagoreader.com/Bleader/archives/2012/08/08/the-orgiast-an-interview-with-joe-dante-part-one]

BEN SACHS AND GABE KLINGER, "The Orgiast: An Interview With Joe Dante (Part 2)," *Chicago Reader*, August 9, 2012 [www.chicagoreader.com/Bleader/archives/2012/08/09/the-orgiast-an-interview-with-joe-dante-part-two]

SCOTT NEUMYER, "A Conversation With Joe Dante," *Slate*, October 1, 2012 [www.slate.com/articles/arts/interrogation/2012/10/joe_dante_s_the_hole_gremlins_director_interviewed.html]

Contributors and Editors

MICHAEL ALMEREYDA (b. 1959) has directed roughly twenty films since the 1980s – narrative features, documentaries and short films. As a screenwriter he collaborated on Wim Wenders' *Bis ans Ende der Welt* (1991) and, together with Jim Robison, on the script for Joe Dante's *The Man with Kaleidoscope Eyes* project. His films include *Another Girl, Another Planet* (1992), a modern-day adaptation of *Hamlet* (2000) with Ethan Hawke, *This So-Called Disaster: Sam Shepard Directs the Late Henry Moss* (2003), *William Eggleston In The Real World* (2005), and the diaristic feature *Paradise* (2008).

NIL BASKAR (b. 1977) has worked as a film writer, organizer and researcher since the mid-1990s. He was co-editor of *Ekran* film magazine and creator of *Terminal*, a monthly show on experimental cinema on Slovenian TV. In 2007, he co-founded *KINO!* magazine and has been a regular contributor since. He has worked for the Slovenian Cinematheque since 2010, where he is in charge of in-house publications. He edited the Slovenian translation of André Bazin's *What is Cinema?* and translated books by Jacques Rancière and Jean-Louis Comolli, among others.

J. HOBERMAN (b. 1948) is a New York-based author and film critic, formerly with the *Village Voice*. His books include *Midnight Movies* (1983, written with Jonathan Rosenbaum), *Vulgar Modernism* (1991), *Bridge of Light: Yiddish Films Between Two Worlds* (1991), *On Jack Smith's "Flaming Creatures" (and other Secret-Flix of Cinemaroc)* (2001), *The Dream Life: Movies, Media, and the Mythology of the Sixties* (2003), *An Army of Phantoms: American Movies and the Making of the Cold War* (2011), and most recently, *Film After Film: Or, What Became of 21ˢᵗ Century Cinema?* (2012).

CHRISTOPH HUBER (b. 1973) grew up in Attnang-Puchheim, Upper Austria, studied Physics at the Technical University of Vienna, and graduated with a thesis about the magneto-inductive characteristics of steel sheets. He is the film editor for the Vienna daily *Die Presse*, a longtime writer of program notes for the Austrian Film Museum, and the European editor of *Cinema Scope*. He has contributed to numerous other publications, curated various film series (usually with other members of the Ferroni Brigade) and co-authored (with Olaf Möller) books about Dominik Graf and Peter Kern.

GABE KLINGER (b. 1982) is a critic, teacher, archivist, curator, and filmmaker. His articles have appeared in *Sight and Sound*, *Film Comment*, *Cinema Scope*, and other publications. He has taught film studies at University of Illinois and Columbia College in Chicago, Illinois, and has worked in the motion picture departments at George Eastman House, MoMA in New York, and the Mary and Leigh Block Museum of Art at Northwestern University. His feature documentary, *Double Play: James Benning and Richard Linklater* (2013), premiered at the 2013 Venice Film Festival.

VIOLETA KOVACSICS (b. 1981) was born in Barcelona, where she writes on film for *La Vanguardia*, *Time Out Barcelona* and *Caimán Cuadernos de Cine*, and teaches the history of silent cinema at ESCAC. She has contributed to more than twenty books, among them volumes on Philippe Garrel, Terence Davies, Don Siegel, Jacques Demy and Georges Franju. She has authored a book on Paris and cinema (*París de cine*), edited a book and programmed a retrospective for the San Sebastián Film Festival. Kovacsics is programmer and chief publications editor for the Sitges Film Festival.

BILL KROHN (b. 1945) has been the Los Angeles correspondent for *Cahiers du cinéma* since 1978. He co-wrote, -directed, and -produced *It's All True: Based on an Unfinished Film by Orson Welles* (1993). His books include *Hitchcock at Work* (2000), *Luis Bunuel: Chimera* (2005), the monographs *Alfred Hitchcock* (2010) and *Stanley Kubrick* (2010), and the work-in-progress "Serial Killer Dreams." He previously published on Joe Dante in *Joe Dante et les Gremlins de Hollywood* (1999). He also reviews films for *The Economist*.

HOWARD PROUTY (b. 1953) gained his unholy knowledge of Joe Dante's life and work as lead researcher for the 1999 Locarno Film Festival retrospective. Since 1986, he has served as Acquisitions Archivist for the Margaret Herrick Library (Academy of Motion Picture Arts and Sciences, Beverly Hills). In this capacity he has been instrumental in bringing to the Academy numerous major archival collections, including the papers of Gregory Peck, W. C. Fields, James Wong Howe, Frank Tashlin, Katharine Hepburn, Charles Brackett, Saul Bass – and, not coincidentally, Joe Dante and Michael Finnell.

DUŠAN REBOLJ (b. 1975) is a writer and translator, living and working in Ljubljana, Slovenia. He's interested in how cinema, as a unique form of expression, intersects with socio-political concerns. He writes a bi-weekly film column for the *Slovenske novice* daily paper, as well as essays for a number of Slovenian publications, primarily *Ekran* film magazine. As translator, he collaborates with the Ljubljana International Film Festival, Slovenian Cinematheque, and the Slovene Art Cinema Association.

JIM ROBISON (b. 1946) is a writer whose works have appeared in *The New Yorker*, *Grand Street*, *The Manchester Review* and elsewhere. He is the winner of a Rosenthal Award from the American Academy of Arts and Letters for his first novel *The Illustrator* (1988) and a Whiting Grant for his book, *Rumor*, a collection of short stories. He collaborated with Michael Almereyda on the screenplay for *The Man with Kaleidoscope Eyes* and co-wrote Almereyda's film *New Orleans, Mon Amour* (2008).

JOHN SAYLES (b. 1950) likes to be known as a storyteller. *Go for Sisters* (2013) is his 18th film, all of which he has also written, and most of which he has edited. He writes fiction, most recently his epic historical novel *A Moment in the Sun* (2011). *Thinking in Pictures,* his book about the making of *Matewan* (1986), is taught in film classes and has never been out of print. Sayles supports his directing career as a "writer for hire" in Hollywood. He has most recently written about KGB assassins, the Tasmanian penal colony, the Rosenberg spy case, the great singer-songwriters Joni Mitchell, Carole King, and Carly Simon, and a famous American brewing dynasty. He directed three music videos for Bruce Springsteen, including *Born in the U.S.A.* He is one of the godfathers – or grandfathers – of the U.S. Independent Film movement. He lives with his producing partner of many years, Maggie Renzi, in upstate New York.

MARK COTTA VAZ (b. 1954) is a *New York Times* bestselling author of more than thirty books, focusing on popular culture and in particular on behind-the-scenes aspects of motion pictures such as visual effects. He has organized several exhibitions at the Cartoon Art Museum in San Francisco where he also served as a board member. Among his most critically acclaimed books are *The Invisible Art: The Legends of Movie Matte Painting* (2002, co-authored with Craig Barron) and the biography *Living Dangerously: The Adventures of Merian C. Cooper, Creator of King Kong* (2005).

List of Illustrations

Pages 11, 12, 17–20, 73, 75 – © Felipe Lima (Los Angeles)

Pages 15 above, 29, 30 below, 33, 36–66, 69 below, 77, 81 above, 87–91, 94, 101–105, 107 above, 109–127, 131–139, 141 above, 143, 145 below, 147–153, 157, 159 above, 160–171, 176–179, 199, 200, 203, 206, 207, 210, 215–228, 239, 245, back cover – Joe Dante collection at the Margaret Herrick Library, The Academy of Motion Picture Arts and Sciences (Los Angeles)

Pages 15 below, 26, 35, 69 above, 71, 82, 84, 97, 99, 141 center & below, 145 above, 159 below, 173 below, 179 below left & below right, 231, 235 right, 241 – Austrian Film Museum, Stills Collection (Vienna)

Page 30 above – Werkstattkino (Munich)

Page 107 below – Park Circus (London)

Page 129 – Viennale / Vienna International Film Festival (Vienna)

Page 173 above & center – ray Filmmagazin (Vienna)

All other photos, mostly in small format and in the filmography, were captured from DVDs.

Acknowledgments

Gabe Klinger: Tremendous gratitude to Peter von Bagh, for organizing the Midnight Sun Film Festival tribute where I re-met Joe for the first time in over a decade; Ashley Fenton, for putting me up (and putting up with me) while I was in Los Angeles to interview Dante and gather materials; Bill Krohn, for providing me with various Dante-related readings, viewings and insights; Elizabeth Stanley and Mark Alan, for their friendly help in all aspects of the preparation and execution of this book; Keetin Cheung and Dan Rybicky, for helping me reach John Sayles; and Andy Rector, Michel Lipkes, Tim Lucas, Eero Tammi, Eugenio Renzi, Patrick Wilson, Don Shay, and Jon Davison.

FilmmuseumSynemaPublikationen

Volume 18
DOMINIK GRAF
Christoph Huber, Olaf Möller
Vienna 2013, 208 pages
ISBN 978-3-901644-48-1
In German

Volume 17
A POST-MAY ADOLESCENCE.
LETTER TO ALICE DEBORD
By Olivier Assayas
Vienna 2012, 104 pages
ISBN 978-3-901644-44-3
In English

Olivier Assayas is best known as a filmmaker, but cinema makes only a late appearance in *A Post-May Adolescence*. This is an account of a personal formation, an initiation into an individual vision of the world; it is, equally, a record of youthful struggle. Assayas' reflective memoir takes us from the massive cultural upheaval that was May 1968 in France to the mid-1990s when he made his first autobiographical film about his teenage years, *L'Eau froide*. The book also includes two essays by Assayas on the aesthetic and political legacy of Guy Debord, who played a decisive role in shaping the author's understanding of the world and his path towards an extremely personal way of making films.

Volume 16
OLIVIER ASSAYAS
Edited by Kent Jones
Vienna 2012, 256 pages
ISBN 978-3-901644-43-6
In English

Over the past few decades, French filmmaker Olivier Assayas has become a powerful force in contemporary cinema. Between his first feature *Désordre* (1986) and such major works as *Irma Vep, Les Destinées sentimentales*, and, most recently, *Summer Hours* and *Carlos*, he has charted an exciting path, strongly embracing narrative and character and simultaneously dealing with the 'fragmentary reality' of life in a global economy. He also brought a fresh perspective to the problem of politics after '68, a subject that he revisits in his memoir *A Post-May Adolescence* and in his film *Après-Mai*. This first English-language monograph on Assayas includes a major essay by Kent Jones, based on his two decades of correspondence with the filmmaker, as well as contributions from Assayas and his most important collaborators. The richly illustrated book also contains 16 individual essays on each of the filmmaker's works.

Volume 15
SCREEN DYNAMICS
MAPPING THE BORDERS OF CINEMA
Edited by Gertrud Koch, Volker Pantenburg, and Simon Rothöhler
Vienna 2012, 184 pages
ISBN 978-3-901644-39-9
In English

This volume attempts to reconsider the limits and specifics of film and the traditional movie theater. It analyzes notions of spectatorship, the relationship between cinema and the "uncinematic", the contested place of installation art in the history of experimental cinema, and the characteristics of the high definition image. Contributors include Raymond Bellour, Victor Burgin, Vinzenz Hediger, Tom Gunning, Ute Holl, Ekkehard Knörer, Thomas Morsch, Jonathan Rosenbaum and the editors.

Volume 14
WAS IST FILM. PETER KUBELKAS ZYKLISCHES PROGRAMM IM ÖSTERREICHISCHEN FILMMUSEUM
Edited by Stefan Grissemann, Alexander Horwath, and Regina Schlagnitweit
Vienna 2010, 208 pages
ISBN 978-3-901644-36-8
In German

Volume 13
ROMUALD KARMAKAR
Edited by Olaf Möller and Michael Omasta
Vienna 2010, 256 pages
ISBN 978-3-901644-34-4
In German

Volume 12
APICHATPONG WEERASETHAKUL
Edited by James Quandt
Vienna 2009, 256 pages
ISBN 978-3-901644-31-3
In English

Apichatpong Weerasethakul is widely praised as one of *the* central figures in contemporary cinema. This first English-language volume on the Thai filmmaker looks at his works from a variety of angles and is extensively illustrated. With contributions by James Quandt, Benedict Anderson, Mark Cousins, Karen Newman, Tony Rayns, Kong Rithdee, and Tilda Swinton. With two interviews and personal essays the filmmaker's own voice is also a strong presence in the book.

Volume 11
GUSTAV DEUTSCH
Edited by Wilbirg Brainin-Donnenberg and Michael Loebenstein
Vienna 2009, 252 pages.
ISBN 978-3-901644-30-6
In English and German

According to Viennese filmmaker Gustav Deutsch, "film is more than film." His own career proves that point. In addition to being an internationally acclaimed creator of found footage films, he is also a visual artist, an architect, a researcher, an educator, an archaeologist, and a traveler. This volume traces the way in which the cinema of Gustav Deutsch transcends our common notion of film. Essays by Nico de Klerk, Stefan Grissemann, Tom Gunning, Beate Hofstadler, Alexander Horwath, Wolfgang Kos, Scott MacDonald, Burkhard Stangl, and the editors.

Volume 10
MICHAEL PILZ. AUGE KAMERA HERZ
Edited by Olaf Möller and Michael Omasta
Vienna 2008, 288 pages
ISBN 978-3-901644-29-0
In German

Volume 9
FILM CURATORSHIP. ARCHIVES, MUSEUMS, AND THE DIGITAL MARKETPLACE
Edited by Paolo Cherchi Usai, David Francis, Alexander Horwath, and Michael Loebenstein
Vienna 2008, 240 pages
ISBN 978-3-901644-24-5
In English

This volume deals with the rarely-discussed discipline of film curatorship and with the major issues and challenges that film museums and cinémathèques are bound to face in the Digital Age. *Film Curatorship* is an experiment: a collective text, a montage of dialogues, conversations, and exchanges among four professionals representing three generations of film archivists and curators.

Volume 8
LACHENDE KÖRPER. KOMIKERINNEN IM KINO DER 1910ER JAHRE
Claudia Preschl
Vienna 2008, 208 pages
ISBN 978-3-901644-27-6
In German

Volume 7
JEAN EPSTEIN. BONJOUR CINÉMA UND ANDERE SCHRIFTEN ZUM KINO
Edited by Nicole Brenez and Ralph Eue, translated from French by Ralph Eue
Vienna 2008, 160 pages
ISBN 978-3-901644-25-2
In German

Volume 6
JAMES BENNING
Edited by Barbara Pichler and Claudia Slanar
Vienna 2007, 264 pages
ISBN 978-3-901644-23-8
In English

James Benning's films are among the most fascinating works in American cinema. He explores the relationship between image, text and sound while paying expansive attention to the "vernacular landscapes" of American life. This volume traces Benning's artistic career as well as his biographical journey through the United States. With contributions by James Benning, Sharon Lockhart, Allan Sekula, Dick Hebdige, Scott MacDonald, Volker Pantenburg, Nils Plath, Michael Pisaro, Amanda Yates, Sadie Benning, Julie Ault, Claudia Slanar and Barbara Pichler.

Volume 5
JOSEF VON STERNBERG
THE CASE OF LENA SMITH
Edited by Alexander Horwath and Michael Omasta
Vienna 2007, 304 pages.
ISBN 978-3-901644-22-1
In English and German

The Case of Lena Smith, directed by Josef von Sternberg, is one of the legendary lost masterpieces of the American cinema. Assembling 150 original stills and set designs, numerous script and production documents as well as essays by eminent film historians, the book reconstructs Sternberg's dramatic film about a young woman fighting the oppressive class system of Imperial Vienna. The book includes essays by Janet Bergstrom, Gero Gandert, Franz Grafl, Alexander Horwath, Hiroshi Komatsu and Michael Omasta, a preface by Meri von Sternberg, as well as contemporary reviews and excerpts from Viennese literature of the era.

Volume 4
DZIGA VERTOV
DIE VERTOV-SAMMLUNG IM ÖSTERREICHISCHEN FILMMUSEUM
THE VERTOV COLLECTION AT THE AUSTRIAN FILM MUSEUM
Edited by the Austrian Film Museum, Thomas Tode, and Barbara Wurm
Vienna 2006, 288 pages, ISBN 3-901644-19-9
In English and German

For the Russian filmmaker and film theorist Dziga Vertov *KINO* was both a bold aesthetic experiment and a document of contemporary life. This book presents the Austrian Film Museum's comprehensive Vertov Collection: films, photographs, posters, letters as well as a large number of previously unpublished sketches, drawings and writings by Vertov including his extensive autobiographical "Calling Card" from 1947.

Volume 3
JOHN COOK. VIENNESE BY CHOICE, FILMEMACHER VON BERUF
Edited by Michael Omasta and Olaf Möller
Vienna 2006, 252 pages
ISBN 3-901644-17-2
In German (part 1) and English (part 2). OUT OF PRINT

Volume 2
PETER TSCHERKASSKY
Edited by Alexander Horwath and Michael Loebenstein
Vienna 2005, 256 pages
ISBN 3-901644-16-4
In English and German
OUT OF PRINT

Volume 1
CLAIRE DENIS. TROUBLE EVERY DAY
Edited by Michael Omasta and Isabella Reicher
Vienna 2005, 160 pages
ISBN 3-901644-15-6
In German
OUT OF PRINT